The Study of
Signed Languages

The Study of Signed Languages

Essays in Honor of William C. Stokoe

David F. Armstrong,
Michael A. Karchmer,
and John Vickrey Van Cleve,
Editors

Gallaudet University Press
Washington, D.C.

Gallaudet University Press
Washington, DC 20002

© 2002 by Gallaudet University
All rights reserved. Published 2002
Printed in the United States of America

Library of Congress Cataloging in Publication Data

The study of signed languages: essays in honor of William C. Stokoe/David F. Armstrong, Michael A. Karchmer, and John Vickrey Van Cleve, editors.

    p. cm.

    Papers presented at a conference honoring William Stokoe's 80th birthday held at Gallaudet University in 1999.

    Includes bibliographical references and index.

    ISBN 1-56368-123-4 (alk. paper)

    1. Sign language—Congresses. 2. Sign language—Research—Congresses. 3. American Sign Language—Congresses. 4. Deaf—Means of communication—Congresses. 5. Deaf—Education—Congresses. I. Stokoe, William C. II. Armstrong, David F. III. Karchmer, Michael A. IV. Van Cleve, John V.

HV2474 .S78 2002
419.7—dc21

2001059781

∞ The paper used in this publication meets the minimum requirements of American National Standard for Information Sciences—Permanence of Paper for Printed Library Materials, ANSI Z39.48-1984.

CONTENTS

List of Contributors — viii

Preface — xi
William C. Stokoe and the Study of
Signed Languages
David F. Armstrong and Michael A. Karchmer

Introduction — 1
Bill Stokoe: An ASL Trailblazer
I. King Jordan

PART I: Historical Perspectives

Introduction — 9
John Vickrey Van Cleve

1 The Curious Death of Sign Language Studies — 13
in the Nineteenth Century
Douglas C. Baynton

2 Historical Observations on the Relationship — 35
Between Research on Sign Languages and
Language Origins Theory
Adam Kendon

3 Modality Effects and Conflicting Agendas Scott K. Liddell	53

PART 2: Language Origins

Introduction David F. Armstrong	85
4 Does Sign Language Solve the Chomsky Problem? Frank R. Wilson	89
5 Continuity, Ethology, and Stokoe: How to Build a Better Language Model Roger S. Fouts and Gabriel S. Waters	100
6 William C. Stokoe and the Gestural Theory of Language Origins Sherman E. Wilcox	118

PART 3: Diverse Populations

Introduction Michael A. Karchmer	133
7 The Impact of Variation Research on Deaf Communities Ceil Lucas, Robert Bayley, Mary Rose, and Alyssa Wulf	137
8 The Impact of Sign Language Research on Black Deaf Communities in America Glenn B. Anderson	161

9 Bilingualism and the Impact of Sign Language   172
   Research on Deaf Education
   Britta Hansen

10 Sign Communication Training and Motor   190
   Functioning in Children with Autistic
   Disorder and in Other Populations
   John D. Bonvillian

11 Gesture and the Nature of Language in Infancy: 213
   The Role of Gesture as a Transitional
   Device En Route to Two-Word Speech
   Olga Capirci, M. Cristina Caselli, Jana M. Iverson,
   Elena Pizzuto, and Virginia Volterra

   Concluding Thoughts
   The Future of American Sign Language   247
   Carol A. Padden and Jennifer Rayman

   Index   263

CONTRIBUTORS

Glenn B. Anderson
Department of Rehabilitation
  Education and Research
University of Arkansas
Fayetteville, Arkansas

Robert Bayley
Bilingual-Bicultural Studies
University of Texas, San Antonio
San Antonio, Texas

Douglas C. Baynton
Department of History
University of Iowa
Iowa City, Iowa

John D. Bonvillian
Department of Psychology
University of Virginia
Charlottesville, Virginia

Olga Capirci
Institute of Psychology
National Research Council (CNR)
Rome, Italy

M. Cristina Caselli
Institute of Psychology
National Research Council (CNR)
Rome, Italy

Roger S. Fouts
Chimpanzee and Human
  Communication Institute
Central Washington University
Ellensburg, Washington

Britta Hansen
Center for Sign Language and
  Sign Supported Communication
Copenhagen, Denmark

Jana M. Iverson
Department of Psychology
University of Missouri—Columbia
Columbia, Missouri

I. King Jordan
Office of the President
Gallaudet University
Washington, D.C.

Contributors

Adam Kendon
Visiting Scholar
Institute for Research in Cognitive
    Science
University of Pennsylvania

Scott K. Liddell
Department of Linguistics
    and Interpretation
Gallaudet University
Washington, D.C.

Ceil Lucas
Department of Linguistics
    and Interpretation
Gallaudet University
Washington, D.C.

Carol A. Padden
Department of Communication
University of California, San Diego
San Diego, California

Elena Pizzuto
Institute of Psychology
National Research Council (CNR)
Rome, Italy

Jennifer Rayman
Department of Education and
    Social Sciences
University of Central Lancashire
Preston, United Kingdom

Mary Rose
Department of Linguistics
Stanford University
Stanford, California

Virginia Volterra
Institute of Psychology
National Research Council
    (CNR)
Rome, Italy

Gabriel S. Waters
Department of Linguistics
University of New Mexico
Albuquerque, New Mexico

Sherman E. Wilcox
Department of Linguistics
University of New Mexico
Albuquerque, New Mexico

Frank R. Wilson, M.D.
Department of Physical Therapy
    and Rehabilitation Science
University of California,
    San Francisco
San Francisco, California

Alyssa Wulf
Department of Linguistics
University of California,
    Berkeley
Berkeley, California

PREFACE

William C. Stokoe and the Study of Signed Languages

David F. Armstrong and
Michael A. Karchmer

The right man in the right place at the right time.

This volume celebrates the work of William C. Stokoe, one of the most influential language scholars of the twentieth century. To understand his impact on both the educational fortunes of deaf people and on the science of language, it is necessary to consider briefly the status of these two related fields in the early 1950s. The almost universal educational goal for deaf people at this time was acquisition of spoken language and the ability to discern speech on the lips—other educational goals, including the acquisition of general knowledge, were arguably secondary to the development of "oral" skills. It was perhaps not coincidental that linguistic science had no interest in the gestural language of deaf people—language was synonymous with speech. This point is well captured in the title of one of the most influential books on linguistics of the first half of the twentieth century, Edward Sapir's *Language: An Introduction to the Study of Speech*. Sapir, writing in the 1920s, dismissed sign languages as substitution codes for spoken languages—speech was dominant (Sapir 1921: 21). The views of "experts" on deaf education in the mid-1950s may be best summed up by Helmer Myklebust, a product of Gallaudet's graduate school.

> The manual language used by the deaf is an ideographic language . . . it is more pictorial, less symbolic. . . . Ideographic language systems, in comparison with verbal systems, lack precision, subtlety, and flexibility. It is likely that Man cannot achieve his ultimate potential through an Ideographic language. . . . The manual sign language must be viewed as inferior to the verbal as a language. (Myklebust 1957: 241–42)

It's all here in this short passage: sign language is equated with the despised, non-alphabetic writing system of a non-Western people (the Chinese), it is said to lack the precision of speech, and it is stated, without any evidence, that deaf people will not achieve their full potential through its use. When Stokoe arrived at Gallaudet in 1955, he was entering an environment that was dominated by thinking like this. His achievements with respect to the value of signed languages were essentially fourfold. Stokoe's first achievement was to realize that the signed language his students used among themselves had all the important characteristics common to spoken languages and that it had the same potential for human communication. His second achievement was to devise a descriptive system that would convince language scholars of these facts. This was what gave him the legitimacy to pursue his third achievement—convincing much of the general public and the educational establishment of the human and educational value of allowing deaf children to communicate in natural signed languages. His fourth grand achievement was then to apply what he had learned from the study of signed languages to the larger problems of the nature and evolution of the human capacity for language.

In his introduction to this volume, I. King Jordan refers to Stokoe as being in the right place at the right time, and we will elaborate on that theme here. Before he arrived at Gallaudet, Stokoe, of course, had had little experience communicating with deaf people and no professional training in the education of deaf children. It is a matter of great interest to understand why Stokoe was able to see these things when the bulk of professionals trained in the relevant areas could not—if we come to even a partial answer to this question, we will have gained a bit of insight into the nature of human genius. With hindsight, it seems obvious that one of the things he had going for him was precisely his *lack* of training (or prejudice) in areas relevant to deafness. He also brought a first-rate mind (an inquiring mind) and training in the study of language generally (he had bachelor's and Ph.D. degrees in English from Cornell). The final ingredients seem to have been his persistence (some would say his obstinacy), his predisposition to question authority, and a well-developed sense of fairness or justice (see Maher 1986, for a discussion of his childhood, his education, and his first years at Gallaudet).

For someone with an open and inquiring mind, and an interest in language and communication, there can be few more stimulating environments than that provided by Gallaudet. Here deaf people communicate among themselves and with hearing people using a great variety of communication systems and codes that we can now recognize, thanks to Stokoe, as ranging from natural signed languages (mainly ASL), to what look like languages of contact between ASL and English, to invented sign codes syntactically modeled on English. During the course of an average day, members of the Gallaudet community are likely to have to negotiate a number of communication situations involving a number of these systems and codes. In this environment, one develops a heightened sense of the range of possible forms that languages can take and a sensitivity to the differences among them.

We have established already that Stokoe was the right person, and now we have located him in the right place. What about the time? Stokoe arrived at Gallaudet just as the civil rights movement was beginning to challenge the traditional caste structure of the United States. As this movement matured during the 1960s, an idea became firmly entrenched in the United States that individuals should not be deprived of legal, civil, educational, or economic rights because of their membership in any particular ethnic, religious, or linguistic group. Ultimately, this idea was extended to include people with physical disabilities. It cannot be completely coincidental that the nascent movement that

Stokoe helped to launch came ultimately to be seen as a civil rights movement in its own right.

What He Did

So what was it exactly that he did? He is often described as having "discovered" ASL or as having "proved" that ASL is a language. A good deal of mythology seems to have sprung up around this question, and we think that, to some extent, Stokoe felt about it the way Columbus should have felt when he was described as having "discovered" America. Just as American Indians had known about the Americas for more than 10,000 years before Columbus arrived, so deaf people had been aware of the "languageness" of their signing and of the benefits that it conferred long before Stokoe came on the scene. They were also "proving" that it was a real language on a daily basis by using it to perform all of the functions that languages usually perform. But just as Columbus had done with respect to the scope of the physical world, Stokoe's accomplishment was to reveal these facts to a larger, skeptical public; and, in doing so, he made a "Columbian" addition to our knowledge of the linguistic world and to our understanding of the human condition.

One aspect of Stokoe's genius was to recognize that it would not be good enough simply to announce the "good news" that sign language was really a language—he would need to show it using the tools of the science of language, the tools of descriptive linguistics. Linguistic science in the mid-1950s was just about to be turned on its head by a young scholar named Noam Chomsky. He launched an intellectual revolution following which language came to be seen more as a cognitive than as a social phenomenon, but that revolution need not concern us here. Stokoe was mainly influenced by an older anthropological linguistics that had as its most urgent goal describing exotic languages that were facing extinction. Anthropological linguists, and anthropologists in general for that matter, had for a half century been trying to overcome Western prejudices that had depicted non-Western languages as somehow inferior to those of Europe. These scholars had developed an armamentarium that could be used to describe any spoken language and commit it to paper.

They had come to realize that all languages have regular structures at a level below that of the individual word—according to the terminology of linguistics, they have sublexical or phonological structure. This structure is based upon systems of contrast—differences in meaning must be based upon perceptible differences in language sounds, as in *bat* and *hat*. It is this sublexical structure that makes phonetic writing possible, and all spoken languages have it. Stokoe's masterstroke was to show that ASL has such a structure and that it too can be written in a phonetic-like script (Stokoe 1960; Stokoe, Croneberg and Casterline 1965). By devising a workable script, he was able to convince other language scholars that ASL employs such a system of linguistic contrast, that it has a regular internal structure, and that is, therefore, not simply ad-hoc pantomime or a corrupt visual code for English. It is beyond the scope of this introduction to describe Stokoe's system (see Armstrong 1999, for a description of the system and a discussion of its historical importance), but it is worth noting that it has held up well, despite numerous attempts to improve upon it, and is still used to transcribe signed languages. Stokoe, along with two deaf colleagues, Carl Croneberg and Dorothy Casterline, used this notation system to compile the first comprehensive dictionary of ASL in 1965.

Having completed this initial descriptive work, Stokoe then set about convincing the larger world of the linguistic qualities of ASL, he took these ideas "on the road" so to speak. At Gallaudet, he put in place several operations that would further bolster the legitimacy of ASL and other signed languages. First, he set up the Linguistic Research Laboratory in 1971 and invited people in from around the world to work on problems in the description and interpretation of signed languages. This provided an institutional home for signed language research. Second, in 1972, he founded the journal *Sign Language Studies* to provide an outlet for publication of increasingly complex and sophisticated scholarly articles on linguistic and other aspects of the signed languages of deaf people. This was at a time when mainstream linguistics journals showed little interest in publishing work from this incipient field.

Stokoe owned, edited, and published this journal himself for more than twenty years, and the journal chronicles the growth and maturation of the fields of signed language research and deaf studies. It is now owned and operated by Gallaudet University Press.

During the early 1970s, Stokoe began to see that his work on ASL might have a larger significance, beyond the development of increasingly complex linguistic studies and the support these were providing for the reform of deaf education. At this time, Stokoe became interested in the newly reinvigorated scientific study of the origin and evolution of the human capacity for language. Because this topic had been the subject of rampant and undisciplined speculation around the turn of the twentieth century, it had fallen out of favor with linguists and anthropologists. Stokoe joined a small group of scholars, including Gordon Hewes, Charles Hockett, Roger Wescott, Stevan Harnad, and Horst Steklis, who began to synthesize new information from paleontology, primatology, neuroscience, linguistics, and, significantly, sign language studies into more coherent scenarios for the evolution of language (see Harnad, Steklis, and Lancaster 1976). During the past quarter century, these scenarios have grown more sophisticated and plausible, due in large part to Stokoe's efforts.

Stokoe concerned himself especially with evolutionary problems that might be solved by postulating a signing stage in human evolution. He participated in several important symposia on this topic, one of which resulted in the book *Language Origins* (Wescott 1974). In order to get this book into print, Stokoe established a small publishing company, Linstok[1] Press, which also took over publication of the journal *Sign Language Studies*. Stokoe came to believe that iconic manual gesture must have played a key role in the transition from non-human primate communication to human language. In making this assertion, he was rediscovering a line of thinking that went back at least to the Abbé de Condillac, an influential figure in the French enlightenment of the

---

1. It is worth noting for posterity that the name "Linstok" was a play on the words "linguistics," "Stokoe," and "linstock," the last referring to a device used to hold a match for firing a cannon.

eighteenth century. According to this line of thinking, the introduction of iconic manual gesture might solve the problem of attribution of meaning to arbitrary vocal signals—iconic gestures which resemble the things they refer to might form a bridge to the symbolic relationship of speech sounds to their referents. This might occur if iconic gestures became paired with non-iconic sounds in reference to objects and events in the environment. But Stokoe went a step beyond this to suggest that iconic manual gestures might also have been involved in the thornier question of how syntax might have originated. This goes to the question at the heart of Chomskyan linguistics which posits syntax as the defining characteristic of human languages—how do languages come to refer not only to objects and events, but to the infinite number of possible relationships among them?

Although Stokoe was no fan of Chomskyan linguistics, there is an interesting parallel between his later thinking and that of Chomsky. We alluded above to the increasing complexity of the linguistics of signed languages. Stokoe began to see in this an unnecessary and ultimately unproductive obscurantism. In response to this trend, he published in 1991, an extraordinarily original article entitled "Semantic Phonology." At the same time, Chomsky was moving in the direction of a "minimalist program" for generative linguistics (Chomsky 1995). According to this program, the number of essential linguistic parameters could be reduced to two: a logical form and a phonetic form. Stokoe proposed that all of the multilayered complexity that had been introduced in linguistic descriptions of signed languages could also be reduced to two parameters: something acting (in the case of manual gesture, a hand) and its action. Stokoe pointed out, moreover, that this acting unit had the essential characteristics of one of Chomsky's elementary sentences, a noun phrase plus a verb phrase. The final link in his chain of reasoning is that use of such iconic manual gestures by early humans might have led to analysis of the agent/action relationship that is inherent to them, leading ultimately to the elaboration of syntax and, hence, language. His views on these and many other issues are summed up in his final major work, a book entitled *Language in Hand,* published posthumously by Gallaudet University Press (Stokoe 2001; and see Armstrong, Stokoe, and Wilcox 1995).

This Volume

This volume contains papers that were presented at the Gallaudet conference honoring Bill Stokoe's eightieth birthday. It is important to emphasize that the fall 1999 conference and this volume originally were planned as a living tribute, not as a memorial to mark his passing. Indeed, Stokoe was very much present at the conference—sitting with family and friends close to the presenters and drinking in every word and sign. In the months that followed, despite rapidly deteriorating health, Stokoe's spirits were buoyed in discussions of the issues raised by each of the presenters. Sadly, the time left to him was all too brief and Bill Stokoe died on April 4, 2000, a few months short of his eighty-first birthday.

It was the intention of the conference's organizers to engage leading scholars in the many scholarly disciplines that his work had influenced, and the wide range of his ideas is represented here. The volume is divided into three major topical sections, bracketed by introductory and closing papers by I. King Jordan and Carol Padden. The sections have to do with the historical context of Stokoe's work, the issue of language origins, and the diverse populations, deaf and hearing, that have benefited from the work he began. Each section is preceded by a brief introduction, and we leave discussion of the individual papers to authors of those introductions. However, we point out that Stokoe's impact is at least partly revealed by the range of time during which the scholars represented in this book have known him and been influenced by him. The range is wide indeed, from deaf scholars such as Jordan and Padden who had known and worked with Stokoe for thirty years or more, to Frank Wilson, author of the widely acclaimed book, *The Hand*, who had known of Stokoe and his work for only a few years before Stokoe's death. The point, of course, is that the work that Wilson drew on in his book was done during the 1990s, when Stokoe was already in his seventies. It is a measure of his full achievement, that he was still doing fresh and original intellectual work forty years after he began.

One final note—the authors of many of the papers were Stokoe's close personal friends, as well as his professional colleagues, and many were aware that they were probably seeing him for the last time at the conference in October, 1999 where the papers were first presented. For this reason, some of the papers present scholarly findings with a personal tone. It was the judgment of the editors, in several cases, that it would be appropriate to retain these personal references in final print form. It is in that spirit that we close this section in the way that Bill Stokoe ended each of his e-mails. It is the way that ham radio operators signal "over and out." Here's to you, Bill—"73."

References

Armstrong, David F. 1999. *Original signs: Gesture, sign, and the sources of language.* Washington, D.C.: Gallaudet University Press.

Armstrong, David F., William C. Stokoe, and Sherman E. Wilcox. 1995. *Gesture and the nature of language.* Cambridge: Cambridge University Press.

Chomsky, Noam. 1995. *The minimalist program.* Cambridge: MIT Press.

Harnad, Stevan R., Horst D. Steklis, and Jane Lancaster. 1976. *Origins and evolution of language and speech.* New York: New York Academy of Sciences.

Maher, Jane. 1996. *Seeing language in signs. The work of William C. Stokoe.* Washington, D.C.: Gallaudet University Press.

Myklebust, Helmer. 1957. *The psychology of deafness.* New York: Grune and Stratton.

Sapir, Edward. 1921. *Language: An introduction to the study of speech.* New York: Harcourt, Brace, and World.

Stokoe, William C. 1960. *Sign language structure: An outline of the visual communication systems of the American Deaf.* Studies in Linguistics: Occasional Papers, 8. Buffalo, N.Y.: University of Buffalo Department of Anthropology and Linguistics.

———. 1991. "Semantic phonology." *Sign Language Studies* 71: 107–14.

———. 2001. *Language in sign: Why sign came before speech.* Washington, D.C.: Gallaudet University Press.

Stokoe, William C., Dorothy Casterline, and Carl G. Croneberg. 1965. *A dictionary of American sign language on linguistic principles.* Washington, D.C.: Gallaudet College Press.

Westcott, Roger. 1974. *Language origins.* Silver Spring, Md.: Linstok Press.

Wilson, Frank. 1997. *The hand: How its use shapes the brain, language, and human culture.* New York: Pantheon.

INTRODUCTION

Bill Stokoe: An ASL Trailblazer

I. King Jordan

I cannot resist starting this volume dedicated to the work of Bill Stokoe with a personal anecdote illustrating an aspect of his character: an aspect that allowed him to become a revolutionary in support of the language rights of deaf people. Back in the 1970s, during my first few years at Gallaudet, Stokoe and I were flying back to Washington from a conference in Chicago. Halfway through the flight, our plane encountered some serious turbulence, including a sudden drop of about a thousand feet. What was Stokoe doing while I was turning green? He was busy making sure to position his glass so that the scotch that had been in it and was now suspended in front of him would fall back into it when the plane settled down. He succeeded of course.

Before we can truly appreciate what Bill Stokoe did, we need to consider what the world was like for deaf people—for us—when he came to Gallaudet in the 1950s. At that time, many—maybe most—deaf people were ashamed of and often hid their deafness, and this was true not only of deaf people but of people with disabilities generally. A decade earlier, even the president of the United States, Franklin D. Roosevelt, felt compelled to hide his inability to walk and the wheelchair or crutches that he regularly used. In those "bad old days," deaf people who used sign language were considered "oral failures." Sign language was not accepted as an appropriate mode of communication for teaching. A majority of schools for deaf children were totally oral.

How bad was it? In an article published in the *American Annals of the Deaf* soon after I began teaching at Gallaudet, my co-authors and I revealed that at the elementary education level, not one school or program in the entire United States acknowledged sign language as its official means of communication. During this period, the preschool operated by Gallaudet's Kendall elementary school was located in one of the college buildings, and a solid wooden fence was erected around its playground. The story at the time was that the fence was there to prevent the young preschoolers from seeing the college students signing to each other. It was also common to hear stories about punishments that were meted out to young children in schools for the deaf who were caught signing. But even though sign language was forbidden in the classroom, it thrived where a considerable part of education always takes place: on the playgrounds and in the dormitories.

The issue of what modes of communication were and were not appropriate was not new when Stokoe arrived at Gallaudet. Sign-based education had been in retreat since the International Congress on Education of the Deaf in Milan in 1880. Throughout Europe and the United States, the goal for both parents and educators was to make deaf children as "normal"—meaning "hearing"—as possible. In practical terms, this meant that no school at any level offered formal education using signing of any kind. Moreover, when a child signed "naturally," that is, in American Sign Language (ASL), it was seen either as "broken English" or as an indication of inferior intellect. Most painful to remember is that because deaf children were denied a language in which they could learn, they were often denied access to the most basic information and experiences. All of us of a certain age can remember story after story showing how the most "progressive" ideas about deaf education during that time were actually the most harmful. Put into practice, those ideas did not educate—they oppressed.

Even some of the brightest deaf leaders internalized and accepted negative definitions of themselves. They "knew" that the hearing world was better than the deaf world. They "knew" they could never hope to have the advantages—the education, the achievements, the careers—that appeared to be so easily acquired in that hearing world. Fortunately, Stokoe was in the right place at the right time to make dramatic changes in those deeply ingrained attitudes. I say the right time because, in the late 1950s and early 1960s, this country was in the midst of upheaval that would have an impact on all cultural and ethnic groups, and ultimately disabled people as well. He could not have come to Gallaudet at a better moment.

To understand how remarkable and unexpected Stokoe's research was, it is necessary to recall that this was a person who had no knowledge of signing at all when he came to Gallaudet. Remember also that in those days, new faculty at the college did not get intensive training in sign language—they were thrust into the classroom and were expected to fend for themselves. Nevertheless, soon after he joined the English Department faculty, Professor Stokoe became intrigued with the communication that was occurring in his classrooms. Because he had an outsider's perspective without all the accepted "baggage" about sign language, he was able to see what others had not. He saw that his students were indeed communicating among themselves about sophisticated ideas. He became fascinated with their fluency and grace, and he soon perceived a contradiction between what he was observing and what he had been told to expect.

Puzzled by this paradox, he began to look more carefully at the behavior itself, behavior that he saw happening all around the campus. In doing this, Stokoe was doing something that few, if any, educators or researchers were doing at the time. He simply looked at what deaf people were doing instead of blindly accepting what hearing (and even some deaf) "experts" said. He also asked deaf people what they were doing, and often the answers he received surprised him. Many of the deaf faculty members, people who communicated easily and fluently with each other and with their students, told him that signing was not language. In fact, when Stokoe argued that sign language *was* a language, many deaf people not only disagreed with him, they criticized him for saying so publicly.

Stokoe was not deterred by this criticism. He continued his detailed observations of deaf people signing and became even more convinced that he was seeing a language in use, a language that was not transmitted by sound but by sight. Because he wanted to test this belief, he began to study the theories and techniques of anthropology and linguistics. His work was revolutionary because he was able to cut through the myths and misconceptions that so pervasively influenced the thinking of the time, even at Gallaudet. As a scholar in stubborn pursuit of the truth, he applied his keen scientific mind to the problem of describing how deaf people on Kendall Green (the Gallaudet campus) communicated with one another. While this seems simple today, it was not in 1960. By doing what he did, he changed our world.

I would like to quote here from David Armstrong's *Original Signs*: "The notion that these sign systems might be languages in the same sense as the world's spoken languages originated with William C. Stokoe, a language scholar who began working at Gallaudet University . . . during the 1950s" (1999, 18). A simple statement with profound implications. Stokoe was the first researcher to apply linguistic principles to the signed communication that was taking place around him. His work resulted in the first demonstration that American Sign Language could be described according to the same principles as those used to describe all languages. What inspired him to do it? I think this is best summed up in a statement written by Sherman Wilcox shortly after Stokoe's death: "His study of language was inspired by his deep understanding that the people who use language come first. His profound respect for Deaf people and their language was the bedrock of his work" (2000, 9).

I indicated earlier that Stokoe had landed in the right place. Of course, it is no accident that his research was conducted at Gallaudet. Gallaudet was then and still is both the center of the world of deaf education, and an institution of higher learning. Stokoe's work represents all that is best about American higher education. In an environment of academic freedom, he was able to pursue what seemed at first glance to be an odd notion—doesn't something have to be spoken to be a language? On a college campus even those who opposed his thinking could not finally obstruct his work. And you can be sure that many educators, both hearing and deaf, did object to his thinking. Stokoe took a centuries-old debate and changed its focus by challenging accepted interpretations of reality. He openly questioned conventional wisdom and refused to be deterred by the naysayers.

Stokoe's research was also possible because Gallaudet was and still is the mecca for the American deaf community. Deaf and hard of hearing people at Gallaudet have always represented a broad spectrum of perspectives. Just as the American deaf community reflects the larger American society, so Gallaudet is a microcosm of the deaf community. Stokoe's research found fertile ground on this campus. Looking back on more than forty years of his research, I find that I cannot fully measure its impact. By legitimizing a language he legitimized a culture. By legitimizing a culture he set the stage for a profound change in the lives of countless deaf people. He shattered the notion best expressed as "deaf world bad, hearing world good." He shattered the paternalistic thinking that had discouraged far too many people from seeking and achieving success.

Although much has changed on the Gallaudet campus since Stokoe first arrived, much has not. Gallaudet had then—and still has today—the largest group of educated deaf individuals to be found in one place anywhere in the world (probably the largest group of deaf people period). Gallaudet was then—and still is—the only university of its kind that the world has so far seen fit to create, a place where visual communication allows every person present to communicate directly with every other person. As a result of Stokoe's work, this ideal has expanded. As a result of his work, students who come to Gallaudet —no matter where they fall on the continuum of deafness or on the spectrum of communication experience—leave with a greater sense of pride in themselves. The coexistence of two languages at the university, ASL and English, continues to raise issues that are difficult and complex, and the university continues to work to resolve them. Just as Bill Stokoe stepped up to the challenge more than forty years ago, we will continue to step up to that challenge today. If the world deaf community owes Stokoe a debt of gratitude, the debt owed by Gallaudet is even greater.

Armstrong writes that Stokoe's "success in winning acceptance of ASL as a natural human language, at least from the scientific community, is one of the great achievements in the behavioral sciences" (1999, 69). As a behavioral scientist, I heartily concur. Without Stokoe's seminal work, the papers in this volume that follow could not have been written. Of course, I must hasten to add that the impact of his work on the community at large has been at least as great as that on the scientific community. Without his work, for example, I am not sure that the Gallaudet community would have had the self-confidence it took to launch the Deaf President Now (DPN) movement, and we might not today be benefiting from all the positive changes that have rippled through our lives as a result.

Stokoe's work is still visible on the Gallaudet campus today. Gallaudet now has a Department of American Sign Language, Linguistics, and Interpretation, a Center for American Sign Language Literacy, and sign language classes for faculty, staff, and students. Gallaudet University Press has revitalized *Sign Language Studies,* the journal Stokoe founded in 1972, returning this irreplaceable periodical to print. In sum, Stokoe's work has resulted in a revolution in communication for deaf people, greater self-esteem, more employment opportunities, and the belief that deaf individuals can pursue and achieve our dreams, whatever they may be.

Bill Stokoe died about six months after the Gallaudet conference celebrating his eightieth birthday. One predominant theme ran through the entire conference, and it can be summed up in these words: "Thank you, Bill, for all you did for the deaf community, for the community of scholars, and for Gallaudet University."

References

Armstrong, David F. 1999. *Original signs: Gesture, sign, and the sources of language.* Washington, D.C.: Gallaudet University Press.

Jordan, I. King, Gerilee Gustason, and Roslyn Rosen. 1976. Current communication trends at programs for the deaf. *American Annals of the Deaf* 121: 527–32.

Wilcox, Sherman E. 2000. Appreciation. *Sign Language Studies* 1: 7–9.

PART I

Historical Perspectives

INTRODUCTION

John Vickrey Van Cleve

Commentators often state that Bill Stokoe was the first scholar to recognize deaf people's signing as a true language, one capable of conveying a broad range of human thought and emotion. This assertion accurately reflects the state of scholarship during the generation in which Stokoe began his work, but it lacks historical perspective. It therefore misinterprets what his work means to the history of ideas. More importantly, such a simplistic and circumscribed view obscures the extent to which the meaning of deafness has been changeable, socially constructed, and therefore capable of further alteration to the benefit of people who are deaf. Careful examination reveals that rich debates about sign language, gesture, and speech once characterized a period that long antedated Stokoe's late twentieth-century studies, a time when philosophers of language took a broad, speculative approach to their subject, one that Stokoe would have embraced.

Chapters in this section by Douglas Baynton and Adam Kendon review the tumultuous history of ideas about signing and signed languages. They show that visual language attracted intense European and American scholarly interest, study, and speculation in the eighteenth and early nineteenth centuries. Sign language sometimes attained a lofty status in this milieu. Some argued that it was the original language, arising before speech; others believed that sign was more expressive than speech, that it better conveyed emotions, or that it was closer to the rhetorical ideal mentioned by classical authors. Yet studies of sign language disappeared—indeed, were even banished—from intellectual discourse as the twentieth century began. Baynton and Kendon thus interpret Stokoe's achievements from the perspective of historical change and context. Each author's perspective is different, demonstrating two aspects of the breadth and importance of Stokoe's vision.

The first chapter, Baynton's "The Curious Death of Sign Language Studies in the Nineteenth Century," focuses on the United States and specifically on attitudes toward signed languages. Baynton asks why sign language was "devalued and discredited at the end of the nineteenth century, to the extent that not only did schools prohibit its use to deaf children, but scholars lost interest in it?" He roots his explanation in national intellectual and social developments, examining changing American attitudes toward religion, science, national identity, and "emotional style." Baynton explains that a language that was once respected, studied, and admired—thus conferring some measure of dignity on its users—acquired wholly negative connotations as an atavistic connection to primitive times and peoples. Once believed to be the key to universal communication, sign language became "a crutch for deaf persons who had failed at oral communication, but not a subject for serious study." This was the situation that Stokoe confronted when he initiated his studies of American Sign Language (ASL) in the late 1950s. Baynton suggests, finally, that similar cultural aversions to sign language persist in the United States today despite Stokoe's efforts.

While the cultural status of people who use sign language in their everyday discourse is central to Baynton's concerns—and was an animating factor for Stokoe as he struggled against educators and linguists—Kendon's immediate focus is somewhat different. He examines the ways sign language and gesture were studied to help understand how language originated. Kendon begins with the eighteenth-century philosopher Giambattista Vico, who reasoned that language started with gestures that had "natural relations" with ideas. For Vico, the signing of deaf people was important because it showed how a language could be expressed with "natural significations."

Vico's thoughts were followed over the next several decades by those of other European philosophers who also saw in sign language important evidence for understanding all human language.

Yet all was different by the end of the nineteenth century. Sign language was no longer seen as having any relevance to important intellectual questions, "issues of theoretical importance," in Kendon's words. The whole study of language origins had been thrown into disrepute. As early as 1866, the Linguistics Society of Paris banned papers on language origins. The London Philological Society did the same in 1872. At about the same time, language became defined in terms of a single modality, speech, and it was believed to require characteristics that signing lacked. This situation remained until the work of Stokoe, his collaborators, and a few other scholars in the late twentieth century challenged these assumptions.

Kendon concludes that the greater understanding of sign languages developed and inspired by Stokoe then led back to a reconsideration of the issues raised by Vico. New examinations showed how behavior could "function *linguistically*, without it necessarily being spoken." Now, with sign language better understood and resurrected to a place of importance, language origins could again be examined, discussed with the help of new evidence supplied by rigorous study of gesture and signed languages.

Scott Liddell argues in his chapter, "Modality Effects and Conflicting Agendas," that the very relation between gesture and signed languages, however, creates both interesting questions and significant problems for modern linguists. Liddell suggests that the presence of iconicity in signed languages and the use of pointing appear to require linguists either to give up their theories about the central properties of language or to decide that sign languages "are not the same kind of entities as spoken languages."

Liddell traces the hold that theory can exert, even in the face of seemingly overwhelming evidence, and concludes that the linguistic study of ASL demonstrates that the theories defining language need alteration. ASL does not fit the theories, but it is a language, albeit a language in a different modality than speech. The problem, Liddell concludes, "is not with ASL, but with faulty conceptions of what language should look like."

The Curious Death of Sign Language Studies in the Nineteenth Century

Douglas C. Baynton

William Stokoe inaugurated modern linguistic research in American Sign Language with his pioneering studies at Gallaudet University in the 1950s. However, while sign language was largely ignored by scholars for the first half of the twentieth century, in the previous century inquiry into the nature of sign language was pursued by instructors at American schools for deaf students. This older tradition of sign language scholarship was brought to an untimely end at the turn of the century. As a result, when Stokoe challenged the prevailing understanding of sign language as a hodgepodge of manually (and poorly) expressed English, pantomime, and nongrammatical gesture, he had to begin anew. The more than fifty-year gap in research meant that Stokoe and his early followers had no foundation in linguistics on which to build. The nineteenth-century study of sign language was so different from modern concerns that Stokoe would have found it of little direct use. Nevertheless, as I hope to show, it is of more than merely antiquarian interest to ask what drove this sustained and serious inquiry into the nature of sign language in the nineteenth century, and, even more important, what brought about its demise.

The obvious and easy answer to the latter question is that "oralism" put an end to it. When schools for the deaf moved increasingly to strictly oral education, banning the use of sign language in most of their classrooms, the number of teachers who knew sign language or had any interest in it decreased drastically. Furthermore, while most hearing manualist teachers through the nineteenth century possessed college degrees in the liberal arts (an especially large number came from Yale), and many saw philosophical inquiry as an important part of their life's work, the oralist teachers who succeeded them conceived of their vocation in more narrow, professional terms. The rise of oralism was accompanied by a transformation in teacher education; by the turn of the century, most teachers of deaf students were no longer college educated, at most having attended a one-year teacher training program, and had little aptitude for, nor interest in, pursuing research into language.[1] The articles published in the *American Annals of the Deaf* at the turn of the century reflected the background and training of this new generation of instructors. While the earlier generation of manualist instructors had written on a wide variety of topics, embracing philology, psychology, philosophy, history, and theology, oralists focused their writing on educational practices—the technical aspects of teaching speech and lipreading, classroom management, and teaching techniques. They transformed the *Annals* into a specialized professional journal of the modern type, narrowly concerned with issues directly related to professional practice.

To say that oralism was behind the decline in sign language research, however, begs the important question of why oralism itself rose to dominance at the time that it did. Oralism was hardly a new idea. German schools were predominantly (though not exclusively) oral throughout the nineteenth century. In America, Samuel Gridley Howe and Horace Mann, both powerful and skilled reformers with large followings, put their reputations in the service of advocating oral education as early as the 1840s. The results of their efforts were negligible. Nor does the advent of oralism in America explain why, until Stokoe, no Gallaudet professors in the twentieth century thought it worthwhile to seriously investigate the means of communication used by their students. Moreover, neither oralism nor the change in the character of instructors at the schools for the deaf can account for the virtual disappearance of research into the sign languages of American Indians and Australian aborigines at about the same time.

Aside from a few cursory investigations (for example, those of John P. Harrington), Plains Indian sign language was largely ignored through the twentieth century until A. L. Kroeber, C. F. Voegelin, and La Mont West began in the 1950s what Kroeber described as a "twentieth-century pick-up of a topic which nineteenth-century students dropped . . . and which for over sixty years has lain neglected." Likewise, as Adam Kendon notes in his essay in this volume, a 1954 article by the anthropologist Mervyn Meggitt was the first important one on Australian aboriginal sign language since the nineteenth century. Meggitt himself cited several studies from the nineteenth century and then commented, in understated fashion, that "at this point there seems to have been something of a lacuna in reports on the presence of sign languages."[2] And while the first significant work on these sign languages all appeared in the 1950s (though Stokoe's was by far the most substantial and significant), it was not until the 1970s and 1980s that this work attracted significant scholarly interest.

Occasional short pieces on sign language did appear here and there earlier in the century. In 1938, *Oceana* published a four-page article (one page of which was illustrations) by C. P. Mountford that described a few signs he had encountered on an anthropological expedition among the Australian aborigines, and generally gave the impression of sign language as a fascinating if not terribly significant curiosity. His citations to previous anthropological descriptions of aboriginal sign language began in the 1870s and ended in 1912. The *Tennessee Archaeologist* in 1947 printed a one-page description of Plains Indian sign language with instructions for making half a dozen signs. And then there was *Communication through the Ages: From Sign Language to Television*, which in its title encapsulated what was seen as the most primitive to the most advanced forms of communication up until 1946.[3]

In 1945, the journal *Man* printed a very brief essay on "Sign Language in Ancient Ceylon," in which the author ranged from the use of "drums and log xylophones . . . among the primitive tribes of India," to fires on hilltops, signal flags, and secret codes. While the author's (barely supported) thesis was that sign language may have been prominent in ancient Ceylon, he thought it important to point out that today "there are children who use it for sport, and dumb people who employ it for making themselves understood."[4] This was the common perception of sign language: a device for people incapable of speech much like drums or smoke signals when distance made speech impossible, an exotic practice among primitives, or a plaything among children who use it "for sport." William Tomkins's *Universal Indian Sign Language,* for example, one of the few books on sign language in the twentieth century, expressed his "earnest hope" that the book would "kindle enthusiasm in the breasts of thousands of boys and girls throughout the world." With its useful chapter on smoke signaling as a bonus, it became the official Indian sign manual for Boy Scouts.[5]

The question, then, is why signed languages were devalued and discredited at the end of the nineteenth century, to the extent that not only did schools prohibit their use to deaf children, but also scholars lost interest in them? It will be no news to most readers of this collection that from that time until the late twentieth century, linguists typically spoke of "language" as though it were synonymous with "spoken language." They may, nevertheless, be interested to know, or be reminded, that one of the first reviewers of Stokoe's 1960 monograph, *Sign Language Structure,* ended a generally skeptical appraisal by suggesting that a "signalling system which does not involve a vocal-auditory channel ... lacks a crucial design-feature of human language."[6] What brought about this extraordinarily blinkered understanding of language?

To ask why sign language was devalued in the twentieth century begs a related question: why was sign language valued and considered worthy of study in the nineteenth? In many ways, the vocabulary and concerns of nineteenth-century sign language scholars appear remarkably similar to those of today. Then as now they argued that sign language was a "natural" language, explored how and to what extent signed language differed from spoken, examined the role of iconicity versus arbitrariness, and debated whether the original language of humanity might have been gestural. The presuppositions, premises, and cultural concerns that they brought to their work, however, were far different from those of researchers today. Even when they reached similar conclusions, the significance and implications of those conclusions were profoundly different.

Linguists today speak of signed languages—American Sign Language, British Sign Language, French Sign Language, etc.—as "natural languages," meaning that they evolved within specific communities and are creations of culture and history, as opposed to such artificial languages as Esperanto, computer languages, or signed English systems. They dismiss as a popular misconception the common belief that there is one universal sign language. Nineteenth-century teachers, on the other hand, did not speak of "sign language," but rather of "*the* sign language." Sign language for them was a universal language that appeared among diverse peoples throughout history. The sign language of American deaf people was the same as that used by the British, Russian, or Chinese deaf, or by American Indians. While they were well aware of the differences among them, they saw these as indications of superficial variations in usage rather than distinct languages.[7]

Like modern linguists, manualist teachers also described sign language as "natural." They did not mean to suggest as linguists do today that it was similar to spoken languages, however, but rather to differentiate it from spoken languages which were seen as artificial and particularistic. Sign language was a natural language because it was universal. Spoken languages were, for them, arbitrary, usually possessing no natural connection to the ideas they expressed. In the distant past words were mimetic, and a few words still retained qualities of onomatopoeia, but most had long ago slipped their moorings with reality and were free-floating signifiers, owing their significance merely to social agreement. Sign language, on the other hand, was a direct expression of nature. Thomas H. Gallaudet explained that the "natural language of signs" was "not an arbitrary, conventional language," but rather "a picture-like and symbolical language, calling up the objects and ideas which it is designed to denote in a portraying and suggestive way, which no oral, written or printed language can do." Sign language, in short, "copies nature."[8] For Benjamin Pettingill, a teacher at the Pennsylvania school, sign language was "a more natural, a more expressive, and, in many respects, a better language" because as "representatives of external and internal nature," gesture signs were "self-interpreting and universally intelligible."[9]

Luzerne Rae, a teacher at Hartford, illustrated how meaning was inherent in visual signs: "a straight line, whether traced on the earth or gestured in the air," is understood everywhere to signify "moral rectitude," while a crooked one stands for the opposite. Such signs, like facial expressions, were universally understood, he explained. Conversely, words typically had "no significance whatever, in themselves alone," and were "to all intents and purposes no better than arbitrary." People learned the words of arbitrary spoken languages only through the use of natural signs: "you pronounce to me, for example, the word aversion. I can get no hint at all in regard to your meaning, until you add the natural sign of the word, which is, the turning away from an object with an expression of dislike upon the countenance." Even after word meanings were learned, they still required the mediation of natural signs for communication, for a word "suggests some natural sign" which we see in our mind's eye.[10] The gap that existed between reality and arbitrary words could be bridged only by natural signs.

We know from contemporary descriptions that the sign language of deaf people in the nineteenth century was composed mostly of signs that we would today describe as arbitrary. It is also clear that sign language required years to learn, that it was not transparent to any who had not learned it, and that it was a highly complex and sophisticated language. Why, then, such descriptions as natural, universally intelligible, and self-interpreting? The manualist teachers of the nineteenth century made a distinction of degree, not of kind, between the complex sign language found in their schools and the simple pantomime of which anyone was capable. Sign language was based upon "imitation and not upon any fixed and arbitrary standard," explained J. A. Ayres, and as such "its precision depends in a great degree upon the skill of him who uses it."[11] The unskilled used "simple, uncultivated signs" while those adept in the art used "cultivated signs." While the latter were more complex and less transparent than pantomime, they were still natural so long as they had been originally derived from pantomimic signs. Pettingill explained that while "all of our signs have some intrinsic significance," nevertheless "for the sake of dispatch we often abridge our signs in conversing with adepts." This abridgement, "of course, diminishes their intelligibility and expressiveness to outside observers who are not familiar with the sign-language."[12] So long as abridged or cultivated signs could be traced to iconic origins, they remained in essence natural. Thus, even if most people could not understand sign language as used by adepts, it remained natural because it always had the potential to be expanded back to its original, more elaborated, and pantomimic form.

This explains why sign language was "self-interpreting," and it explains nineteenth-century accounts of deaf people conversing in "natural signs" with American Indians or with deaf people from foreign lands.[13] It explains how, in 1839, Gallaudet conversed with the Amistad rebels, the Africans who revolted and brought the Cuban slave ship *Amistad* to the northeastern United States where they were imprisoned to await trial. Gallaudet visited them in the prison at Hartford, where he reportedly "carried on a conversation of considerable length" through "natural signs," eliciting from them "information respecting the families they had left in Africa, besides some particulars of their own recent history."[14] These conversations occurred not in sign language per se but by using the expanded or elaborated form of the signs—that is, through the practiced and skillful use of pantomime. The manualist description of sign language as natural arose, then, not from any transparent iconicity in the language as typically used, but from a belief that, unlike words, most signs retained essential ties with their iconic origins.

Sign language syntax was also thought to be more natural than that of spoken languages. The Reverend Collins Stone, a teacher at the Hartford school, explained that sign language followed the natural order of thought rather than the "inverted and arbitrary forms of written language." Rather than "the subject coming first, and the action, quality and object following," as in artificial languages, when the deaf person sought to express something, "the object first attracts his attention, then its qualities, and afterward the other circumstances connected with it." Consequently, when a deaf person attempted to write English, "unless great care is exercised, his sentences are constantly running in the order of his thoughts."[15]

As Benjamin Talbot, superintendent of the Iowa school, explained, the "order of signs . . . is really not the order of language, but the order of thought." For example, unlike English, in sign language the adjective usually followed the noun. Can anyone, Talbot asked, "think of such a thing as a black?" Before thinking of a quality one must first conceive of the object it describes, he insisted. "You can readily think of a black horse, a black table, or a black hat; but the idea of that something, whatever it is, necessarily comes first."[16] The Reverend John Keep of the Kentucky school provided another example: "Suppose, for example, that I strike a board. I do not strike the vacant air, seeing nothing, and having no idea of anything before me, until after I have struck, when, suddenly, a board rises up to receive the blow. I first see the board, I intend to strike it, and, with it before my sight, I strike. In exact conformity with this necessary order of nature and of fact, in describing this in signs, I say, 'I a board strike.'"[17]

Another indication of the naturalness of sign language was its facility for the expression of emotion. The enthusiasm for sign language in the nineteenth century in part was a reflection of a culture that valued depth of feeling and sincerity of emotion. Evangelicals of the Second Great Awakening, the evangelical revival that swept antebellum America, considered emotions rather than thought to be crucial to religious experience and conversion. Moreover, they believed reason alone was too feeble to restrain the dangerous weakness and desires to which humans were prone.[18] Already in the eighteenth century, "New Light" evangelicals were known and condemned by their traditional Calvinist critics for immoderate displays of emotion. As a disapproving observer of an evangelical preacher wrote, "He began in a low and moderate Strain . . . but towards the Close of the Sermon . . . he began to raise his Voice, and to use many extravagant Gestures."[19] By the mid-nineteenth century this style of preaching had become commonplace. Most teachers in the schools for the deaf were themselves evangelical Protestants, a great many were ministers, and they generally shared these values. For Gallaudet, for example, abstract knowledge was not the primary goal of education; rather, "the heart is the principal thing which we must aim to reach."[20] Lucius Woodruff of the American Asylum echoed Gallaudet, insisting that "the heart is the noblest part of human nature, giving direction and imparting energy to the other faculties ... all education should begin here." For Harvey Peet, head of the New York school, it was the "emotions which make man superior to the brute creation."[21]

Gallaudet and his fellow ministers and teachers also shared the long-standing belief that gestures better expressed emotion, and speech the intellect. Harvey Peet explained that "a language of articulation and intonation wakes sympathetic chords in the ear and brain; a language of gesture and expression equally speaks to the sympathies." Speech was linked to "reason," gesture to "the passions."[22] While manualists disagreed on whether oral language better communicated abstraction, all maintained that sign language was superior for the expression of the emotion; as Gallaudet put it, "the heart claims as its peculiar and appropriate language that of the eye and countenance, of the attitudes, movements, and gestures of the body."[23] Manualist teachers differed from other ministers in that they wielded a language of gestures rather than merely supplemental gestures, but in either case gestures were thought capable of expressing emotion more forcefully, and of arousing greater emotion, than could be done by voice alone.

Manualist teachers believed that the benefits of sign language could extend far beyond the school for the deaf, even in nonreligious contexts. In the academies and colleges they attended before becoming teachers, oratory was considered to be at the heart of education and civic life. Their classical education taught them that the power to move audiences was outward evidence of inner virtue, and they maintained that American oratory would be much improved if augmented by gestural signs. "How much greater power their eloquence would have," Gallaudet suggested in 1848, if only orators would "act out [their] thoughts as well as speak them." It was "greatly to be regretted," he believed, "that much more of this visual language does not accompany the oral ... in all our social intercourse."[24] The Reverend J. Addison Cary, of the New York Institution, contended in 1850 that sign language was already becoming familiar to the public through "its exhibition in the classroom and on public occasions," and that the "art of public speaking has been and will be still further improved by the cultivation of the language of signs."[25] Gallaudet also claimed wider benefits than the enrichment of American oratory. If sign language were "vastly more cultivated than it is, and employed in the early training of children and youth in our families, schools, and other seminaries of learning," he wrote, "we should find its happy results in all the processes of education, on all occasions where the persuasions of eloquence are employed, and in the higher zest which would be given to the enjoyments of social life." The language of signs could "supply the deficiencies of our oral intercourse [and] perfect the communion of one soul with another," bringing "kindred souls into a much more close and conscious communion than . . . speech can possibly do."[26]

The historian Karen Halttunen has described a popular antebellum set of values that she calls the "cult of sincerity." Antebellum advice books admonished their readers to cultivate "a faithful correspondence between the heart and the lips, the feelings and the words, the inward consciousness and the outward expression." True sincerity required that "every aspect of social behavior should transparently display the contents of the heart." This emphasis on honest and transparent expression arose from anxiety over the growing anonymity of urban life and the concomitant breakdown of traditional forms of social control. One advice manual described the countenance of Adam before the Fall as "the tablet upon which all he felt and thought was written"; he would have felt "no need of oral speech for the conveyance of his ideas," for the "wonderful play of the innumerable muscles of his face and lips" were in "perfect correspondence with all his feelings and thoughts, and gave to them all full and beautiful utterance."[27] Personal beauty likewise depended upon a transparent honesty, according to Halttunen, for as women's magazines advised, "in a woman of true beauty, 'the body charms because the soul is seen.'" This attitude made popular a style of dress intended to "reveal the feelings of its wearer" and to "reveal her soul." Conversely, the use of cosmetics was condemned as an attempt at disguise or misrepresentation. True beauty in a woman "was not the deceitful product of surface work, but the transparent outward reflection of her inner mind and heart; she was beautiful because she was sincere."[28]

These values, often the very words, were repeated in manualist descriptions of sign language. As Gallaudet phrased it, sign language encouraged the "transparent beaming forth of the soul." Sign language was the "beautiful language of signs" because it gave people "the power to have the inmost workings of their souls . . . *beam out* through the eye, countenance, attitude, movement and gesture." Those who would learn sign language had to be prepared "to have the soul speak out freely in their looks and movements."[29] The Reverend J. Addison Cary, a teacher at the New York school, urged ministers to make use of "the eye, the face, head, arms, hands, in short, the whole person, and not merely the *tongue,* to indicate the operations of the ethereal agent within." Words alone could not inspire love nor sway the heart; but if the "interior spirit finds an index in the hand and eye," he wrote, "and paints upon the countenance as upon canvas its minutest conceptions," then, while "sparks radiate from every part . . . will he, filled with the spiritual fire of heaven, be radiant with a divine light, and emit an influence on all assembled, at once thrilling and irresistible."[30]

God and Nature were inextricably bound up together in antebellum thought, and Evangelicalism was therefore closely associated with nineteenth-century Romanticism. Just as Evangelicals saw the emotions as the key to understanding the glories of God, so did Romantic writers portray emotional response as the key to understanding the beauty of nature.[31] Manualists admired sign language for its beauty, one of the highest ideals not only of Romantics but of the ancient philosophers they studied in college. They avowed that "for beauty and effective expression it is not surpassed by any language ever yet spoken or used."[32] Sign language was as often referred to as the "beautiful language of signs" as it was the "noble language of signs"; both were stock phrases in the manualist rhetoric and they signified similar values. Affirming that "the heart is the noblest part of human nature," Lucius Woodruff praised the "power over the hearts of our pupils which this beautiful language gives us."[33] When they spoke of sign language as a "singularly beautiful and impressive language," and claimed that it possessed "a beauty and charm not surpassed by the painted landscape or the scenery of the stage," they were paying the highest compliments they knew how to bestow.[34] The Reverend Henry B. Camp wondered "whether the language of *signs* or of the *articulate voice* would, in itself, be preferable, so graphic and beautiful is the former in comparison with the latter."[35] Gallaudet believed sign language to be so precious that no one should teach deaf children "if he does not cherish and cultivate it to the highest degree of force, beauty and grace which it is possible for him to reach."[36]

Sign language as deaf people use it employs not just the hands but the face, and before the scientific acceptance of evolutionary theory in the late nineteenth century, it was commonly believed that the ability to consciously use facial expression was uniquely human. Sir Charles Bell, for example, author of *The Anatomy and Philosophy of Expression* in 1806 and foremost authority of his time on the physical expression of emotions, expressed the common creationist belief that humans were created with specific muscles intended for the sole purpose of expressing emotional states, a gift from the Creator to permit human souls to communicate with one another unimpeded by artificial convention.[37] The manualist educator Charles Turner was therefore in the mainstream when he claimed that "man alone possesses the distinctive faculty of *expression*." His observation that facial expression was "an indispensable concomitant" to sign language, and that sign language owed "its main force and beauty to the accompanying power of expression," was intended as high praise.[38] Gallaudet similarly marveled that "the Creator furnished us ... an eye and countenance, as variable in their expressions as are all the internal workings of the soul."[39] The expressions of the face, as a means of communicating feelings and thoughts, were seen as both distinctly human and wonderfully eloquent. Teachers of this generation, for example, delighted in telling of sign masters who could recount Biblical tales using only facial expression so skillfully that deaf audiences could identify the stories.[40]

Manualists also believed that sign language was natural in the sense that it was closer to God—this they meant quite literally, for they believed that sign language was the original language of humanity. During the eighteenth and nineteenth centuries the origin of language had become an important topic of philosophical discussion in both Europe and America, and many speculated that humans had used gestural language before turning to spoken language.[41] The teachers in the schools for the deaf interpreted this theory in terms of biblical history. According to the creationist narrative of nineteenth-century America, humanity had come into the world in essentially its present form but had degenerated morally and intellectually since the Creation. The theory that sign language preceded speech was seen therefore as an indication of its superiority over modern, degenerate languages. The past implied superiority, not inferiority for them. Sign language, as the first language, was a gift from God, while speech was a product of human invention after the Fall. Neither natural nor a direct expression of the soul or of the heart, speech was instead an expression of the intellect, inherently more suited to falsehood, dissimulation, and artificial sophistication. Speech was degenerate language.[42]

This complex constellation of meanings associated with the notion that sign language was natural would take on much different, indeed nearly opposite, significance in the scientific age of the late nineteenth and early twentieth century. If to the earlier generation "original language" had meant "closer to the Creation," in the early Darwinian age, when evolution was usually interpreted as simple progress akin to climbing a ladder, it meant merely "closer to the apes." Humanity had risen from a low point rather than fallen from a high estate, and was the end product of history rather than its beginning. Antiquity was no mark of honor, but rather one of inferiority. Sign language was transformed from a noble and beautiful language into a language low on the evolutionary scale, antedating even the most "savage" spoken language. Nature came to be seen as something that humans were trying to transcend. Emotions were no longer the higher and finer expressions of the human soul, but rather the involuntary outpourings of humanity's more primitive, more animal nature.

Language scholars began to promulgate a kind of "linguistic Darwinism," arguing that inferior languages were periodically replaced by superior ones in the "struggle for existence." Gestural communication had suffered an early defeat in that struggle. The American philologist William Dwight Whitney, for example, believed that human communication once consisted of "an inferior system of . . . tone, gesture, and grimace," and it was through the "process of natural selection and survival of the fittest that the voice has gained the upper hand." The British anthropologist Edward B. Tylor noted that "savage and half-civilized races accompany their talk with expressive pantomime much more than nations of higher culture," indicating to him that "in the early stages of the development of language, ... gesture had an importance as an element of expression, which in conditions of highly-organized language it has lost." Garrick Mallery of the Smithsonian Institution, an expert on American Indian sign languages, believed that the "most notable criterion" for distinguishing between "civilized" and "savage" peoples was to be found in the "copiousness and precision of oral language, and in the unequal survival of the communication by gesture signs which, it is believed, once universally prevailed."[43]

The language used by deaf people was increasingly associated with "savages," who themselves had lost the aura of "nobility" that earlier Romantics had attributed to them and were now seen merely as losers in the evolutionary struggle. Tylor wrote of "the gesture-signs of savages and deaf-mutes." Darwin referred to the gestural communication "used by the deaf and dumb and by savages." Mallery suggested that "troglodyte" humans communicated "precisely as Indians or deaf-mutes" do today. A contributor to *Science* suggested that sign language was relied upon by "the less cultured tribes, while the spoken language is seen in its highest phase among the more civilized," adding that sign language was used "in the training of the deaf and dumb." A *New York Evening Post* article on the gestures of Italian immigrants noted that "among most savages the language of gesture is extensive," that this was commonly taken as a "sign of feeble intellectual power," and that deaf people communicated in the same way.[44]

Educators of the deaf began to echo the same ideas, saying that sign language was "characteristic of tribes low in the scale of development," and that the sign language of deaf people "resembles the languages of the North American Indian and the Hottentot of South Africa." They began to argue that "as man emerged from savagery he discarded gestures for the expression of his ideas," and that it was about time that deaf people discarded them as well. They avowed that as spoken language was the "crown of history," to permit deaf children the use of sign language was to "push them back in the world's history to the infancy of our race."[45] Sign language suggested not only the lower human but the nonhuman as well. Critics charged that sign language was nothing more than "a set of monkey-like grimaces and antics," told deaf students that "you look like monkeys when you make signs," and that "it is apish to talk on the fingers." They scoffed that "these signs can no more be called a language than the different movements of a dog's tail and ears which indicate his feelings."[46]

The significance of the common notion that gestures were more expressive of emotion, and speech more suited for the intellect, was now much changed. Unlike the manualists who had believed that it was the emotions that set humans apart from the animals, to the oralist generation it was the ability to reason, and to express reason through speech, that distinguished the human species from all others. If reason was distinctly human, emotion came to be seen as a mere holdover from our animalistic or primitive past, part of our "natural" inheritance. Darwin associated lack of emotional control with childhood, insanity, and the lower stages of evolutionary development, contending also that the expression of an emotion by gesture intensifies it, while control of the gesture controls the emotion. A writer in *Science* wrote of students at a school for the deaf as "inmates making faces, throwing their hands and arms up and down. . . . The effect is as if a sane man were suddenly put amidst a crowd of lunatics." Given the theory of the time that insanity was a kind of reversion to an earlier stage of evolution, the metaphors were closely related.[47]

The changed emotional style of the late nineteenth century (heralding the attitude of cool detachment that became standard for twentieth-century Americans) was reflected in an increasing disdain for the romantic temperament of France, home of the "manual method." Caroline Yale of the Clarke School pointed out with ill-concealed disdain that "this sign language was used by the French for years, and possibly suited them temperamentally."[48] Conversely, oralist teachers spoke of their admiration for Germany, the undisputed leader in scientific endeavor and intellectual center for the oralist cause—just as American scholars of the time studied in Germany to acquire prestigious advanced degrees, so did oralist educators make pilgrimages to Germany to study technique.[49] Oralists made sure to remind their listeners at every opportunity of the respective points of origin of the two methods. In letters and articles Alexander Graham Bell took pains to mention that the sign method was "known as the French system while the oral method was known as the German system." Oralists took to referring to sign language as "the De l'Epée sign language."[50] Sign language, they implied, was the invention of a nation associated in America with effete emotionalism, romanticism, and, like sign language, glories belonging to a past age.

An important change in attitudes toward facial expression was also underway, signaled by Darwin's *The Expression of the Emotions in Man and Animals*. Expression, for Darwin, was not a God-given gift, a mark of humanity, nor the outward expression of the unique workings of the human soul, as it had been for the manualist generations. Darwin convincingly demonstrated that humans shared many expressions in common with animals, and that the origins of human expression were to be found in their animal ancestors.[51] In short, facial expression was no longer distinctly human, but, like gesture, a mere vestige of our animal past.

Writers for more popular audiences were soon commenting on the "special facility" that apes have for "the more lowly forms of making one's self understood"—that is, the "gesture-language" and the "facial muscles as a means of expression."[52] Teachers of the deaf quickly picked up on the new knowledge as well, and attached their own special significance to it. An anonymous letter to the *American Annals of the Deaf*, signed "A Disgusted Pedagogue," criticized the use of sign language in the schools because it caused teachers to "grimace and gesticulate and jump."[53] Advocates of pure oralism ridiculed signers for their "monkey-like grimaces."[54] Facial expression and gestures both were called the "rudimentary and lower parts of language," as opposed to speech, the "higher and finer part."[55]

In this climate, interest in sign language waned considerably. As a relic of a stage of development left behind, sign language seemed to have little relevance to the modern world. Research into sign language became mere antiquarianism, of no pressing interest to a progressing world. Throughout the twentieth century, sign language remained a quaint curiosity, something for Boy Scouts to play at along with the making of moccasins and campfires, and a crutch for deaf people who had failed at oral communication, but not a subject for serious study.

And so it remained—until the work of William Stokoe. Interest in other sign languages revived at about the same time, indicating a changing cultural climate in regard to the body, emotional expression, and the question of "primitiveness" versus "civilization." Emotional expression was once again encouraged, a sign of mental health rather than the opposite, and a characteristic of advanced human beings. Psychotherapy shifted from an emphasis on the intellect to the expression of repressed emotion. The fine arts and music began to favor warm expression over cool detachment, and both dance and theater experimented with forms that celebrated the natural and unadorned body.

It was Stokoe's great achievement to see in American Sign Language the necessary elements of a true language—a natural language, in the modern sense of the word—and to resurrect the scholarly study of signed language. Stokoe's work revived sign language research as a legitimate field of inquiry. Today, there is still considerable hostility toward sign language. It would be of more than academic interest to know if those parents and teachers of deaf children who are most averse to sign language share any particular cultural beliefs in common. That is, if a culturally dominant set of attitudes toward the body, toward the place of humanity in the greater scheme of things, toward gesture and emotional display, were behind the turn against sign language at the start of the last century, are similar sets of attitudes (or analogous clusters of different attitudes) behind the resistance of a minority today? And if those attitudes should gain prominence, what then might become of deaf education, of sign language research, and of sign language programs in our universities? And how can we guard against another turn of the cultural wheel? How can we ensure that another Stokoe, a hundred years from now, will not have to start again?

Notes

1. See Edward Miner Gallaudet, "Our Profession," *American Annals of the Deaf* [hereafter cited as *Annals*] 37 (January 1892): 1–5; Edward P. Clarke, "An Analysis of the Schools and Instructors of the Deaf in the United States," *Annals* 45 (April 1900): 235–36.

2. A. L. Kroeber, "Sign Language Inquiry," *International Journal of American Linguistics* 24 (January 1958): 1–19, quote from p. 2; C. F. Voegelin, "Sign Language Analysis, On One Level or Two," *International Journal of American Linguistics* 24 (January 1958): 71–77; La Mont West, "The Sign Language: An Analysis" (Ph.D. diss., Indiana University, 1960). Mervyn Meggitt, "Sign Language Among the Walbiri of Central Australia," *Oceana* 25 (September/December 1954): 2. See also the two-volume collection of reprinted articles on aboriginal sign languages, D. Jean Umiker-Sebeok and Thomas A. Sebeok, eds., *Aboriginal Sign-Languages of the Americas and Australia* (New York: Plenum Press, 1978).

3. C. P. Mountford, "Gesture Language of the Ngada Tribe of the Warburton Ranges, Western Australia," *Oceana* 9 (December 1938): 152–55. Paul C. Ziemke, "The Indian Sign Language," *Tennessee Archaeologist* 3 (1947): 30–31. Alfred Still, *Communication Through the Ages: From Sign Language to Television* (New York: Murray Hill, 1946).

4. N. D. Wijesekera, "Sign Language in Ancient Ceylon," *Man* 45 (March/April 1945): 46–47.

5. William Tomkins, *Universal Indian Sign Language of the Plains Indians of North America* (New York: Dover Publications, 1969 [1929]). J. Schuyler Long's dictionary of American Sign Language, *The Sign Language: A Manual of Signs* (Washington, D.C.: Press of Gibson Brothers, 1910) was a descriptive work rather than an analytical one, and while he evinced respect for the language, Long nevertheless felt compelled to point out that it "is manifestly imperfect when compared with written or spoken language." Long also "strongly condemned" the "haphazard, slipshod manner of using signs," by which he meant ASL syntax, and urged that "the English order should be followed as nearly as possible."

6. Herbert Landar, review of *Sign Language Structure: An Outline of the Visual Communication Systems of the American Deaf* by William Stokoe, *Language* 37 (April/June 1961): 271.

7. See, for example, Thomas H. Gallaudet, "The Natural Language of Signs," *Annals* 1 (October 1847): 59; Collins Stone, "Address Upon the History and Methods of Deaf Mute Instruction," *Annals* 14 (April 1869): 107–8.

8. Stone, "Address Upon the History," 107; J. C. Covell, "The Nobility, Dignity, and Antiquity of the Sign Language," *Proceedings of the Seventh Convention of American Instructors of the Deaf, 1870* (Indianapolis, 1870), 135; R. H. Kinney, "A Few Thoughts on the Universality and Power of the Language of Signs," *Proceedings of the Fifth Convention of American Instructors of the Deaf, 1858* (Jacksonville, Ill., 1858), 85; Thomas H. Gallaudet, "Natural Language of Signs," 58, and "The Natural Language of Signs—II" *Annals* 1 (January 1848): 91.

9. Benjamin D. Pettingill, "The Sign Language," *Annals* 18 (January 1873): 6, 10–11.

10. Luzerne Rae, "The Philosophical Basis of Language," *Proceedings of the Third Convention of American Instructors of the Deaf, 1853* (Columbus, 1853), 157–62.

11. J. A. Ayres, "An Inquiry Into the Extent to Which the Misfortune of Deafness May be Alleviated," *Annals* 1 (April 1848): 223.

12. Pettingill, "Sign Language," 3.

13. See, for examples, "Institution Items: Pennsylvania Institution," *Annals* 19 (January 1874): 48–49; Warring Wilkinson, "The Development of Speech and of the Sign-Language," *Annals* 26 (January 1881): 171; Garrick Mallery, "The Gesture Speech of Man," *Annals* 27 (April 1882): 75; Stone, "Address upon the History," 107–8; William Turner, "Discussion," *Proceedings of the Third Convention of American Instructors of the Deaf, 1853* (Columbus, 1853), 73.

14. Lucius Woodruff, "Primary Instruction of the Deaf and Dumb," *Annals* 1 (October 1847): 54.

15. Collins Stone, "On the Difficulties Encountered by the Deaf and Dumb in Learning Language," *Proceedings of the Third Convention of American Instructors of the Deaf, 1853* (Columbus, 1853), 129, 135; see also Turner, "Discussion," 72–73; Harvey P. Peet, "Preliminary Remarks—Signs Versus Articulation," *National Deaf-Mute Gazette* 2 (February 1868): 6. Woodruff, "Primary Instruction," 51–52.

16. Benjamin Talbot, "Discussion," *Proceedings of the Seventh Convention of American Instructors of the Deaf, 1870* (Indianapolis, 1870), 60.

17. John R. Keep, "Natural Signs—Shall They be Abandoned?" *Annals* 16 (January 1871): 22.

18. Jean Matthews, *Toward a New Society: American Thought and Culture, 1800–1830* (Boston: Twayne Publishers, 1991), 42.

19. Robert A. Gross, *The Minutemen and Their World* (New York: Hill and Wang, 1976), 20.

20. Gallaudet, "Natural Language of Signs," 88–89.

21. Lucius H. Woodruff, "Moral Education of the Deaf and Dumb," *Annals* 3 (January 1851): 66. Harvey Peet, *Proceedings of the Ninth Convention of American Instructors of the Deaf, 1878* (Columbus, 1879), 300.

22. Harvey P. Peet, "Notions of the Deaf and Dumb Before Instruction," *Annals* 8 (October 1855): 9.

23. Gallaudet, "Natural Language of Signs," 88–89.

24. Gallaudet, "Natural Language of Signs—II," 80.

25. J. Addison Cary, "On Significant Action in the Pulpit," *Proceedings of the First Convention of American Instructors of the Deaf, 1850* (New York, 1850), 175.

26. Gallaudet, "Natural Language of Signs—II," 80–81, 92.

27. See Karen Halttunen, *Confidence Men and Painted Women: A Study of Middle-Class Culture in America, 1830–1870* (New Haven, Conn.: Yale University Press, 1982), 41–42, 51–52, 60.

28. Halttunen, *Confidence Men,* 71, 83, 89–90.

29. "Natural Language of Signs—II," 80–81, 92.

30. Cary, "On Significant Action," 171–75.

31. On the convergence of nineteenth-century Protestantism with Romanticism, see Perry Miller, *Errand Into the Wilderness* (Cambridge: Harvard University Press, Belknap Press, 1956), 208–11.

32. Turner, "Discussion," 73.

33. Woodruff, "Moral Education," 66, 69; see also Gallaudet, "Natural Language of Signs—II," 93.

34. Gallaudet, "Natural Language of Signs—II," 88–89; Cary, "On Significant Action," 171; see also J. Addison Cary, "Deaf-Mute Idioms," *Proceedings of the Second Convention of American Instructors of the Deaf, 1851* (Hartford, Conn., 1851), 103.

35. Henry B. Camp, "Claims of the Deaf and Dumb Upon Public Sympathy and Aid," *Annals* 1 (July 1848): 211.

36. Gallaudet, "Natural Language of Signs—II," 89; see also J. Van Nostrand, "On the Cultivation of the Sign Language," *Proceedings of the Third Convention of American Instructors of the Deaf* (Columbus, 1853), 43; see also Camp, "Claims of the Deaf," 211.

37. For a review of nineteenth-century writings on expression, see the introduction to Charles Darwin, *The Expression of the Emotions in Man and Animals,* (Chicago: University of Chicago Press, 1965); Sir Charles Bell, *The Anatomy and Philosophy of Expression as Connected with the Fine Arts* (London: George Bell and Sons, 1885 [1806]), 1–26; Gallaudet, "Natural Language of Signs—II," 80; see also Robert J. Richards, *Darwin and the Emergence of Evolutionary Theories of Mind and Behavior* (Chicago: University of Chicago Press, 1987), 230–34.

38. Charles P. Turner, "Expression," *Annals* 1 (January 1848): 77.

39. Gallaudet, "Natural Language of Signs—II," 81.

40. See, for example, Turner, "Expression," 77–78.

41. Gordon W. Hewes, "Primate Communication and the Gestural Origin of Language," *Current Anthropology* 14 (February/April 1973): 5; Alf Sommerfelt, "The Origin of Language: Theories and Hypotheses," *Journal of World History* 1 (April 1954): 886–892; James H. Stam, *Inquiries into the Origin of Language: The*

Fate of a Question (New York: Harper and Row, 1976); Renate Fischer, "Language of Action," in Fischer and Lane, eds., *Looking Back: A Reader on the History of the Deaf Community and Their Sign Languages* (Hamburg: Signum, 1993), 429–55.

42. Pettingill, "The Sign-Language," 9; Remi Valade, "The Sign Language in Primitive Times," *Annals* 18 (January 1873): 31; Peet, "Notions," 10; Covell, "Nobility, Dignity, and Antiquity," 133–36.

43. William Dwight Whitney, *The Life and Growth of Language: An Outline of Linguistic Science* (New York: D. Appleton and Co., 1876), 291; Edward B. Tylor, *Researches into the Early History of Mankind* (New York: Henry Holt and Co., 1878 [London, 1865]), 15, 44, 77–78; Garrick Mallery, "The Gesture Speech of Man," *Annals* 27 (April 1882): 69; Garrick Mallery, *Introduction to the Study of Sign Language Among the North American Indians as Illustrating the Gesture Speech of Mankind* (Washington, D.C. 1880), reprinted in D. Jean Umiker-Sebeok and Thomas A. Sebeok, eds., *Aboriginal Sign-Languages of the Americas and Australia*, vol. 1 (New York: Plenum Press, 1978), 13.

44. Edward B. Tylor, "On the Origin of Language," *Fortnightly Review* 4 (April 15, 1886): 547. Charles Darwin, *The Expression of the Emotions in Man and Animals* (Chicago: University of Chicago Press, 1965), 61. Mallery, *Introduction*, 12–14. Joseph Jastrow, "The Evolution of Language," *Science* 7 (June 18, 1886): 556. Ernest Ingersoll, "Gestures in Mulberry Bend," *New York Evening Post* (July 10, 1897): 12. The reporter was noting a common attitude, but he himself disagreed with the modern disdain for gesture.

45. J. C. Gordon, "Dr. Gordon's Report," *Association Review* 1 (December 1899): 206; Gardiner G. Hubbard, "Proceedings of the American [Social] Science Association," *National Deaf Mute Gazette* 2 (January 1868): 5; J. D. Kirkhuff, "Superiority of the Oral Method," *Silent Educator* 3 (January 1892): 139; Susanna E. Hull, "Do Persons Born Deaf Differ Mentally from Others Who Have the Power of Hearing?" *Annals* 22 (October 1877): 236.

46. Pettingill, "The Sign-Language," 4; Sarah Harvey Porter, "The Suppression of Signs by Force," *Annals* 39 (June 1894): 171; R. W. Dodds, "The Practical Benefits of Methods Compared," *Annals* 44 (February 1899): 124; John Dutton Wright, "Speech and Speech-Reading for the Deaf," *Century Magazine* (January 1897): 332–34.

47. Jastrow, "Evolution of Language," 556. B. Engelsman, "Deaf Mutes and their Instruction," *Science* 16 (October 17, 1890): 220. Darwin, *Expression of the Emotions,* 154, 365. See also Sander L. Gilman, *Disease and Representation: Images of Illness from Madness to AIDS* (Ithaca: Cornell University Press, 1988), 129–32.

48. Caroline A. Yale, *Years of Building: Memories of a Pioneer in a Special Field of Education* (New York: Dial Press, 1931), 48.

49. Jane L. Russel, "Observation of Oral Work in German Schools," *Proceedings of the Fifteenth Convention of American Instructors of the Deaf, 1898* (Washington, 1899), 153.

50. "Teaching Deaf Mutes," *Detroit Tribune*, 9 March 1895, and "Save the Deaf School," *Daily Eastern Argus*, 19 January 1894 and 2 March 1894, in Alexander Graham Bell Family Papers, Library of Congress, container 178, Deaf-Day Schools, Michigan file. Z. F. Westervelt, "The Colloquial Use of English by the Deaf," *Proceedings of the Twelfth Convention of American Instructors of the Deaf, 1890* (New York, 1890), 113.

51. Darwin, *Expression*, 10.

52. Jastrow, "Evolution of Language," 555–56.

53. Anon., "The Perversity of Deaf-Mutism," *Annals* 18 (Oct. 1873): 263.

54. Cited by Pettingill, "The Sign-Language," 4.

55. Samuel Gridley Howe, et al., *Second Annual Report of the Board of State Charities* (Boston, 1866), liii–liv.

2

Historical Observations on the Relationship Between Research on Sign Languages and Language Origins Theory

Adam Kendon

The Neapolitan philosopher, Giambattista Vico, in his *Scienza Nuova* of 1744, formulated what was, at that time, a highly original theory of the origin of language, according to which articulate spoken language had its origins, first of all, in the human capacity for imagination or *fantasia*. Through the *fantasia*, images were created which, at first, were transformed into actions that represented them. These mimetic actions were either gestural or they were inscribed in sand, on rock, or on some other surface, and it was only later that a connection was established between visual signs and aural forms, which then could become the beginnings of words. The further process, by which visual representations of the images created by the *fantasia* came to serve also as signs

---

A version of this chapter was presented to the Fifteenth Annual Meeting of the Language Origins Society, Naples, Italy, 2–6 July 1999.

for more general concepts or for other things than just themselves, came about through Metaphor.

Vico, thus, saw the linguistic sign as being derived by processes of metaphorical extension from representations of images created by the imagination that were primarily visual. These representations were either gestures or inscriptions. In the beginning, in Vico's view, humans were mute and communicated by gesture, not by speech. He writes, "The first language in the first mute times of the nations must have begun with signs, whether gestures or physical objects, which had natural relations to the ideas to be expressed" (401).[1]

In another passage he writes,

> The philosophers and philologists should all have begun to treat the origins of languages and letters from the following principles: (1) The first men of the gentile world conceived ideas of things by imaginative characters of animate and mute substances. (2) That they expressed themselves by means of gestures or physical objects which had natural relations with ideas; for example, three ears of grain, or acting as if swinging a scythe three times, to signify three years. (3) That they expressed themselves by a language with natural significations. (431)

Among the observations Vico adduces in support of his position are observations of "mutes" (as he calls them) who, as he says, "make themselves understood by gestures or objects that have natural relations with the ideas they wish to signify" (225). Thus deaf people and their signing was of great pertinence for him. He does not elaborate any observations on deaf signing, however, and his ideas about the origins of language did not, in his time, nor indeed until relatively recently, have wide impact (see Danesi 1993).

A more widely influential approach to the problem of language origins, which also regards the first form of language to be a form of action or gesture, also begins in the eighteenth century. Indeed, it begins in the same decade of that century in which Vico's book was published, but in Paris, and the philosopher dominating this beginning was John Locke. Here, the development of ideas about language origins began with such thinkers as Condillac and Diderot, who believed the phenomena of the gesturing of deaf people was of particular theoretical significance.

John Locke taught that all knowledge is derived only through the senses. This approach provided a starting point for a natural explanation of the origin of human nature, including the problem of the origin of language. One of the questions debated at that time was this: If all knowledge comes only through the senses, how is an individual's knowledge restricted if one or more of the senses are missing? Stated another way, Does a blind man's knowledge of objects perceived only through touch differ from the knowledge of another man who can only see? Those who were born deaf were of particular interest for they seemed to present a natural example of human beings restricted in the kinds of sensations they can receive. There was, accordingly, a great interest in deaf people and in the common observation that deaf people used gestures of all sorts to communicate.

Of particular relevance here is the work of Condillac. In his *Essay on the Origin of Human Knowledge* ([1756] 1971), which was written as an extension of ideas originally developed by John Locke, Condillac proposed that language begins when one human exploits the capacity of another to appreciate the *intent* that governs an action, such as a reach for a desired object. Thus, for Condillac, language began in the reciprocation of overt actions, making its first form a language of action. This led Condillac to write about the language of gesture, both as this was practiced in the pantomimes of antiquity and as it might be observed among deaf people.[2] Likewise of relevance here is some of the work of Denis Diderot, in particular his *Lettre sur les sourds et muets* ([1751] 1904), in which he argues that a man born deaf can develop a natural language of gesture. According to Diderot, study of this natural language, which had not been overlaid by the structures of a conventional language, could perhaps lead to an understanding of the natural progression of thought.

The *philosophes* belief that the gestural expressions of deaf people were truly symbolic representations that made possible the kinds of expression of thought that spoken language also made possible, led others, most notably Abbé Charles Michel de L'Epée, to recognize that these natural signs could be used to reach and to develop the *minds* of deaf children. Epée and his successor, Abbé Roch Ambroise Sicard, adapted and added to the signs already in use in Paris, creating a system of "methodical signs" through which they taught deaf students to read and write languages such as French and Latin (see Siegel 1969).

Thus gesture, in general, and signs, in particular, were established as legitimate and important objects of investigation because of the light their study could throw on the nature and origin of language and on the nature of the relationship between thought and expression. Interest in the idea of a universal language was widespread in the eighteenth century and, for a time, gesture and the signing of deaf people were seen as an ideal medium for the creation of such a language.[3] Sicard, for example, strongly advocated this.[4] Joseph-Marie Degerando, however, was critical of this idea. In a commentary on sign language (*Des signes et de l'art de penser*, Paris, 1800), he wrote that sign language, at least in the form advocated by Sicard (which required complex sequences of elementary signs to express complex ideas), could never become a universal language since, as soon as such sequences became abbreviated, as was inevitable, they lost all natural ties to their meanings and became forms with meanings established by convention. Because of this, sign language in one community would diverge from sign language in another community. This criticism notwithstanding, the idea that gesture language could form the basis for a universal language persisted for a long time.

By the end of the eighteenth century the importance of studying gesture and sign languages for a number of issues of theoretical importance was well established. This interest continued in the nineteenth century. Edward Tylor (1865) wrote a thorough review of what was then known of both the sign languages of deaf people and the gestural expressions reported by ethnographers and others from various parts of the world. He regarded gesture as important for what it can reveal about the way the human mind operates in creating symbols.

> The Gesture-language and Picture writing, insignificant as they are in practice in comparison with Speech and Phonetic writing, have this great claim to consideration, that we can really understand them

as thoroughly as perhaps we can understand anything, and by studying them we can realize to ourselves in some measure a condition of the human mind which underlies anything which has as yet been traced in even the lowest dialects of Language, if taken as a whole. Though, with the exception of words in which we can trace the effects either of direct emotion, as in interjections, or of imitative formation, as in 'peewit' or 'cuckoo,' we cannot at present tell by what steps man came to express himself in words, we can at least see how he still does come to express himself by signs and pictures, and so get some idea of this great movement, which no lower animal is known to have made or shown the least sign of making. (Tylor 1878, 15)

Later writers likewise studied gesture and sign languages for the insight they could provide on the fundamental process by which the act of signification came to be achieved. Garrick Mallery gathered a large amount of material on the sign languages used by the Plains Indians of North America. In his report he argues, citing numerous authorities, that there are strong reasons for believing that there is a deep, intimate, and ancient connection between gestures and words. This connection, he writes,

> was so early and intimate that gestures, in the wide sense indicated of presenting ideas under physical forms, had a direct formative effect on many words; that they exhibit the earliest condition of the human mind; are traced from the remotest antiquity among all people possessing records; are generally present in the savage stage of evolution; survive agreeably in the scenic pantomime, and still adhere to the ordinary speech of civilized man by motions of the face, hands, head and body, often involuntary, often purposely in illustration or for emphasis. ([1881] 1972, 285)

Mallery did not believe that the signs and gestures he described, whether for the Indians or for other groups, were primitive, for he recognized that they had undergone many changes since the first emergence of gesture languages. Nor did he argue that the extent to which gestures are used is necessarily connected to any lack in the development of articulated speech. He suggests, rather, that whether a group of people use gesture extensively or not "depends," as he puts it, "more on sociologic conditions of the speakers than upon the degree of copiousness of their oral speech" (Mallery [1881] 1972, 35).

Mallery argues, however, that expression in gesture is a fundamental aspect of the human language capacity, and as a part of this argument he draws in references to the signing of deaf people. It is interesting that he argues that the signs even of the most untutored native-born deaf-mutes are to be understood as constituting a "real language." The "conclusive proof" of this is that it is only through the medium of signs that such a person is capable of acquiring a highly developed language such as English or French. He points out, "no one can learn a foreign language unless he had some language of his own, whether by descent or acquisition, by which it could be translated, and such translation into the new language could not even be commenced unless the mind had been already in action and intelligently using the original language for that purpose" (Mallery [1881] 1972, 277).

Wilhelm Wundt, in the section of his monumental *Volkerpsychologie* ([1921] 1973) devoted to language, includes a whole chapter on gestures.[5] In this discussion, he surveys the various kinds of gesture languages, from the gesture language of deaf people to that found among the American Indians, as well as the elaborate gestures reported by Andrea de Jorio (1832) for the Neapolitans (which Mallery also quoted from extensively). Wundt offers a comprehensive classification of the various forms of gestural expression and an interesting and farsighted discussion of grammar and syntax in the sign languages of deaf people (this evidently in part based on his own observations). He concludes that "natural gestural communication" under the right conditions develops spontaneously and shows a fundamental similarity in modes of expression. Yet, at the same time, it can be modified both by the introduction of artificial forms and by the force of social tradition, so that in certain circumstances we may find systems of gestural communication in which forms exist that may no longer have evidence of their natural origin. Wundt says that "gestural communication" is a very incomplete form of language, but just for that reason it is "the most instructive form." He suggests that in its development it "represents . . . all the stages of man's intellectual evolution" ([1921] 1973, 148–49). Wundt believed that gestural expression had its beginnings in "expressive motions" but that it transformed into a socially organized system of expression. It is, thus, a kind of bridge between the biological and instinctive, and the developed forms of language. For this reason it is of particular importance to study it.

Over the period of a century and a half, from the middle of the eighteenth century until the beginning of the twentieth century, the importance of the study of gesture and sign languages for understanding the nature of language became well established, and the main outlines of its character as a mode of expression emerged. A consensus widely shared was that gesture, though it was not always seen as preceding speech as the first form of linguistic expression, nevertheless was thought to have led the way, in the sense that more elaborate forms of expression would have first developed gesturally.

In all of this, the signing of deaf people was seen as a crucial datum. From Vico in Naples and Condillac and Diderot in Paris, to Tylor in Oxford, Garrick Mallery in Washington, and Wundt in Leipzig, the signing of born-deaf people seemed proof of the point that linguistic expression was a natural and spontaneous feature of humans, that language in the first place was a matter of the imaginative creation of imagistic representations, and that the study of sign languages and gesture could show us how the acquisition or development of a form of language takes place. It was not that these modes of expression were seen as more primitive, but rather, as Wundt saw, that gestural communication could reveal, in a way that spoken expression could not, the various stages in the growth of a language. It was this, then, that made the study of gesture and sign language seem central to any attempt to elaborate a theory of language.

All this, then, was in place by the end of the nineteenth century. Yet it was then that attention turned away and development in the study of gesture and sign language came more or less to a halt. The promise that the study of gesture and sign language held out for the understanding of the nature and origin of language and the relationship between language and thought, appears to have been forgotten. It was not to be rediscovered until the second half of the twentieth century.

What caused this promise to be forgotten, or, neglected? Several factors were involved. First of all, the issue of how to account for the origin of language itself became something that serious scholars avoided discussing. It had become apparent that one man's speculations were as good as another's. As Tylor said, it was clear "that there is as little use to be a good reasoner when there are no facts to reason upon, as it is to be a good bricklayer when there are no bricks to build with" (1865, 56). By 1866 the Linguistics Society of Paris had written into its by-laws a ban on all papers on the subject of language origins, and the London Philological Society followed with much the same kind of ban in 1872 (Stam 1977).

Soon after this, signing as a medium of instruction for deaf students fell into disrepute, with the consequence that there was no further encouragement for the serious study of sign language. At the International Congress on Education of the Deaf in Milan in 1880 the proponents of using sign in deaf education were roundly defeated by the German oralist approach. According to Wundt, whereas the French approach of using sign was the more psychologically fitting, the oralist approach of the Germans was more ethical. It was argued very strongly that if deaf people could be taught to speak they could much more easily fit into everyday life than they could if they only used signs. This argument, combined with new methods based on a detailed analysis of processes of speech-articulation, which bore the prestige of high German science, was enough to carry the day (Facchini 1983).

Another factor was a change in the approach to the study of language. In the nineteenth century, along with the first efforts toward the reconstruction of Indo-European and the discovery of what appeared to be rules of linguistic change (for example, the various Sound Laws), linguists focused their study on the *history* of language. In the early twentieth century a new paradigm was established, in which the study of the history of language was sharply divided from the study of language as a structured system. This developed following the posthumous influence of Ferdinand de Saussure's *Cours de linguistique generale*.[6] Saussure, in formulating what he called *semiologie,* saw the possibility of a general science of signs. The study of language was but a branch of this, and thus the study of gesture could have been included. However, the main reason for taking an interest in gesture had been its connection to language origin and development. Since these issues were no longer the focus of linguists' attention, there was a decline in interest in the phenomena of gesture and sign. Further, Saussure's insistence on the "arbitrariness of the linguistic sign" seemed to rule out of the linguist's purview anything that did not seem to have this property of arbitrariness. This meant that systems involving sign and gesture, where iconicity seems to be very important, tended to be dismissed as "not really language" and so ceased to command the serious attention of students of language.

Sign languages soon came to be regarded as, at best, a loose collection of gestures or, perhaps, as a simple back formation from spoken language. Likewise gestures were no longer taken seriously as objects of study, for they did not appear to conform to the rigorous structures that spoken languages were deemed to have. It is remarkable how widespread and persistent these attitudes came to be. Thus when Mervyn Meggitt, a well-known student of the Walbiri of central Australia, published a paper on Walbiri sign language, he felt it necessary to defend himself against the possible charge that such a topic might be no more than of dilettante interest (1954, 3). Indeed, in this connection, it is notable that Meggitt's contribution of 1954 was the first work on Australian Aboriginal sign languages since the late nineteenth century, and no other major work on them appeared again until 1988 (Kendon 1988). Similarly, despite the substantial work of Garrick Mallery on the sign languages of the Plains Indians of North America, no further serious work was undertaken on these sign languages until La Mont West attempted a structural analysis of one form of these sign languages in 1960. Like Meggitt's paper on Walbiri sign language, however, this was an isolated study, and none of its results have ever been published in book form. More than three decades went by before anyone else attempted to examine these sign languages (Farnell 1995).

The rediscovery of the promises offered by the study of sign language and gesture for an understanding of the nature and origins of language began, at least in North America, in 1970. It was in this year, at the meeting of the American Anthropological Association in San Diego, that Gordon Hewes first presented his now famous paper,

"Primate Communication and the Gestural Origin of Language," which was later published, with extended peer commentary, in *Current Anthropology* in 1973. Hewes showed in this paper that a great accumulation of ethological facts, neurological facts, and paleontological facts relevant to the study of language made it possible to develop a scenario for the origin of language that was no longer based upon whimsy and imagination.

Support for Hewes' argument came from the work of Allen and Beatrice Gardner, who had raised Washoe, a chimpanzee, in their home and taught her American Sign Language. Over the course of just a few years, Washoe acquired a vocabulary of 80 to 100 signs that she was able to use to name objects and initiate requests, as well as to respond to requests made to her in sign by her caretakers. Even more impressive, she had occasionally spontaneously created a sign and had combined signs as if she was able to use these symbolic expressions in a *productive* fashion.[7]

One of the earliest commentaries on the Gardners' work was written by Jacob Bronowski in collaboration with Ursula Bellugi (1970) who, just a year or so before, had been working with Roger Brown at Harvard on the acquisition of language in children. This work had been precipitated in part by the claims of Noam Chomsky and also of Eric Lenneberg that humans developed language in a particular way, according to biological principles, and, specifically, the grammar of a language was innate.[8] These claims prompted a new look at the phenomena of child language acquisition. Brown (1973) was one of the pioneers in analyses that focused on the syntactic properties of early child utterances. Bellugi, as a participant in this work, was already much interested in the biological roots of language. In 1969, she and her husband Edward Klima went to visit the Gardners and Washoe in Reno, Nevada. She wrote of this visit:

> We became interested in the wily chimpanzee, who was presented to us the first evening in her filmy nightgown and stocking cap. We had never paid attention to a human signing, much less a chimpanzee, but we were duly impressed with what her trainers, the Gardners, reported she was "saying." From that visit came a paper in 1970 with

Jacob Bronowski, called "Language, name and concept." One aspect of that paper was a comparison between the reported accomplishments of the chimpanzee in sign language and hearing children learning spoken language, because nothing was known at the time of deaf children learning sign language (surely a more appropriate comparison for Washoe). (Bellugi 1981, 157)

Soon after this visit, Jonas Salk invited Bellugi to set up a small research unit at the Salk Institute for Biological Studies (where Bronowski was a Fellow). The Gardners' work with Washoe suggested to her that a study of the acquisition of sign language by deaf children of deaf parents would be an appropriate point of departure. This led to the realization that very little was actually known about the structure of any sign language such children might be learning and so it was necessary, first, to begin a study of this. Bellugi's research soon gained attention and many young scholars were attracted to the laboratory she started. Within a few years, a number of important publications on sign language appeared, many of which were written or edited by members of this laboratory. Other publications of importance did precede those that ensued from the work at the Salk Institute, but there seems little doubt that this laboratory played a very important role in creating the momentum for the modern interest in sign language.[9] A detailed history of this would be well worth writing.

It must not be supposed, however, that the modern view of sign language began in this period. The first serious modern study of sign language had been published more than a decade earlier. This was William Stokoe's *Sign Language Structure* (1960). Within five years, Stokoe and his colleagues published *A Dictionary of American Sign Language on Linguistic Principles* (1965).[10] These works together clearly demonstrated that American Sign Language was a fully articulated language with a structure that could be analyzed on levels analogous to the levels of phonology, morphology, and syntax of spoken language. It has always interested me that these works attracted relatively little notice at the time they were published. It was only after the Gardners' work with Washoe, with its broad implications about the biological roots of language, that sign language once again received serious attention from more than just a small circle of scholars. Once others, such as Bellugi, began to study sign language systematically, Stokoe's claims in his initial publications were quickly confirmed. By the middle of the following decade the main outlines of a basic understanding of the nature of sign language had become established.[11]

So what have been the implications of this newer and more sophisticated understanding of sign languages for language origins theory? Perhaps the most important was the firm demonstration that *modality of expression* does not have to be a part of the definition of language. Even using this term in a quite strict sense, it is clear that the principles of vocabulary organization, morphological structure, and syntactic processes familiar to us from spoken languages, can all be found in sign languages. At the time that the modern debate about language origins began, many scholars, including Charles Hockett, assumed that for a communicative system to be a *language* it would have to be spoken.[12] The demonstration that primary sign languages are languages in the full-fledged sense made a very strong case for the view that the capacities for language in human beings do not require the capacity for speech. The anatomical and neurological specializations for *speaking* emphasized by Lenneberg and others could be regarded as a somewhat separate and possibly even a later product of evolution. It came to be seen that while we may address ourselves to the origin of *speech*, it is but a refinement into one mode of behavior of an already established *language* function. The research on sign language opened up the question of how behavior could come to function *linguistically* even when it did not involve speech.

One of the places where the implications of this realization have been most fully and recently worked out is in the work of William Stokoe in collaboration with David Armstrong and Sherman Wilcox (see Armstrong, Stokoe, and Wilcox 1995). Whereas syntactic organization had long been seen as something that arises after a vocabulary of lexical items has been established, Stokoe and his colleagues saw syntactic organization as a late abstraction from the fundamental structures of purposeful actions. These authors pointed out that in visible manual action of any sort there is already something that can be analyzed as an expression of a relation, and hence a sort of syntax.

The Saussurean tradition insists that, to be linguistic, a sign must be arbitrary; but Stokoe and his colleagues see the recognition of iconic and indexical relations as being at the very heart of the process that leads to and constitutes language. This can be much more readily appreciated if one takes, as one's starting point, language as fashioned from gestures that produce visible actions, rather than language fashioned from gestures that produce audible signals. It is also clear, if one draws on the most recent insights into the richly nuanced character of visible action that is used in primary sign languages, that the complexity of iconic representation made possible in visible gesture is what permits elaboration of syntax beyond the simplest relational structures. Thus, syntax is the result of a long process of analysis or "unpacking" of inherently relational modes of expression.

In the view of Stokoe and his colleagues, actions that function in a linguistic fashion—those that are semiotic and serve to symbolize relationships between concepts—first emerged in visible actions. This does not mean that full-fledged signed languages developed first, followed by spoken language. Rather, vocal gestures could also have played a role in symbolic communication from an early stage. These vocal gestures, however, are not fundamentally different from manual gestures. And while the burden of symbolic communication indeed has shifted heavily on to the use of such vocal gestures, this does not constitute a radical *qualitative* shift. Language, according to Stokoe and his colleagues, always was and is to this day a symbolic system fashioned from gesture. The shift to spoken language is but a shift towards using the audible consequences of mouth gestures as a vehicle for symbolization, away from exclusive reliance on the visual consequences of manual gestures.

Fundamental to the vision of Stokoe and his colleagues appears to be the creation of visible actions that serve as iconic representations of their referents. The capacity for perceiving analogies between the forms of visible action and the forms of other actions or the forms of things, and the capacity to see analogies between the relational structure of actions and relational structures of events in the world is fundamental. This seems not too different from the Vichian scenario which I mentioned at the outset. Thus we seem to be returning to where we began.

As one reviews the history of theories of language origins (especially those that spring from the view that language emerged through a process by which practical acts became transformed into symbolic acts) and considers how these symbolic acts, in the process of becoming established as socially shared communicative actions, acquired the properties of arbitrariness, contrastiveness, and other features so often cited as characteristic of language, it is striking how little this line of thought has changed. What has changed is that the support for such a line of thought is so much greater than ever before. This is clearly due to the much greater understanding of the nature of sign languages that we have today. As I have tried to show here, this increase in understanding has come about as a consequence of the philosophical issues raised by the phenomena of "gesture talk" among deaf people. Thus there is, and always has been, a reciprocal relationship between the study of sign language and the elaboration theories of language origin.

Notes

1. All quotations are from the translation of Bergin and Fisch (1984). Passages are identified by paragraph numbers.

2. For a lucid account of Condillac's ideas with regard to the origin of language, see Wells (1987).

3. On gesture and the idea of a universal language, see Knowlson (1975). See also Knox (1990).

4. Roch Ambroise Sicard, *Cours d'instruction d'un sourd-muet de naissance pour servir à l'éducation des sourds-muets: Et qui peut être utile à celle de ceux qui entendent et qui parlent.* (Hambourg: Chez Fauche, Librarire, 1799) and *Theorie des signes pour l'instruction des sourds-muets* (Paris: A l'Imprimerie de l'Institution des Sourds-Muets, sous la direction d'Ange, 1808). See Knowlson (1975, 220–21).

5. The quotations here are from chapter 2. See Wundt ([1921] 1973).

6. Ferdinand de Saussure. *Cours de linguistique generale.* Paris: Payot 1916. 2d ed. 1922. English translation by Roy Harris (1983).

7. Gardner and Gardner (1969) is the first published report of this study.

8. See Lenneberg (1967); for an early formulation of the idea of the Language Acquisition Device, see Chomsky (1965).

9. Perhaps the most conspicuous and most widely disseminated publication that followed from the work at the Salk Institute was Klima and Bellugi's *Signs of*

Language (1979). This was a collaborative work and many who contributed to it went on to become prominent sign language researchers in their own right. Another important publication that owed much to the excitement created at Salk was *Understanding Language through Sign Language Research,* a collection of papers from the first conference on Sign Language and Neurolinguistics, held in Rochester, New York, in 1976, and edited by Patricia Siple (1978). Other publications less directly related to the work at Salk, or independent of it, include Schlesinger and Namir (1972), Friedman (1977) and Peng (1978). In both Schlesinger and Namir and in Peng the connection is maintained with problems of language origins and the importance of the linguistic work with apes. Gordon Hewes contributed to both of these volumes.

10. Stokoe wrote the dictionary with Dorothy Casterline and Carl Croneberg. A new edition was issued in 1978 by Linstok Press, the publishing company Stokoe created.

11. The literature stemming from modern research on primary sign languages is now very large indeed. While this is not the place to discuss it, those looking for modern starting points from a linguistic point of view are referred to Valli and Lucas (1995) for American Sign Language and Sutton-Spence and Woll (1999) for British Sign Language.

12. See, for example, Hockett and Asher (1954). Hockett later revised his view. See his very valuable essay "In Search of Jove's Brow" (Hockett 1978).

References

Armstrong, David F., William C. Stokoe, and Sherman E. Wilcox. 1995. *Gesture and the nature of language.* Cambridge: Cambridge University Press.

Bellugi, Ursula. 1981. The acquisition of a spatial language. In *The development of language and language researchers: Essays in honor of Roger Brown,* edited by Frank S. Kessel. Hillsdale, N.J.: Lawrence Erlbaum Associates.

Bergin, Thomas Goddard, and Max Harold Fisch, trans. [1744] 1984. *The new science of Giambattista Vico.* 3d ed. and *Practic of the new science.* Ithaca, N.Y.: Cornell University Press.

Bronowski, Jacob, and Ursula Bellugi. 1970. Language, name, and concept. *Science* 168 (3932): 669–73.

Brown, Roger. 1973. *A first language: The early stages.* Cambridge: Harvard University Press.

Chomsky, Noam. 1965. *Aspects of the theory of syntax.* Cambridge: MIT Press.
Condillac, Etienne Bonnot de. [1756] 1971. *An essay on the origin of human knowledge.* Translated by Thomas Nugent. Facsimile Reprint, Gainesville, Fla.: Scholars' Facsimiles and Reprints.
Danesi, Marcel. 1993. *Vico, metaphor and the origin of language.* Bloomington: Indiana University Press.
De Jorio, Andrea. 1832. *La mimica degli antichi investigata nel gestire napoletano.* Naples: Fibreno.
Diderot, Denis. [1751] 1904. Lettre sur le sourds et muets (Letter on deaf mutes). In *Diderot's early philosophical works,* edited and translated by Margaret Jourdain. Chicago: Open Court Publishing.
Facchini, G. Massimo. 1983. An historical reconstruction of the events leading to the Congress of Milan in 1880. In *SLE '83: Sign language research,* edited by William C. Stokoe and Virginia Volterra. Rome: Istituto di Psicologia del Consiglio Nazionale delle Ricerche; Silver Spring, Md.: Linstok Press.
Farnell, Brenda. 1995. *Do you see what I mean?* Austin: University of Texas Press.
Friedman, Lynn H., ed. 1977. *On the other hand: New perspectives on American Sign Language.* New York: Academic Press.
Gardner, R. Allen, and Beatrice T. Gardner. 1969. Teaching sign language to a chimpanzee. *Science* 165 (3894): 664–72.
Harris, Roy. 1983. Translation of *Course in general linguistics* by Ferdinand de Saussure. London: Duckworth.
Hewes, Gordon W. 1973. Primate communication and the gestural origin of language. *Current Anthropology* 14: 5–24.
Hockett, Charles F., and Robert Ascher. 1964. The human revolution. *Current Anthropology* 5: 135–68.
Kendon, Adam. 1988. *Sign languages of aboriginal Australia: Cultural, semiotic and communicative perspectives.* Cambridge: Cambridge University Press.
Knowlson, James R. 1965. The idea of gesture as a universal language in the 17th and 18th centuries. *Journal of the History of Ideas* 26: 495–508.

Knox, Dilwyn. 1990. Late medieval and renaissance ideas on gesture. In *Die Sprache der Zeichen und Bilder: Rhetorik un nonverbate Kommunikatio in der friihen Neuzeit,* edited by Volker Kapp, 11–39. Marburg: Hitzeroth.

Lenneberg, Eric H. 1967. *Biological foundations of language.* New York: John Wiley and Sons.

Mallery, Garrick. [1881] 1972. *Sign language among North American Indians compared with that among other peoples and Deaf-Mutes.* Reprint, The Hague: Mouton.

Meggitt, Mervyn. 1954. Sign language among the Walbiri of Central Australia. *Oceania* 25: 2–16.

Peng, Fred C. C., ed. 1978. *Sign language and language acquisition in man and ape.* AAAS Selected Symposia Series, no. 16. American Association for the Advancement of Science. Boulder, Colo.: Westview Press.

Radutzky, Elena, ed. 1992. *Dizionario bilingue elementare della lingua italiana dei segni.* Rome: Edizioni Kappa.

Saussure, Ferdinand de. [1922] 1983. *Cours de linguistique generale* (Course in general linguistics). 2d. ed. Translated by Roy Harris. London: Duckworth.

Schlesinger, Izchak M., and Lila Namir, eds. 1978. *Sign language of the Deaf: Psychological, linguistic and sociological perspectives.* New York: Academic Press.

Siegel, J. P. 1969. The Enlightenment and the evolution of a language of signs in France and England. *Journal for the History of Ideas* 30: 96–115.

Siple, Patricia L., ed. 1978. *Understanding language through sign language research.* New York: Academic Press.

Stam, James H. 1976. *Inquiries into the origin of language: The fate of a question.* New York: Harper and Row.

Stokoe, William C. 1960. *Sign language structure: An outline of the visual communication systems of the American Deaf.* Studies in Linguistics, Occasional Papers no. 8. Department of Anthropology and Linguistics. Buffalo, N.Y.: State University of New York at Buffalo.

———. 1978. *Sign language structure. The first linguistic analysis of American Sign Language.* Rev. ed. Silver Spring, Md.: Linstok Press.

Stokoe, William C., Dorothy C. Casterline, and Carl G. Croneberg. 1965. *A dictionary of American Sign Language on linguistic principles.* Washington, D.C.: Gallaudet College Press.

Sutton-Spence, Rachel, and Bencie Woll. 1999. *The linguistics of British Sign Language: An introduction.* Cambridge: Cambridge University Press.

Tylor, Edward B. 1865. *Researches into the early history of mankind and the development of civilization.* London: John Murray.

———. 1878. *Researches into the early history of mankind and the development of civilization.* Rev. ed. London: John Murray.

Valli, Clayton, and Ceil Lucas. 1995. *Linguistics of American Sign Language: An introduction.* Washington, D.C.: Gallaudet University Press.

Wells, G. A. 1987. *The origin of language: Aspects of the discussion from Condillac to Wundt.* LaSalle, Ill.: Open Court Publishing.

West, La Mont. 1960. The sign language: An analysis. 2 vols. Vol. II: Dialects. Ph.D. diss., Indiana University.

Wundt, Wilhelm [1921] 1973. *The language of gestures.* Translated by J. S. Thayer, C. M. Greenleaf, and M. D. Silberman. Approaches to Semiotics. Reprint, The Hague: Mouton.

3

Modality Effects and Conflicting Agendas

Scott K. Liddell

Beginning with the work of William Stokoe, scholars studying American Sign Language (ASL) have maintained that ASL is a naturally developed, human language. A number of important social and educational issues depend on this conclusion. The fact that sign languages are produced by the hands, arms, and body and are perceived visually, however, could influence the nature of the language. These influences, or modality effects, make sign language research both interesting and challenging. At times, these two issues—that sign languages are indeed languages and that their mode of production and reception may affect the nature of the language—appear to be in conflict. Determining that sign languages differ from spoken languages in some property seen as central to what defines language may lead to the conclusion that sign languages are not the same kind of entities as spoken languages. The presence of iconicity and gesture in ASL are examples of why the conflict arises. This chapter argues that abandoning unwarranted assumptions about the characteristics of language resolves this apparent problem.

Theory-Driven Conclusions: The Uniformitarian Principle

To illustrate the power of theory over data, it is instructive to look at the case of the Barringer Crater, located in the desert east of Flagstaff, Arizona. In the late 1800s chunks of silver were found lying near the crater, which was approximately three-quarters of a mile in diameter (see figure 3.1). An accurate analysis of the composition of these chunks revealed that they contained 7.9 percent nickel, a percentage consistent with that previously found in metallic meteorites.[1] In 1891, a geologist from the United States Geological Survey (USGS) studied the crater and concluded that it had a volcanic origin, in spite of a lack of evidence of volcanism. Grove K. Gilbert, also of USGS, was studying craters on the moon and in 1892 presented a paper to the Washington Philosophical Society claiming that the craters on the moon were indeed formed by the impact of meteorites. Then, in 1896, he published a paper in which he claimed that the crater in Arizona was produced by a volcano. He reached this conclusion after his analysis using a magnetometer found no evidence that a huge meteorite was lodged anywhere inside the crater. He also calculated that the volume of the rim was roughly sufficient to fill the crater. That being the case, there would not be room for both a huge meteorite and the material from the rim inside the crater. In his view, this eliminated the possibility of a meteorite as the cause of the crater. This type of crater was said to be formed by a "cryptovolcanic process" (Lewis 1995, 33); somehow, volcanic activity had created the crater but had left no trace.

In 1902 a mining engineer named D. M. Barringer and his physicist friend, Benjamin Tilghman, began making trips to the crater in order to study it and, hopefully, get rich from the metals to be found there. They found that the surface of the desert around the crater contained a mixture of meteoric materials and rocks ejected from the crater, millions of tons of finely pulverized silica, meteoric iron in the

---

1. This story of the reluctance to accept Meteor Crater, Arizona, as resulting from an impact crater comes from Lewis (1995, 30–36) and from the Barringer Meteorite Crater web site (http://www.barringercrater.com/).

Figure 3.1. A satellite photograph of the Barringer Crater taken by D. Roddy, courtesy of Meteor Crater Enterprises and available online at http://antwrp.gsfc.nasa.gov/ap971117.html

rim and the surrounding plane, and the absence of any evidence of volcanic activity.

A new type of quartz glass also was discovered at the crater. In 1908, George P. Merrill concluded that this quartz glass could have been produced only by intense heat—much greater than the heat found in a volcano. Merrill also demonstrated that the rock beds below the crater were undisturbed by volcanic activity.

Barringer presented papers to the Academy of Natural Sciences in Philadelphia in 1906 and 1909 in support of his meteor impact theory, but his work was not received well. In fact, during his 1909 address "some persons could scarcely conceal their derisive thoughts. Nevertheless, with vocal encouragement from Thomson in the audience, Barringer ploughed through his paper, painful though it must have been for him, until he completed it" (Abrahams 1998).

Table 3.1 lists the data known about the crater in 1909. A checkmark under the origin theory indicates that the theory is consistent with the data. An objective look at table 3.1 reveals that the impact origin theory is consistent with all the known evidence at that time,

TABLE 3.1. Comparison of Evidence on the Origin of the Barringer Crater

DATA KNOWN IN 1909	IMPACT ORIGIN	VOLCANIC ORIGIN
Presence of a crater	✓	✓
Absence of volcanic rocks	✓	
Large quantities of meteoric iron with 7.9% nickel	✓	
Surrounding earth with a mixture of rocks and meteoric materials	✓	
Millions of tons of pulverized silica	✓	
Reversed order of rock deposits	✓	
Quartz glass requiring very high temperatures to be formed	✓	
Undisturbed rock bed below crater	✓	

Note: The information in this table comes from Lewis (1996) and the Barringer Meterorite Crater web site http://www.barringercrater.com.

while the volcanic origin theory is virtually unsupported. Although evidence was overwhelming, the impact theory was not widely accepted at that time, demonstrating the power of theory over data. Barringer's conclusion that the crater resulted from the impact of a meteorite directly contradicted the Uniformitarian Principle, which stated that "catastrophes were not only unimportant factors in geological change, they were nonexistent" (Lewis 1997). This widely held principle of nineteenth-century geology ruled out impact from meteorites as a possible cause for large craters on the earth. The only other natural phenomenon known to be able to produce a crater of that size was a volcano. Since the theory ruled out the impact of a meteorite, simple deduction led to the conclusion that a volcano must have produced the crater.

In 1920, meteorite fragments were discovered inside the crater. This, along with all the previously known evidence, finally led to the general acceptance of the conclusion that the crater was caused by the impact of a meteorite. Today, a NASA web site, the Astronomy Picture of the Day, states that, "In 1920, [the Barringer Crater] was the first feature on Earth to be recognized as an impact crater. Today, over 100 terrestrial impact craters have been identified."

What Was At Stake?

The Uniformitarian Principle developed in response to the view that cataclysmic events were responsible for the current state of the earth and that the earth was young. Conceding that the crater had an impact origin would allow cataclysmic events back into the picture and potentially could reopen the issue of whether the earth was billions of years old or only a few thousand years old. Thus, much was at stake in recognizing the impact origin of the crater.

Beliefs About Spoken and Signed Languages

In 1955, Bill Stokoe was hired to teach in the English Department at Gallaudet College (later Gallaudet University). Despite the fact that faculty were expected to communicate through signs, misconceptions about American Sign Language (ASL) were also deeply held at Gallaudet.[2] One common misconception saw ASL as a system of gestures with limited expressive ability. Another saw ASL as an attempt to manually produce spoken English by means of signs representing English

---

2. I suspect that at least part of the reason for the misconceptions held by teachers is that they were not trained to use ASL. Rather, they were taught ASL vocabulary (not grammar) and were expected to produce the ASL vocabulary while speaking English. This practice is called *Simultaneous Communication*. As a result, although the faculty signed as part of Simultaneous Communication, in general, faculty did not know or use ASL.

words. At the same time, in the field of linguistics there was a strong belief that language could only be produced by means of the vocal tract. Outside of linguistics there were also widely held beliefs inconsistent with regarding ASL as a language. When Stokoe began to closely observe his students communicate using ASL, what he saw appeared to be in conflict with these deeply held views.

Confronted with a choice between accepting the theories and widely held beliefs about ASL or the evidence he could see in front of him, Stokoe described the evidence. In *Sign Language Structure: An Outline of the Visual Gestural Communication System of the American Deaf* (1960), he presented considerable data that ASL has the characteristics found in any language. Had Stokoe been studying the grammatical properties of a previously unknown spoken language, the readiness to accept it as a language would have been different. Even if Stokoe had discovered a radically different grammatical property of a spoken language, there still would have been no question about the linguistic status of that spoken communication. Despite Stokoe's demonstration of the grammatical properties of ASL, however, the forces of theory and widely held misconceptions were too powerful, and his proposal did not receive serious consideration at first. Accepting that ASL was a language would have required giving up strongly held views.

By the late 1970s many more linguists and psychologists had been attracted to the study of ASL. They were soon convinced that ASL was a language and were conducting research on various aspects of its grammar and finding parallels in the structure of ASL and spoken languages. For example, Stokoe had proposed that signs are constructed of meaningless parts. This is a clear parallel with spoken languages, where words are also composed of meaningless parts. Stokoe proposed the term *cherology* as the signed equivalent of phonology in spoken language analysis. He proposed that three meaningless parts combine to form a meaningful sign: (1) the place at which the sign is produced, (2) "what acts" (a hand in a particular orientation), and (3) one or more movements. Multiple movements could occur simultaneously, sequentially, or both.

At that time, there were still significant differences between analyses of the phonology, morphology, and syntax of ASL and what one would expect in a spoken language. The cherological structure proposed by Stokoe, for example, is unheard of in the analysis of spoken languages. All spoken languages put phonological segments (consonants and vowels) together sequentially to produce words.

Two quite distinct conclusions could follow from the difference between ASL and spoken languages. The first is that the difference is due to a "modality effect." That is, the physical differences between the two articulatory systems results in a difference in language structure. ASL, in this view, would still be regarded as a language, but an effect of the visual modality on languages would have been discovered. A second conclusion is also possible—sign language cherology and spoken language phonology are so different that signing should not be in the same category as spoken language.

Studies of ASL morphology in the 1970s also were showing that repeated and modified forms of signs added important aspectual meanings to verbs and adjectives. But how do these form changes compare to morphological processes in spoken languages? Fischer (1973) and Fischer and Gough (1978) adopted Stokoe's model of sign structure and treated these changes as parallel to reduplication in spoken languages. Klima and Bellugi (1979) also adopted Stokoe's model, but proposed augmenting it by adding features to the three "aspects" he had proposed. Under this analysis, modulations are feature-changing rules. Both reduplication and feature changing rules are common in the analysis of spoken languages. The fact that these rules operated on signs structured differently from spoken words still made the aspectual forms seem different from morphological forms found in spoken languages, but segmenting signs temporally into phonological segments eliminated the major phonological difference between nonsegmental cherology and phonology (Liddell 1982, 1984a). Temporal segmentation also provided a means to address the analysis of aspectual forms of signs using phonological segments. The various aspectual forms then could be analyzed in terms of segmented, morphological frames that incorporate features from the verb root (Liddell 1984b).[3] This is similar in

---

3. Most of these forms additionally involve reduplication rules.

some respects to what has been shown to occur in Semitic morphological processes (McCarthy 1979).

Two additional aspects of signing still have the potential to show significant differences between signing and speech, however. First, a high proportion of ASL signs appear to be iconic. Linguists have adopted the view that one of the defining characteristics of language is that its words must be arbitrary. That is, there should be no motivated relationship between the form of a word and its meaning: spoken words should not sound like what they mean; signs must not look like what they represent. If words must be arbitrary and not iconic, then the perceived iconicity of ASL signs would count against the language status of ASL.

The second problematic aspect of signing, for which there is no direct parallel with speech, is that many signs can be directed in space; that is, pointing occurs. The tongue does not meaningfully point at things in the environment during speech. Once again, the fact that the hand does point at things as it produces some signs could be viewed as counting against the language status of ASL. The following sections provide a more detailed analysis of these two aspects of signing.

Iconicity

Since the days of Saussure it has been axiomatic that proper linguistic forms are arbitrary. That is, the form of a word and its meaning have no inherent connection except that they have been arbitrarily paired in the lexicon. Saussure formalizes this lack of motivation as "Principle I: The Arbitrary Nature of the Sign."

> The bond between the signifier and the signified is arbitrary. Since I mean by sign the whole that results from the associating of the signifier with the signified, I can simply say: the linguistic sign is arbitrary. (Saussure 1959, 67)

Saussure does not treat this principle as either new or surprising, and in fact, goes on to say that no one disputes it. If it is taken simply as an observation about the nature of most words of a typical spoken language, it is reasonably accurate and easy to accept. However, this is not simply an observation. It is stated as a principle that if correct, produces an arbitrary lexicon.

There are exceptions to this principle. The *choo-choo* in *choo-choo train* bears an obvious relationship to the release of steam from steam-driven locomotives. Similarly, it is easy to see the relationship between the release of compressed gasses and the sounds of the words *poof* and *puff*, or the sound produced by drinking from a bottle and *glug glug glug*. These words exhibit onomatopoeia since the sounds of these words resemble sounds relatable to the meanings of these words. Examples of onomatopoeia are quite easy to find. English instances include such terms as: *pop, beep, boom, boing, buzz, chug-a-lug, chirp, cheep, clack, clang, cuckoo, ding-dong, drip, hiss, hum, kaboom, kerplunk, kablooey, knock, ping, pitter pat, pitter patter, ping pong, plop, rat-a-tat, roar, splat, swish, tap, thud, tinkle, whir,* and *whoosh*.

Words exhibiting onomatopoeia can be found in any spoken language. As a class, they constitute a set of exceptions to the idea that the relationship between the form of a word and its meaning is arbitrary. Although they are fully established lexical forms, they are nevertheless treated as marginal or exceptional because they do not conform to Saussure's principle. Some commentators suggest that their contribution to language is dubious. Bolinger (1975) states that "language has become an almost purely conventional code, with a few exceptions listed as curiosities" (1975, 217). That is, words exhibiting onomatopoeia do not participate in this purely conventional code. Westcott (1971) suggests that the difference in coding has implications for the ability to precisely encode meaning.

> Linguistic icons, though less precise than linguistic symbols, are more easily understood by those with imperfect mastery of the language in which they occur. Just as threat-signals, despite their imprecision, are understood across species boundaries in a way in which courtship-signals are not, so also are onomatopoeic forms appreciated, if only vaguely, by foreigners in a way in which other forms are not. (1971, 426)

The words that exhibit onomatopoeia in the lexicon of a spoken language exist in clear violation of Saussure's principle. If his principle were correct such words should not exist. Although violations of fundamental principles would seem to require explanation, words exhibiting onomatopoeia are generally described merely as exceptions to the rule. It has been claimed that words exhibiting onomatopoeia are primitive (Bolinger 1975, 217) and will eventually lose this nonarbitrariness through processes of historical change (see Saussure 1959, 69; Frishberg 1975, 717). But what is to be done when one is faced with a language where iconic words do not constitute a small set of exceptions within an otherwise arbitrary lexicon? There have been four distinct approaches to the issue of the iconicity of signs.

Signs Are Not Iconic

One approach denies that signs are iconic. This is accomplished through redefining the term *arbitrary*. For example, in describing a specific set of signs, Frishberg (1975) argues that since the signs are produced with handshapes, locations, and movements specific to ASL they are really not iconic. Wilbur (1987, 164) discusses ASL, Brazilian Sign Language, Greek Sign Language, and Spanish Sign Language and notes that all have chosen distinct ways to produce signs meaning "cat." Two of the signs involve whiskers as part of the imagery of the sign while the other two appear to involve petting or stroking a cat. In discussing these signs, and others, Wilbur argues that "the different formations of the signs themselves are not predictable from knowledge of cats or tree structure and in this sense the signs are as arbitrary as spoken words" (Wilbur 1987, 164).

The same logic applied to the English *cock-a-doodle-do*, the French *cocorico*, and the Japanese *kokekkoko* would result in the conclusion that these words are also not iconic (Mandel 1977). Each language has chosen to represent the sound made by a rooster in different ways, consistent with the phonologies of the respective languages. The fact that these words are made up of phonemes of their respective languages and differ from one another is a separate issue than whether they are iconic. Deciding whether a word is iconic is not based on whether the word has a phonological representation. Rather, it depends on the existence of some nonarbitrary relationship between the form of the word and its meaning.

Iconicity Is Present—A Modality Difference

A second approach recognizes the iconicity of signs, but treats it primarily as a modality effect. DeMatteo (1977) examines a number of sign types, including classifier predicates and concludes that iconicity and visual imagery are significant aspects of signs in ASL. Mandel (1977) not only accepts the iconicity of signs in ASL, but provides an extensive categorization of types of iconic devices used in ASL signs. Both Mandel and DeMatteo consider the iconicity of ASL to be a reflection of a modality difference. Mandel suggests that there may be a problem with Saussure's claim that the relationship between the form and meaning of a word must be arbitrary.

> There seem to be some linguists who do not consider iconicity a significant factor in ASL, at least at the lexical level. . . . On the contrary, it is Saussure's claim that requires support. Experience has supported it, by and large, in oral languages; but once we cross so important a line as the difference between the vocal-auditory and the gestural-visual channels, we must be prepared to encounter facts and patterns at variance with our previous experience. (Mandel 1977, 61–62)

Iconicity Is Present—But Not Important

A third approach recognizes the iconicity of signs, but minimizes its importance. For example, Hoemann (1975) and Klima and Bellugi (1979) performed experiments aimed at determining to what degree naïve hearing subjects had access to the meaning of signs based on their form. In one experiment, nonsigners were asked to guess the meanings of 90 signs. None of the subjects were able to guess the meanings of 81 of the 90 signs. The meanings of the remaining nine signs were guessed by some subjects. Klima and Bellugi conclude that in general the meaning of a sign is not self-evident from the form of the sign. In another study naïve hearing subjects were shown ASL signs and asked to select the correct meaning as a multiple-choice task. In general, subjects performed at a chance level. For 12 of the 90 signs presented, however, the majority of subjects selected the correct meanings. In a third study, naïve hearing subjects were presented with signs and their meanings, but were now asked to provide an explanation for the form of the sign. In order to carry out this task, the hearing subjects would have to recognize the iconicity of a sign and then describe the basis for the iconicity. For many of the signs, nonsigners were able to agree on an iconic motivation for the signs. Klima and Bellugi conclude that many ASL signs do indeed have a representational aspect.

Frishberg examines historical changes of signs in ASL. She concludes that "signs change away from their pantomimic or imitative origins to more arbitrary shapes" (1975, 700), and that "in general, signs have become less transparent, pantomimic, and iconic; they have become more arbitrary, conventionalized, and symbolic" (1975, 718). This conclusion is consistent with the general notion that iconic signs are somehow more primitive and will eventually become purely arbitrary signs.

Wilbur cites the lack of importance of iconicity in the acquisition of morphology as additional evidence of iconicity's overall insignificance to ASL:

> The literature on deaf children's early acquisition of sign language repeatedly demonstrates that the presence of iconicity in ASL contributes little if anything to the overall development of sign morphology, although there may be an effect for individual lexical items. (Wilbur 1987, 207)

All the approaches described here recognize that many signs are iconic and also recognize that linguistic theory does not view iconicity in a positive light.[4] The lack of significance found for iconicity, in some sense, excuses its presence.

---

4. Cognitive linguistic theory does not have this negative view of iconicity and onomatopoeia.

Saussure's Principle Is Wrong

The fourth way of dealing with the iconicity issue has been to argue that Saussure's claim is incorrect (Liddell 1990, 1992). This approach recognizes that many signs are iconic but argues that iconicity is not an indication that the signs are somehow primitive or less precise than noniconic signs. I argue that languages, spoken or signed, strive for iconicity and other types of motivated forms. The point made by Frishberg that iconic signs are composed of arbitrary, meaningless parts (as are noniconic signs) demonstrates that they have all the properties of a symbolic word. That is, they have a phonological form consistent with the phonological structure of ASL while also exhibiting iconicity.

The notion that words exhibiting onomatopoeia or iconic signs are somehow more primitive and less precise than arbitrary symbols is unfounded. The examples of both types examined in this chapter all exhibit arbitrary correspondences between an abstract phonological form and a meaning. They are distinguishable from purely arbitrary words in that some aspects of their form are relatable to the lexically fixed meaning, thereby leading to the ability to form images that lead to an enhancement of that meaning (Liddell 1992).

If, as I claim in Liddell (1990, 1992), iconicity is desirable, why do words exhibiting onomatopoeia in spoken languages comprise only a relatively small proportion of the lexicon? Here we have arrived at a modality difference. The difference is not that sign languages are iconic and spoken languages are not. Rather, iconicity is desirable in either type of language, but the potential for onomatopoeia in spoken languages is limited by the auditory modality. That is, in order for a spoken word to exhibit onomatopoeia there must be a nonarbitrary relationship between the form of the word—its sound—and its meaning. This is possible only if the meaning of the word is about something that makes a sound. In a visual modality, iconicity is present when there is a relationship between the visual form of the sign and its meaning. Since there are so many more things that are visible, or can be represented with a visible image, than make sounds, the potential for iconicity is much greater in a signed language.

Taub (1997) argues that both signed and spoken languages exhibit iconicity at various levels. She distinguishes "pure" iconicity with "metaphorical-linked" iconicity and develops an analogue-building model of how iconic items arise in both spoken and signed languages. Such mechanisms help to demonstrate some of the benefits of iconicity.

Models of grammar that pay no attention to iconicity have nothing to say when a signer uses iconicity to creatively produce a new form. Okrent (1997) discusses one such example. The sign OPPRESS is made with an open B handshape pressing down on an S handshape. If one conceives of the upper hand as corresponding to an oppressor and the bottom hand as corresponding to those oppressed, the sign is iconic. Those denying the iconicity of OPPRESS might simply characterize its iconicity as an invention of the analyst. Okrent examines a spontaneous instance of a nonce sign meaning, "become unoppressed." This signer produced the sign with a rapid upward and outward movement of the "oppressing" handshape away from the "oppressed" handshape. This would be an example of metaphor-linked iconicity in Taub's analysis. This invention makes perfect sense from an iconic-metaphoric perspective. It is both creative and dramatic. Someone believing that OPPRESS is not iconic would be limited to saying that the invention was pronounced with some of the characteristics of OPPRESS, but with a different movement. Observing this formational difference does not begin to address the motivation for the creative invented sign.

If having words that sound like what they mean was desirable, spoken languages should have capitalized on opportunities to construct words exhibiting onomatopoeia. The 26 words naming the letters of the English alphabet make an interesting test case because the characters these words signify are associated with speech sounds due to their use as elements of a phonetically based orthographic system. Thus, English had 26 opportunities to create (or destroy through processes of historical change) onomatopoeic words in its names for the alphabetic characters. According to my analysis, 23 of the 26 words that name letters of the alphabet currently exhibit onomatopoeia. The exceptions are the words naming "h," "w," and "y." The sound of the vowel in the word naming the character "a," for example, is the same vowel sound found in words like *lake, rake, fake, lame,* and *pain.* This correspondence

Modality Effects and Conflicting Agendas

is not perfect, since the letter "a" also appears in words like *American, Antarctica, Africa,* and *Australia* where the initial vowel sounds differ from the vowel sound in the word naming "a," but the correspondence is sufficient to demonstrate that the name of the letter is not arbitrary. Similar evidence demonstrates that all of the names for vowels show onomatopoeia. Demonstrating that the names of consonants also show onomatopoeia is equally straightforward.

The onomatopoeia exhibited by the names of the first three letters of the alphabet is illustrated in table 3.2. The English word for the written symbol "a" is pronounced $[e^I]$. The English word *say* is written with that letter and pronounced $[se^I]$. The sound of the name of the letter appears in the sound of the word written with that letter.[5] Similarly, the English word for the written symbol "b" is pronounced [bi]. The English word *boss* is written with that letter and pronounced [bas]. The sound in the name of the letter appears in the word written with that letter, demonstrating that the forms of these words is not arbitrary, but is based on sounds related to the meanings of the words.

Of the 26 opportunities for onomatopoeia in naming the letters of the alphabet, English demonstrates onomatopoeia in 88 percent. Apparently, when the opportunity for onomatopoeia presents itself, it is often exploited. Similar analysis of the names for the characters of the Thai alphabet shows that 98 percent show onomatopoeia. There is one character that has no associated sound, and could therefore, by definition, not show onomatopoeia. The same exploitation of the possibility for onomatopoeia can be seen in other alphabetic systems as well.

What Is at Stake?

Recall that the age of the earth was tied to the Uniformitarian Principle. What is tied to the claim that words should be arbitrary? Within the field of generative linguistics, I can think of no principles of phonology, morphology, or syntax that hinge on (or are even related to) the

---

5. Claire Ramsey informed me that an elementary school student teacher told her that letters of the alphabet "say their names" when a word is pronounced. The *a* in *pay*, for example, says its name when *pay* is pronounced.

TABLE 3.2. Onomatopoeia in the Names of the 26 Characters in the English Alphabet

WRITTEN SYMBOL	ENGLISH NAME FOR THE SYMBOL	WRITTEN WORD CONTAINING THAT WRITTEN SYMBOL	PHONETIC FORM OF THE SPOKEN WORD WRITTEN WITH THAT SYMBOL
a	[e^I]	say	[se^I]
b	[bi]	boss	[bas]
c	[si]	cell	[sɛl]

arbitrariness of signs. Within cognitive linguistics, iconicity (and more generally, motivated forms) are already recognized at various levels of the grammar.

Not accepting the normalcy of iconicity, however, does have a cost. Those who hold Saussure's principle to be correct will continue to view sign languages and their users as deficient. In spite of the lack of a theoretical cost to accepting iconicity, I suspect that it will require a long time for the normalcy of iconicity to be widely accepted within the field of linguistics.

Pointing

Historically, most linguistic analysis has been focused on aspects of the speech stream that can be treated as discrete units for analytical purposes. This is evident in the distinction between aspects of the speech stream considered to be linguistic and those considered to be paralinguistic. The term *paralinguistic* was developed to describe vocal articulations that are meaningful but outside the linguistic system. Since linguistic and paralinguistic elements both occur as a normal part of speech, addressees simply understand the message without attending to the linguistic-paralinguistic distinction.

Meaningful actions or gestures of the body have also been seen as outside the linguistic system. McNeill (1992) credits Kendon (1972, 1980) with discovering the unity between speech and gesture. In his own work, McNeill presents considerable, convincing evidence that "gestures are an integral part of language as much as are words, phrases, and sentences—gesture and language are one system" (1992, 2). These arguments have had little influence on sign language research. The theoretical bias in linguistic theory that devalues gesture has motivated ASL researchers to see pointing gestures not as gestures but as manifestations of linguistic units.

Pointing Is Not Pointing

Pointing that accompanies speech is treated as outside the linguistic system. Such pointing can be directed in virtually any direction. However, when sign language linguists have analyzed signs that point in unlimited numbers of directions depending on the location of the things being pointed at, they have seen this activity as driven by linguistic units rather than by gesture (see, among others, Woodward 1970; Lacy 1974; Friedman 1975; Fischer and Gough 1978; Klima and Bellugi 1979; Kegl 1985; Liddell 1984a; Padden 1988, 1990; Liddell and Johnson 1989; Lillo-Martin and Klima 1990; Engberg-Pedersen 1993; Neidle et al. 1995; Janis 1995; Bahan 1996; Brentari 1998; Meir 1998).

In general, the proposals can be characterized in the following way. A location in space becomes associated with a referent (physically present or not). That physical location is a linguistic unit, typically a morpheme. That morpheme is attached to the directional sign by using its location features as the place of articulation of the sign. Thus, when the sign is articulated at or toward that spatial location, the hand is merely carrying out articulatory instructions. In other words, the pointing so obvious to the unsophisticated observer is not really pointing at all because the hand is merely carrying out articulatory instructions. Moving the hand toward a spatial locus is no different than moving the hand toward the forehead in producing the sign KNOW.

Armstrong, Stokoe, and Wilcox (1995) address the issue of gesture in ASL from a different perspective. They note that the spoken language signal is produced by gestures within the vocal tract. Similarly, the sign language signal is produced by gestures of the head, arms, hands, and body. In both modalities gestures of the body produce the language signal. The only difference is which body parts are producing the gestures. From this perspective, both spoken and signed languages are equally gestural. But Armstrong et al. do not distinguish between the fixed nature of linguistic elements and the nonfixed nature of pointing and demonstrating gestures.[6] This is still an important distinction to make, even in the case of signed languages. I will use the criterion of variability in order to distinguish between fixed, symbolic lexical units and acts of pointing or demonstrating.

Instances where the signer points at things while signing are extremely common in ASL discourse. For example, the signer might point with one hand while producing a sign with the other hand. More commonly, however, the hand producing the sign simultaneously points at something during the production of the sign. This is most evident when the entity is physically present. For example, the signer could direct the sign FIFTEEN with the back of the hand extended toward the addressee then move the hand close to the chest and produce the sign TWELVE. In the context of a game, this would be understood to be a description of the score of the game: fifteen points for the addressee, twelve points for the signer. Directing the sign FIFTEEN toward the addressee associates the value fifteen with the addressee (Powell 1984). Similarly, producing the sign TWELVE near the chest associates the value twelve with the signer. The pointing nature of this signing could hardly be more obvious. Neither could the variability of its directionality. The directionality of the numeral sign depends completely on the location of the addressee. If the addressee is seated to the left of the standing signer then FIFTEEN would be

---

6. Throughout the remainder of this chapter I will use the term *gesture* to mean the actions of the face, head, arms, and hands in either pointing or demonstrating. I will not use the term to describe the actions of articulators in producing fixed lexical elements.

directed downward and to the left, toward the addressee. Regardless of the location of the physically present addressee, the sign will point toward the addressee.

A large number of grammatical categories allow this kind of pointing, including numerals, pronouns, determiners, nouns, adverbs, adjectives, and at least two categories of verbs. Of these, the signs that have received the most analytical attention have been verbs. Verbs in some spoken languages may inflect to provide information about their subjects or objects. This is typically referred to as subject agreement or object agreement. Although very limited in English, (1) provides an example of subject agreement.

(1) That boy walks to school everyday.

The suffix—*s* on the verb *walk* marks the fact that the subject of the verb (the phrase, *that boy*) is both third person and singular. The suffix—*s* is only added when the subject is third person singular and the verb is present tense. Analysts have seen a parallel between subject and object agreement and the directionality of some verbs in ASL. As a result there have been numerous proposals about the directionality of ASL verbs spanning almost thirty years. Multiple problems arise with such grammatical analysis of verb directionality. I have described these problems in some detail in Liddell (1990, 1994, 1995, 1998) and Liddell and Metzger (1998). First, directional signs appear to be able to be directed in an unlimited number of directions. Each possible direction would (presumably) carry with it a different meaning. This would lead to the conclusion that ASL has an unlimited number of agreement affixes, each with its own distinct phonological shape, controlling the directionality of verbs. Such a proposal has both phonological and semantic problems. First, there are no phonological proposals capable of describing the variable directionality. Consequently, there is currently no adequate means of describing the phonological form of any sign that uses space. The issue of meaning is equally problematic. Directing a verb to the left expresses different information than directing the same verb to the right. Presumably, this difference is accounted for by having different affixes attached to the verb. These affixes would then account for the differences in meaning. In order for this to work, the meanings of all the possible directional affixes would need to be made clear, but no one has yet been able to identify the phonological form of a spatial agreement affix and what it would mean. This has led me to conclude that, "an act of faith is required to hold onto the idea that spatial loci are grammatical entities with morphological and phonological substance" (Liddell 2000).

The problems with morphological analysis of directional signs do not end with being unable to describe morphemic affixes. There is a crucial distinction to be made here between meaning and reference. The subject of the sentence and the person or thing to which the subject refers are not the same thing. The subject of (1), *that boy*, is a grammatical constituent composed of two words. The entity to which the subject refers in this case is a male human made of flesh and blood. The particular boy the speaker intends the sentence to be about is not part of the sentence; in other words, the boy himself is not the subject of the sentence. However, the sentence is about him and it is important for the addressee to know which person the sentence is about. The speaker can assist the addressee in making this connection by pointing at the boy while saying *that boy*. By doing so, the speaker makes it clear that the phrase refers to that particular boy. Since the phrase *that boy* is the subject of *walks*, and since that boy has been associated with a particular boy through pointing, the addressee now knows which particu-lar boy runs everyday. The function carried out by pointing toward the boy is to connect some entity outside the sentence with the meaning of the sentence. In this case the actual boy is connected with the subject of the verb *walk*.

Pointing Is Pointing

Directing the sign FIFTEEN toward the addressee in signing the score of a game conveys the information that the addressee has fifteen points. The signer is making an association between the value fifteen and the person the sign is directed toward. By directing the sign toward the addressee, the signer indicates that the value is to be associated with the addressee.[7] Directing the sign TELL toward the addressee accomplishes the same basic function. The meaning of the verb TELL involves some entity providing information to some other entity through an act of telling. At this abstract semantic level the two entities involved are highly schematic. Langacker (1987, 1991) refers to these semantic entities as the verb's *trajector* and *landmark*. The trajector and landmark are part of the semantic representation of the verb TELL.

The ongoing task of any addressee is to make connections between the meanings expressed in the semantic representation of an utterance and the real or hypothetical entities the utterance is about (Fauconnier 1994, 1997). By directing the sign TELL toward the addressee, the signer associates the addressee with the verb's landmark (its semantic object). This is illustrated in table 3.3, where I have made a distinction between the lexical unit TELL, the pointing, and the entity being pointed at.

Exactly the same distinction applies to (1), where the speaker points while speaking the words, *that boy*. Here the same three parts in table 3.3 are equally apparent. The actual boy being talked about in (1) is not part of the semantics of the phrase *that boy*, but by pointing during the production of *that boy* the speaker makes a connection between the linguistic utterance and the actual boy.

Once this function is understood, it becomes clear that the pointing seen in the so-called agreement verbs carries out the same function as the pointing that could accompany the spoken English phrase, *that boy*. It directs the addressee's attention toward physically present entities to be associated with the meaning of the sentence (Liddell 2000).

Signs also can be directed in space when the relevant entity is not physically present. Such cases have been described as resulting from a grammatical mechanism involving a verb and affixes. The same phonological, semantic, and functional problems manifest themselves

---

7. Padden (1990) treats the directionality of nouns and adjectives as resulting from pronouns that have cliticized to the noun or adjective. Presumably, she would treat numerals the same way. This proposal suffers from the same lack of phonological substance described in the text for agreement analyses.

TABLE 3.3. Pointing that Links Linguistic Symbols with External Entities

LINGUISTIC UNITS	POINTING	EXTERNAL ENTITIES
TELL	⟶	External entity receiving the information
That boy	⟶	External entity to be associated with the meaning of the phrase, *that boy* (i.e., its referent)

in this situation as when the signer directs a sign toward a physically present entity. The solution in these cases involves the recognition that humans can conceptualize situations different from the current physical reality. In other words, the signer acts as if some absent entity were actually present. Treating the entity as if it were present means that it exists in some location in the environment of the signer. Although the entity is not physically present it is, nevertheless, conceptually present. I have called such conceptually present entities *surrogates* (Liddell 1995). Since the surrogate is conceptually present, the signer simply directs signs toward the surrogate. No new principles (or affixes) are needed. The function of directing signs toward surrogates is exactly the same as the function of directing signs toward physically present entities. In both cases the signer makes an association between the semantic representation of an utterance and some entity external to that representation.

Signers have other options for making missing entities conceptually present. One of the most common ways is to associate the entity with a volume of space. This is commonly referred to in the literature as "establishing an index" or "associating a referent with a locus." These descriptions imply that there is a point in space associated with the missing referent. Actually, it is most common to have a three-dimensional volume of space associated with the missing referent. I refer to this volume of space as a *token*. The token often has a significant height. For example, if the token is associated with a standing human then the token could be roughly a foot tall. Tokens are typically placed ahead of the signer at about the level of the trunk. By associating the token with a particular entity, the signer makes the entity conceptually present. That is, for the purposes of the discourse, the entity is conceptually present in the form of the token. Since the token is conceptually present, the signer can direct signs toward it.

A single generalization applies to all these cases: Signers direct signs at present entities. Such entities may be physically present (real things and real people), or conceptually present (surrogates and tokens).[8] This analysis entails that signers conceptualize space in specific ways that make nonphysically present entities conceptually present. Signers are then able to direct signs toward those conceptualized-as-present entities. Just as real people and things are not part of a grammatical representation, neither are the conceptualized-as-present entities. The mechanism that guides the hand in these cases is the ability to point. Signers know where things are and direct signs toward them through the ability to point. The handshapes, orientation of the hand(s), the type of movement (straight, arc) are linguistically defined. The directionality of the signs is not linguistically defined. It is variable, depending completely on the actual or conceptualized location of the entity the sign is directed toward.

What Is at Stake?

For the past several years, I have been describing the inadequacies of grammatical attempts to explain the directionality of signs in ASL. There are more than fifteen distinct proposals attempting to provide grammatical explanations for verb directionality. Only one, Liddell and Johnson (1989), attempts to provide a phonological system of representation capable of encoding spatial loci. Even this complex system is inadequate to the task. None of the other proposals provides any means of

---

8. There are other ways of making things conceptually present, but I will not discuss them in this chapter. The principle of directing signs toward such conceptually present entities applies in the same way to all these cases.

phonological representation.[9] During the same period, I have been developing a theoretical framework for describing the pointing nature of signs that depends on the cognitive ability to point at things. If things are physically present, pointing at them is straightforward. If the things are not physically present, they must be conceptualized as present. In either case, the signer simply directs a sign toward a present entity.

Gestural analysis accurately describes how signs are produced and provides a plausible explanation for the mechanism responsible for directing signs (see table 3.4). Very strong parallels can be demonstrated between the conceptualizations I propose for ASL discourse and the types of conceptualizations needed for spoken language discourse (Liddell 1998). However, in spite of the descriptive, phonological, semantic, and functional problems associated with a grammatical treatment of verb directionality, the idea that grammatical elements control the directionality of verbs is tenaciously held. This is not because the ASL data demand it or because agreement analyses are compelling. The idea that directionality is controlled by a grammatical mechanism is held because of a theoretical bias that values a grammatical analysis more highly than a gestural analysis.

In contrast with the iconicity issue, where accepting iconicity as normal carries virtually no cost to grammatical theory, there is a lot riding on the grammatical versus gestural interpretation of directionality. Virtually all grammatical parallels between verb directionality and grammatical phenomena in spoken language will have to be abandoned. Likewise, all conclusions about acquisition of directional signs will need to change from a grammatical interpretation of the facts to a gestural interpretation of the same facts. Even how one views the nature of ASL will need to change. It will require seeing ASL as a language in which grammatical elements and gestural elements coexist, both providing essential parts of signed messages. In this sense, the ASL data provides unexpected evidence in support of this view of spoken languages (see Kendon 1972, 1980; McNeill 1992).

---

9. Padden (1988) provides descriptive devices such as "In direction of addressee," but given that the addressee could be anywhere, such a description is not phonological.

TABLE 3.4. The Merits of a Gestural Analysis and a Grammatical Analysis

	GESTURAL ANALYSIS	GRAMMATICAL ANALYSIS
Uses prefixes, suffixes, clitics, etc.		✓
Children first learn non-directional forms of verbs and only later learn to to direct them[a]	✓	✓
Works with physically present entities	✓	
Plausible conceptual structures when entities are not physically present	✓	
Works with missing entities	✓	
Conceptual structures needed apply equally well with demonstrations	✓	
Provides a conceptual framework and accurately describes how signs are directed during "role shifting"	✓	
Conceptual parallel with pointing co-present with speech	✓	
Conceptual structures needed independently for spoken language	✓	

a. When this chapter was presented as a paper at the conference honoring William Stokoe, this characteristic of ASL acquisition was not in the table. Elissa Newport suggested that it should be considered as evidence in favor of a grammatical analysis. Actually, this acquisition fact is consistent with either analysis. Let us begin with the assumption that the order of acquisition tells us that the directed form is more 'difficult' to acquire than the non-directional form. A grammatical analysis would attribute the difficulty to combining morphemes. A gestural analysis would attribute the difficulty to the need to learn to overlay a gesture on top of a linguistic sign as well as the increased complexity of the conceptualizations that underlie the use of the directed forms of signs.

Conclusion

Theories have a powerful influence on how those in a given field see and understand the data in front of them. Linguists and psychologists carry with them expectations about what a language should be like and, just as important, what should not be part of linguistic signs. If one assumes that all such expectations are correct, then ASL presents serious problems. But one of the reasons for studying a signed language, as opposed to a vocally produced language, is to learn something new. These issues of iconicity and gesture should not be viewed as problems in the analysis, but as opportunities to learn something about language in general. The problem is not with ASL but with faulty conceptions of what language should look like.

References

Abrahams, Harold. 1998. Introduction to Daniel Moreau Barringer and the battle for the Impact Theory, by Carla Barringer Rabinowitz. Available online: ⟨http://www.barringercenter.com/adventure⟩

Armstrong, David F., William C. Stokoe, and Sherman E. Wilcox. 1995. *Gesture and the nature of language.* Cambridge: Cambridge University Press.

Bahan, Benjamin. 1996. Nonmanual realization of agreement in American Sign Language. Ph.D. diss., Boston University.

Bolinger, Dwight. 1975. *Aspects of language.* 2d ed. New York: Harcourt, Brace, Jovanovich.

Brentari, Diane. 1998. *A prosodic model of sign language phonology.* Cambridge: MIT Press.

DeMatteo, Asa. 1977. Visual imagery and visual analogues in American Sign Language. In *On the other hand: New perspectives on American Sign Language,* edited by Lynn H. Friedman, 109–36. New York: Academic Press.

Engberg-Pedersen, Elisabeth. 1993. *Space in Danish Sign Language: The semantics and morphosyntax of the use of space in a visual language.* International Studies on Sign Language and Communication of the Deaf, vol. 19. Hamburg: Signum-Verlag.

Fauconnier, Gilles. [1985] 1994. *Mental spaces.* Reprint, Cambridge: Cambridge University Press.

———. 1997. *Mappings in thought and language.* Cambridge: Cambridge University Press.

Fischer, Susan. 1973. Two processes of reduplication in American Sign Language. *Foundations of Language* 9: 469–80.

Fischer, Susan, and Bonnie Gough. 1978. Verbs in American Sign Language. *Sign Language Studies* 18: 17–48.

Friedman, Lynn. 1975. Space, time, and person references in American Sign Language. *Language* 51: 940–61.

Frishberg, Nancy. 1975. Arbitrariness and iconicity: Historical change in American Sign Language. *Language* 51: 676–710.

Janis, Wynne. 1995. A crosslinguistic perspective on ASL verb agreement. In *Language, gesture, and space,* edited by Karen Emmorey and Judy Reilly, 195–223. Hillsdale, N.J.: Lawrence Erlbaum Associates.

Kegl, Judy. 1985. Locative relations in American Sign Language word formation, syntax, and discourse. Ph.D. diss., Massachusetts Institute of Technology, Cambridge.

Kendon, Adam. 1972. Some relationships between body motion and speech. In *Studies in dyadic communication,* edited by Aron Wolfe Siegman and Benjamin Pope, 177–210. New York: Pergamon Press.

———. 1980. Gesticulation and speech: Two aspects of the process of utterance. In *The relationship of verbal and nonverbal communication,* edited by Mary Ritchie Key, 207–27. The Hague: Mouton.

Klima, Edward S., and Ursula Bellugi et al. 1979. *The signs of language.* Cambridge: Harvard University Press.

Lacy, Richard. 1974. Putting some of the syntax back into semantics. Salk Institute. Typescript.

Langacker, Ronald W. 1987. *Foundations of cognitive grammar. Vol. 1: Theoretical prerequisites.* Stanford: Stanford University Press.

———. 1991. *Foundations of cognitive grammar. Vol. 2: Descriptive application.* Stanford: Stanford University Press.

Liddell, Scott K. 1980. *American Sign Language syntax.* The Hague: Mouton.

———. 1982. THINK and BELIEVE: Sequentiality in American Sign Language Signs. Paper presented at the Linguistic Society of America, University of Maryland, College Park.

———. 1984a. THINK and BELIEVE: Sequentiality in American Sign Language Signs. *Language* 60: 372–99.

———. 1984b. Unrealized-inceptive aspect in American Sign Language: Feature insertion in syllabic frames. In *Papers from the 20th Regional Meeting of the Chicago Linguistic Society*, edited by J. Drogo, V. Mishra, and D. Teston, 257–70. Chicago: University of Chicago Press.

———. 1990. Lexical imagery in signed and spoken languages. Paper presented at Theoretical Issues in Sign Language III, Boston, Mass., 18 May.

———. 1992. Paths to lexical imagery. Washington, D.C.: Gallaudet University. Typescript.

———. 1994. Tokens and surrogates. In *Perspectives on sign language structure: Papers from the Fifth International Symposium on Sign Language Research* [vol. 1], edited by Inger Ahlgren, Brita Bergman, and Mary Brennan, 105–19. Durham, U.K.: The International Sign Linguistics Association.

———. 1995. Real, surrogate, and token space: Grammatical consequences in ASL. In *Language, gesture, and space*, edited by Karen Emmorey and Judy S. Reilly, 19–41. Hillsdale, N.J.: Lawrence Erlbaum Associates.

———. 1998. Grounded blends, gestures, and conceptual shifts. *Cognitive Linguistics* 9 (3): 283–314.

———. 2000. Indicating verbs and pronouns: Pointing away from agreement. In *The signs of language revisited: An anthology to honor Ursula Bellugi and Edward Klima*, edited by Karen Emmorey and Harlan Lane, 303–20. Mahwah, N.J.: Lawrence Erlbaum Associates.

Liddell, Scott K., and Robert E. Johnson. 1989. American Sign Language: The phonological base. *Sign Language Studies* 64: 195–277.

Liddell, Scott K., and Metzger, Melanie. 1998. Gesture in sign language discourse. *Journal of Pragmatics* 30: 657–97.

Lillo-Martin, Diane, and Edward S. Klima. 1990. Point out differences: ASL pronouns in syntactic theory. In *Theoretical issues in sign language research*, edited by Susan Fischer and Pat Siple, 191–210. Chicago: University of Chicago Press.

Mandel, Mark. 1977. Iconic devices in American Sign Language. In *On the other hand: New perspectives on American Sign Language*, edited by Lynn H. Friedman, 57–107. New York: Academic Press.

McCarthy, John. 1979. Formal problems in Semitic phonology and morphology. Ph.D. diss., Massachusetts Institute of Technology, Cambridge.

Meir, Irit. 1998. Thematic structure and verb agreement in Israeli Sign Language. Ph.D. diss., Hebrew University of Jerusalem.

Neidle, Carol, Dawn MacLaughlin, Judy Kegl, Benjamin Bahan, and Debra Aarons. 1995. Overt realization of syntactic features in American Sign Language. Paper presented at Syntax seminar, University of Trondheim, Norway, May.

Okrent, Arika. 1997. The productive use of conceptual metaphor in ASL: How form and meaning can be connected without the bond of convention. Washington, D.C.: Gallaudet University. Typescript.

Padden, Carol A. 1988. *Interaction of morphology and syntax in American Sign Language.* New York: Garland Publishing.

———. 1990. The relation between space and grammar in ASL verb morphology. In *Sign language research: Theoretical issues,* edited by Cecil Lucas, 118–32. Washington, D.C.: Gallaudet University Press.

Powell, Faith. 1984. How to score points in ASL. Washington, D.C.: Gallaudet University. Typescript.

Rabinowitz, Carla Barringer. 1998. Daniel Moreau Barringer and the battle for the Impact Theory. Available online: ⟨http://www.barringercenter.com/adventure⟩

Saussure, Ferdinand de. [1922] 1959. *Course in general linguistics.* Translation of *Cours de linguistique generale* by Wade Baskin. Edited by Charles Bally and Albert Reidlinger. New York: Philosophical Library.

Taub, Sarah F. 1997. Language in the body: Iconicity and metaphor in American Sign Language. Ph.D. diss., University of California, Berkeley.

Wescott, Roger W. 1971. Linguistic iconism. *Language* 47: 416–28.

Wilbur, Ronnie. 1987. *American Sign Language: Linguistic and applied dimensions* 2d. ed. Boston: College Hill Press.

Woodward, James. 1970. Personal pronominalization in American Sign Language. Georgetown University. Typescript.

PART 2

Language Origins

INTRODUCTION

David F. Armstrong

When Stokoe began to become interested in the question of language origins in the early 1970s, he was entering a field that had lain fallow, at least with respect to serious scholarship, for a century or more. In the Western world, of course, the primary influence on our thinking about the origin of language has come from the Bible. However, with the advent of Darwin's *Origin of Species*, Western thinking increasingly focused on materialist explanations for the origins of biological phenomena, including human beings and aspects of human behavior, language included. According to Darwin, in *The Origin of Species*, "Much light will be thrown on the origin of man and his history." In the latter half of the nineteenth century, speculation about the origin and evolution of language, or the biological capacity for it, became so rampant and undisciplined that the Linguistic Society of Paris in 1866 banned all discussion of it (Hewes 1996). A passage in the Society's bylaws states the following: "The Society will accept no communication concerning either the origin of language or the creation of a universal language." A contemporary philologist, Max Müller, characterized some of the dominant language origins theories of the time with derisive epithets: the bow-wow theory, the ding-dong theory, the pooh-pooh theory, the yo-he-ho theory (Hewes 1996, 583).

The nature of the bow-wow theory is fairly obvious—speech sounds were thought to be originally onomatopoeic. According to Gordon Hewes (1996, 583), an anthropologist and historian of language origin theories:

> The pooh-pooh theory asserted that language originated in emotional cries—an idea advanced in the eighteenth century by Rousseau among others. The yo-he-ho theory saw the basis for language in cooperative work-songs or chants ... Müller himself preferred the ding-dong theory, which claimed that a kind of psychic resonance existed between certain combinations of sounds and natural objects. The 'mouth-gesture' theory ... derived articulate speech from approximations by the tongue and other parts of the vocal tract to replicating movements of the hands and fingers in gestural communication. Only this last (and by no means convincing!) model derived spoken language from an already existing non-vocal language.

The theories discussed by Müller all had to do with the origin of *speech*. Others speculated about the origin of *language* as having begun with some sort of gestured or signed communication. Speculation of this sort predated Darwin by a considerable margin, and it was done by such as the Enlightenment French *savant*, the Abbé de Condillac.

Since the Linguistic Society of Paris decided to ban discussion of the topic in 1866, respectable science had tended to steer clear of the topic. It was just too speculative, too resistant to hypothesis testing in the usual scientific fashion. In fact, there was very little evidence available, from the fossil record for human evolution, from comparative studies of other primate species, or from neuroscience to support theories about the evolution of language. By the early 1970s this situation had begun to change—evidence from the fields mentioned above had become available that could be used to construct theoretical frameworks. In addition, the field of linguistics had been energized by the theories of Noam Chomsky, and these, in turn, had led to increased study of the neurological underpinnings of human language use. Stokoe himself provided one of the final keys—the idea that language could be expressed in a medium other than speech, and this could be tied back to earlier speculation concerning the role of gesture in the evolution of language.

Karchmer and I discussed some of Stokoe's ideas on the role of gesture in the evolution of language earlier in this volume, and I will not repeat that discussion here—the chapters that follow elaborate extensively on those ideas. However, it is worth noting here that Stokoe was very much opposed to what he saw as the anti-evolutionary formalism of Chomsky, although some of Chomsky's ideas on phrase-structure grammar had a strong influence on Stokoe's thinking. Frank Wilson and Roger Fouts discuss the division that has developed in theories of language origins between adherents of Chomsky, who think that language must have arisen very rapidly and must have been enabled by specific genetic mutations affecting brain structure, and those who posit a more general, more gradual approach. They describe how Stokoe's theoretical work supports a more gradual evolution of language through a gestural stage. Sherman Wilcox expounds on Stokoe's notion of "semantic phonology" and shows how this little understood idea solves many problems in linguistics generally, as well as in the study of language origins.

Reference

Hewes, Gordon W. 1996. A history of the study of language origins. In *Handbook of human symbolic evolution,* edited by Andrew Lock and Charles R. Peters. Oxford: Oxford University Press.

4

Does Sign Language Solve the Chomsky Problem?

Frank R. Wilson

Over the course of several years, when I was preparing to write a book about the role of the hand in human life, I began to formulate the following idea: all humans are born with a brain that expects the hand to be the prime bodily mediator of discovery, invention, and communication (Wilson 1998). I began my book with a simple question that had come to me in the course of more than a decade of treating musicians who had injured their hands. The question was: Why are musicians always so upset when they cannot work? For musicians, playing is not only real work but *hard* work, and yet for them, time off (even if it is *paid* time off) is uniformly unwelcome. Obviously, if musicians are simply emotional about everything—they are professional emoters, one might say—one could ignore their distress over interruptions in the daily routine. But there is more to it than that: musicians devote their lives to self-expression and are unusually liable to upset when physically unable to exercise their hard-won skills. When they are instrumental musicians rather than vocalists, obviously, their achievements depend upon the hands.

What about other examples of people whose professional work has an expressive component and depends upon skilled hand use? What about sculptors and painters, goldsmiths, machinists and blacksmiths, and other performing artists like jugglers, magicians, and puppeteers? These people, too, are passionate about their work. In the course of interviewing a number of such individuals, inquiring not only about their careers but about childhood interests, teachers, family support, and so on, I learned that for some people, at least, the hand is not merely a practical tool for making a living, but a master teacher and interpreter of the world, and the primary means of expressing ideas and feelings about it and of effecting change in it. There are certainly rudiments of this hand-based relation to the world in all of us, but these were people who, often when they were quite young, had staked their future on what they wanted to do with their hands, seeking inclusion in a professional community that defines itself on the basis of a specialized skill and sphere of knowledge.

The more stories of this kind I heard, the more powerfully I was struck by the parallels in the developmental path of all of these young people. It did not seem to matter whether it was music or fixing cars or quilting or juggling or building things out of wood or clay—a remarkable force was set loose when these young people began creating something personal with their own hands. Of course these were not the stories of the average child in our society, who grows up in a world that has largely reduced the hand to an incidental role in educational and working life. Given the way most of us live our lives, these stories—even when they were told by successful surgeons—made me feel as if I had stumbled across something akin to a Big Foot colony in the wilds of the Pacific Northwest. Whatever they were, they looked suspiciously like a behavioral or cognitive missing link in the human evolutionary story, a hidden subspecies of humans whose intelligence was geared to a time when we were tool users—which is to say, before we became device managers and computer users.

I finally convinced myself that these were not throwbacks at all, but rather unusually transparent expressions of the inborn tendency of most if not *all* humans to have a brain that expects the hand to be the prime bodily mediator of experience and communication. It was evident that the claim of a special relationship between hand and brain in human cognition would be scorned by every cognitive scientist who believes that intelligence is a descriptive term for the brain's computing power, but it was something of a surprise to discover the implications of these childhood stories for the rarified world in which questions about language origin are seriously debated. But as soon as I decided to follow the hand-brain relationship as far back in history as it has been traced, it was inevitable that I would encounter human ancestors who depended upon gestural communication, and that I would have to ask how the systematic use of signs in populations of evolving hominids might inform our understanding of the emergence of language as a defining human behavior.

When our earliest ancestors began life on the ground, neither the hand nor the brain were what they are today. Lucy, an *australopithecine* female who lived three million years ago, had several un-apelike anatomic features in the hand. As minor as these alterations to ancestral anatomy were—an increase in the length of the thumb compared to the fingers and the ability to rotate the index and middle fingers on their long axis—they gave Lucy's clan the biomechanics needed for some new grips and hand movements. Most important of these was the "3-jaw chuck"—a grip that permits an irregularly shaped stone to be held tightly between the thumb, index, and middle fingers. This grip is identical to that used by a baseball pitcher for an overarm pitch. Such a grip, of course, would have been extremely useful if the skill of throwing could be mastered for purposes of hunting or defense. No one knows how much aggressive or defensive overarm throwing the *australopithecines* actually did, nor do we know exactly when subsequent changes in the anatomy of the hand occurred or how they may have been exploited by Lucy's descendants, but we do know that over the span of several million years, those of Lucy's descendants who learned to take advantage of the hand came to dominate the bipedal world of the hominids and eventually outlasted all their competitors. When our ancestors came down from the trees, in other words, an upright walking posture had not merely relieved the forelimbs of their primary role in locomotion but had opened the door to a completely novel domain of perception, action, and *interaction* based in the hands, and *our* ancestors were the ones who walked through that door (Marzke 1983, 1996).

It is now widely acknowledged by anthropologists, archeologists, and cognitive scientists alike that the biological success of humans has largely been due to an increasing dependence on tools (Tattersall 1995; Schick and Toth 1993; Donald 1991). This success story is centered in the hand, beginning with Lucy's 3-jaw chuck. Subsequent structural changes, mainly on the side of the hand opposite the thumb, allowed improved finger-to-finger contact and a greatly expanded range of both power and precision handling movements in manipulation of objects. There is still no accepted timetable for these later changes in hand structure, but the archeological record makes it clear that the exploitation of this potential to improve tools and tool use came very slowly. Stone knapping is the deliberate chipping of rocks to make cutting tools that became a widespread practice about two million years ago. Somewhat more elaborate stone tools first appeared at about the time the worldwide migration of *Homo erectus* began a half a million years later. But the same tools that these pioneers carried with them across the entire face of the globe over a span of a full million years remained essentially unchanged for that entire period. Our earliest ancestors had restless legs, it seems, but were thoroughly contented with the modest state of their technology.

However difficult it may be for us to imagine this degree of indifference of human ancestors to tools and gadgets, we should not really be surprised. After all, it is highly unlikely that the brain would have been capable of controlling the novel and increasingly complex movements of the evolving hominid hand *before* the hand itself was physically capable of varying the hand grips and individual finger movements that are now part of our repertoire. From a neurological and evolutionary perspective the conservative position must be that the brain developed these control capabilities very gradually and modified them over time as experience with the hand defined its long-term role in hominid survival. And because of the extremely slow pace of genetic change at the species level, a very long period of time would have been required to ensure that each new member of our species would arrive with an inborn potential for skilled hand use, plus the urge to take things apart and put them back together again.

In the first half of this century, anthropologists had not yet accepted that brain, body, and behavior could evolve in concert, or as a corollary that the structure and function of brain and hand can only have *co*-evolved. On the contrary, it was taught that the human hand was simply a primitive structure that had been elevated to importance in life by the gift of a larger and more advanced brain. But we now know better, and indeed it could be argued just as forcefully (and narrowly) that the truth verges on the opposite: that it was the newly configured hand—and the uses to which it could be put—that leveraged an ancient and highly successful simian brain into what it is now. Co-evolutionary theory leads us to see the process as reciprocal and complementary, without telling us anything about the specifics. But this conceptualization also leads us to a profoundly important inference about the modern brain: namely, that it diverges from other primate brains mainly in its having acquired a host of specialized neural operations to support sensorimotor and cognitive activities involving the hand. It is at this point that we find ourselves questioning a few pivotal constructs of cognitive science and linguistics, and headed for a minor fender-bender with Noam Chomsky's theory of language.

The account I have just given of hand-brain co-evolution is actually a quite conservative attempt at reconstruction of an unknown hominid past that extends from an era of novel biomechanics and behaviors to a complex present marked by endlessly ramifying realms of action, cognition, and communication. But how does this reconstruction relate to the "Chomsky problem?" There is one part of Chomsky's linguistics that has given cognitive science and evolutionary theory its grandest case of indigestion: How can a biologic trait as complex as language have become a species level, heritable trait without a biologic or behavioral antecedent? But that is exactly what he has postulated. In an interview published in the *New York Times,* Professor Chomsky said "Imagine that some divine superengineer, in a single efficient stroke, endowed humans with the power of language where formerly they had none" (Fox 1999). In an earlier interview, in 1992, when asked whether the evolutionary history of language could be traced, he had said "I don't think we have a prayer of answering it on the basis of anything that's now understood" (Chase 1992). Unless he has changed his mind in the last few years, Professor Chomsky still doubts that evolutionary theory can provide an adequate account of the origins of human language.

Somehow—quite possibly because I am naïve—I do not feel quite so defeated by this question. I see no difficulty at all creating a perfectly tenable evolutionary explanation for language. To begin with, it seems to me that the celebrated discontinuity paradox is actually something of a sham. First of all, whatever language-like abilities humans and living apes may share, these similarities cannot in any case support a claim of ape-to-human evolution in language because humans and apes diverged from their common ancestor millions of years before human language emerged. This does not mean that humans and apes cannot be compared as to commonly derived skills in communication, reasoning, or tool use—of course they can. But humans are the only surviving representatives of the hominid line, so we are obliged to seek an account of the unique linguistic adaptations of *Homo sapiens* among the shards left by the australopithecines and *their* descendants.

The anthropologist Peter J. Reynolds makes clear that the celebrated discontinuity argument is not merely irrelevant but obstructive. This is because assertions of a discontinuity between ape and human language obscure clear-cut and highly significant *continuities* in language and tool use in both ape and hominid lines. To put Reynolds' case in its briefest possible form, "the linguistic constructions of apes are analogous to their object constructions, and the absence of grammar and function words in ape sign language should come as no surprise given that these animals lack analogous abilities in tool-using skills" (Reynolds 1993).

Reynolds argues that human tool-making and language-making advanced as an integrated cognitive and behavioral adaptation in the hominids—they *co-evolved*. Most important, hominid tool manufacture and use cannot have been a solitary activity, except perhaps at the very beginning, two million or so years ago. As tools themselves became more complex constructions and as they came to be used for the manufacture of more complicated objects (weapons, clothing, shelters, and the like), they required the cooperation of individuals working in groups, which is to say, the exploitation of diverse skills and knowledge within in a stable social context. And by the time *Homo erectus* had settled large parts of the planet, cooperative tool use in hunting and sheltering had become an essential underpinning of their survival strategy. This extraordinary revolution had taken place many thousands of years—hundreds of thousands of years, actually—before speech as we know it can have become part of the hominid behavioral repertoire.

Reynolds forces us to keep our attention on the hominids as we look for adaptations leading to language, where in fact there is no discontinuity problem whatever. There is no need to claim that a completely formed language module of occult origin inserted itself into the human brain when we were still primitive communicators, thus transforming us into language-competent creatures. There is no need to do this, that is, unless one insists that speech and language are discrete, "modular" adaptations (or "instinctive" behaviors, in Pinker's language). But they are not. Walking and standing and reaching and grasping are instinctive in humans, requiring neither the example nor the instruction of others. Language development, however quickly and systematically it unfolds, still requires exposure to others who can demonstrate it, and with whom it can be practiced.

If language *per se* was not evolving as a heritable trait in hominids, what was? I submit that it was an entire suite of cognitive, inventive, and communicative potentials associated with vastly more complex uses of the hand. I illustrate this claim concerning the inherent legibility of rehearsed movement (including hand movement) by recalling a period in my residency training when I assisted a neurosurgical operating team. The senior surgeon was a deliberate man, unusually strict about operating room protocol, obsessive about preventing wound infections, and absolutely fanatic about preserving as much normal brain tissue as possible when he was operating. Normally, four or five people worked together on his team, plus an anesthesiologist who had to follow everything that happened during the operation in order to act promptly should there be changes in the patient's condition. Everyone at the table was dressed in long gowns and masks. In addition, the chief surgeon himself wore a sort of modified snorkel apparatus that was connected to a vacuum air line, whose purpose was to keep his own exhaled breath from drifting over the surgical site. He looked like a modern astronaut rigged for a space walk. His operations typically lasted anywhere from six to ten hours and he never shifted his standing position once he had begun.

Despite all of these peculiarities, to my mind none was quite so remarkable as the fact that, to the best of my recollection, this surgeon *never* spoke a word during any of his operations, nor did he permit anyone else to speak. Just for a moment, imagine yourself standing at this operating table, doing your part to assist through a long and difficult operation. How would you know what the surgeon was doing? How would you know what *you* were supposed to do, or when you were supposed to do it? I can tell you how it was done: everyone watched the surgeon's hands and what he was doing with the operating instruments. These were not naive observers. Their own professional knowledge of brain anatomy and surgical technique, their complete familiarity with the team strategy for removing tumors, and their instant grasp of the significance of every nuance of movement of the leader's arms, wrists, hands and fingers, made his assistants equal and fully informed participants in the ongoing and richly informative *but completely silent* conversation that began with the first touch of a scalpel to the patient's forehead and did not conclude until the last suture was securely in place many hours later.

What kind of language was this? I would be tempted to call it a San Francisco dialect of mainstream operative neurosurgical sign language. No one invented this language, named it, or even considered it to be a language as such. It just came into being in this particular community, where it thrived for a number of years and eventually became the principal operating room language of residents who trained on this particular team at this particular time. Its deep structure, its conjoined semantics and syntactics, were absolutely typical of every human language that has ever existed, whether spoken or signed, and its emergence can be understood as the natural outgrowth of shared expertise, cooperative labor, the association of skilled movement with complex knowledge and intentionality, and of the innate capacity of each individual initiated into the rituals of neurosurgical work to construct his or her own meaning from the signs being exchanged between those present.

How, then, do formalized signed languages such as ASL fit specifically into this scheme? All that remains to make the picture complete is to remember that skilled hand use develops in all humans out of a combination of trial and error, observation, instruction, and rehearsal. The old joke: "How do you get to Carnegie Hall? Practice, practice, practice!" illustrates this point. But it is not only expertise in execution—the elimination of inconsistencies and the achievement of fluency—that comes with movement rehearsal. Musicians practice the same movements over and over again to achieve expressive effects in performance. Tennis and basketball players, among others, engage in prolonged movement rehearsal for the same neuromuscular reasons as do musicians. However, because any skilled competitor can decipher an opponent's strategy by observing the flow of postures, gestures, and facial expressions that accompany skilled play, the expert competitive athlete must have learned to *disguise* anything in his or her skilled movements that could reveal thinking, intentions, or feelings.

Note that the skilled movements of athletic performance defy classification along any linguistic spectrum that divides gestures into those that are iconic and those that are opaque, or fully coded. The practiced movements of the skilled artist or athlete are inherently transparent to others who share the skill and understand how the game, or the music, is played. Moreover, they are expressive—that is, they can be read—regardless of the communicative intent of the person making the gestures. Why? Because humans have an innate potential to associate complex bodily movements in a familiar environment with cognitive state and intentionality.

William Stokoe, David Armstrong, and Sherman Wilcox have addressed the complicated problem of gestural origins, use, and meaning in a number of their recent publications, arguing among other things that some animals are capable of finding "true language, with syntax as well as vocabulary, in gestural activity" (Armstrong et al. 1995: 197). I fully agree with this claim, and might make bold enough to push it just a bit further: habitual movements, whether overtly imitative or not, are dynamic reflections of mental state and intention and as such are available to any observer as signs to be interpreted. Ordinary movements like combing the hair and brushing the teeth (which neurologists call *praxic movements*) send messages, and virtually everyone can read them. But there is another class of movements that arise through repetition carried out specifically for the purpose of refining their execution. We do not have an official term for these movements, but perhaps they should be called *super-praxic*. The gestures of the skilled musician qualify for inclusion in this class of movement, as do those of the skilled athlete, surgeon, juggler, chef, painter, or the deaf person who makes sentences with hands, arms, face, and indeed with the rest of the body.

What is critically important about all such gestures is that they can *always* be recognized by knowing observers, irrespective of the intent of the author of those gestures. All of our ordinary praxic movements are signs for whatever they accomplish, and praxic movements have been a component of gestural communication among primates for millions of years. So what is new? What is distinctive about human language? I suggest that what we humans now formally refer to as language benefits in a critical way from this ancient and originally opportunistic mode of gestural communication that grew into an exclusive behavioral potential in humans with the advent of the neurologic potential for super-praxic capacities in the hominid hand.

This hand, unprecedented in its manipulative powers (and in that aptitude ours alone), can create an infinite variety of complex physical structures out of a limited set of undifferentiated units. Because our ancestors not only exploited the hand in social contexts but staked their survival on cooperative tool use, every new human arrives with the potential to use the hands in this same way, which leads me to the following conclusion:

> To the extent that stereotyped skilled movements could be (and with significant benefit increasingly were) appropriated by observers to infer mental or intentional states of others whose actions were of interest, the generative potential of the movements of the hand must to the same degree have been appropriated as the foundation for the generative potential of a system of communication.

Lately this conceptualization seems less like fantasy and more like reality, because the more we learn about manual praxis and signed languages, the more striking are the congruities we find in their respective ontogeny, phenomenology, and neural underpinnings.

If Peter Reynolds is right, the long history of human tool use in social settings explains the creation of both the cognitive and neural basis for formal languages, in multiple modalities. Human language, in other words, derives from and shares the same semantic, syntactic, and generative rules that govern the behavior, transformation, and recombination of physical objects by the synergistic actions of human hand and human imagination. And for as long as humans continue to devise and perfect hand-based skills, you can be sure there will be a continued elaboration and refreshing of the human repertoire of languages.

References

Armstrong, David F., William C. Stokoe, and Sherman E. Wilcox. 1995. *Gesture and the nature of language.* Cambridge: Cambridge University Press.

Donald, M. 1991. *Origins of the modern mind: Three stages in the evolution of culture and cognition.* Cambridge: Harvard University Press.

Chase, Naomi. 1992. Naomi Chase interviews Noam Chomsky. ZNet Archives (April).

Fox, M. 1999. A changed Noam Chomsky simplifies. *New York Times.* (December).

Marzke, M. 1983. Joint functions and grips of the *Australopithecus afarensis* hand, with special reference to the region of the capitate. *Journal of Human Evolution* 12: 197–211.

———. 1996. Evolution of the hand and bipedality. In *Handbook of human symbolic evolution,* edited by Andrew Lock and Charles R. Peters. Oxford: Oxford University Press.

Reynolds, Peter J. 1993. The complementation theory of language and tool use. In *Tools, language and cognition in human evolution,* edited by K. Gibson and Tim Ingold. Cambridge: Cambridge University Press.

Schick, K., and N. Toth. 1993. *Making silent stones speak: Human evolution and the dawn of technology.* New York: Simon and Schuster.

Tattersall, I. 1995. *The fossil trail: How we know what we think we know about human evolution.* Oxford: Oxford University Press.

Wilson, Frank R. 1998. *The hand: How its uses shapes the brain, language, and human culture.* New York: Pantheon.

5

Continuity, Ethology, and Stokoe: How to Build a Better Language Model

Roger S. Fouts and Gabriel S. Waters

Our perspective of the world determines how we behave in the world. If we thought the world was flat, we would certainly avoid trying to sail around it. If we thought the earth was the center of the universe, we might try to get to another planet but without much success. While geocentric models are now part of our scientific history, we are in the middle of a major change in perspective with regard to our species' place in nature and our relationships with other organic beings. A great deal of evidence has been accumulated in the more than 150 years since Darwin that is stimulating and supporting this change. In *The Origin of Species,* Darwin proposed four basic principles that we consider today as the driving force behind speciation. They are (1) the variability of organisms within a species, (2) differential reproductive success due to selective pressure on these variations, (3) successful varieties are passed on to subsequent generations, and (4) in each generation more offspring are produced than will survive (Darwin [1859] 1991). The synthesis of these four principles provides a robust framework for the creation and testing of hypotheses (Freeman and Herron 1998).

In stark contrast to the Darwinian worldview are the Platonic and Cartesian worldviews in which "man" is superior to all other beings including women. The Greek view is the more traditional chain of being approach, which is rather like a ladder on which the inferior creatures are placed below the superior male human. Descartes's view was slightly different in that a definite gap or difference in kind existed between man and the defective automata below him. It was still a chain of being that ordered our fellow animals in descending fashion on a scale of imperfection, but these imperfect automata were quite distinct and different in kind from man because they lacked reason and being machines they were incapable of thought as well as feeling.

Plato's notion of the "Ideal" is the basis of "man's" arrogant assumption of superiority, which implicitly carries with it the notion of "Not Ideal," just as the notion of "perfect" carries with it the notion of "imperfect." From Plato's student, Aristotle, comes a companion concept in the law of contradiction. It states that "A cannot be both B and non-B," therefore "A must be either B or non-B." This is the Law of the Excluded Middle, or more correctly the fallacy of the excluded middle. This bivalence provides us with the false sense of "certainty" and "absolute prediction." True and False become our absolutes. Even Aristotle saw problems with this since a few pages earlier in his *Metaphysics* he recognized that "more" or "less" are still present in the nature of things. But it was Plato's "Ideals" that caught on and led to "essentialism," which was one of the main barriers to the theory of evolution.

Essentialism held that each species is completely distinct from all other species and is based on an eternal static essence. The variations were nothing more than imperfections of the underlying ideal model. This model placed permanent gaps in the phylogenetic scale. As it turned out these gaps were really gaps in the mind and scholarship of humans. Today this archaic superstitious notion still survives. Science still implicitly clings to the arrogant notion that we are somehow different and superior to the "have-nots."

Darwin's principle that all biological functions vary in degree rather than kind is certainly accepted with regard to the blood and bone, but the mind still remains embattled, and at the center of that battle is language. Language has a long tradition as being the defining trait of human primates dating back to the ancient Greeks. This tradition has persisted through the rise and fall of many a paradigm despite a surprising lack of scientific study concerning its place in nonhuman animals (Seyfarth and Cheney 1997). In fact, one could argue that even today many theorists hold to the uniqueness of human language in spite of strong empirical evidence to the contrary (Gardner and Gardner 1989).

Glottogenesis and Gesture

Hypotheses on the origin of human language, or *glottogenesis*, have traditionally fallen into two groups, both with ties to Darwinian or Platonic theory. These camps are best defined as gradualists and punctuationalists. While the gradualists propose a slow incremental progression of language capabilities, the punctualationists suggest that language appeared rather suddenly with the evolution of modern *Homo sapiens*. A belief or disbelief in a gestural stage within the origin of language also marks these two groups (Armstrong, Stokoe, and Wilcox 1994).

It is quite possible that the failure to accept the notion of a gestural stage in glottogenesis has forced the hand of those who believe in a punctuated model. The apparatus required for speech did not appear in the human lineage until 200,000 years ago with the emergence of *Homo sapiens* (Fouts and Mills 1997). Time constraints inherent in this model simply do not allow for a gradual evolution of language. The result is a theory that must rely on the rapid development of a complex suite of behaviors based on a single morphological structure. A structure that, as Stokoe (1983) points out, does not necessarily add much to the communicative repertoire present in other primates; their systems of communication that already include arms, hands, faces, frontally faced eyes and voices.

Now We Have It and You Don't

It is next to impossible to begin a discussion on language evolution or acquisition without a mention of the Cartesian linguist Noam Chomsky. Chomsky's influence is apparent in the fact that he currently ranks in the top ten cited writers in the humanities, much less in language studies (Pinker 1994). Chomsky's theory applies to a discussion of the evolution of language in that he claims that grammar is innate and the structures responsible for language can be conceived as a language "organ" (Pinker 1994). One would think that this would place him squarely in the ranks of Darwinian theory, after all Darwin ([1859] 1991) himself stated that natural selection "can act on every internal organ, on every shade of constitutional difference, on the machinery of life" ([1859] 1991, 61). This would intuitively seem to be a strong base on which Chomsky could place his theory, yet he is a vocal opponent of Darwin, not only in regard to language but also natural selection as a mechanism for evolution. Chomsky goes as far as to say that natural selection "does not say much about how new qualities can emerge" (Cziko 1995).

Since Chomsky introduced his theory of language, some of his followers have tried to correct his disdain for natural selection by incorporating some evolutionary ideas into his work. However, the queasy feeling left in the stomach of a Darwinian after reading Chomsky's statement will not quickly fade upon this synthesis. Steven Pinker (1994) criticized Chomsky's elimination of natural selection in an attempt to show his theory of innate grammar in the light of instinctual behavior. Unfortunately, in the process of praising Darwin's theory for eliminating the theological Chain of Being argument, Pinker systematically refutes the related concept of continuity of organic beings. With the elimination of continuity of beings Pinker misses the point Darwin ([1859] 1991) made when he stated, "how infinitely complex and close-fitting are the mutual relations of all organic beings" ([1859] 1991, 59). Darwin was referring to the relatedness of the beings themselves and that they are in a state of constant interaction within their environment.

The current language origin theories that are based on a rapid vocal development of speech build their foundations on Chomsky's notion of the language "organ." This language organ, as proposed by Chomsky and his followers, is essentially a metaphor for the structures within the brain that facilitate speech (Pinker 1994). By utilizing the concept of an organ in a discussion of language origins, proponents of a punctuated evolution accomplish two things:

1. They can make analogies to other complex organs as a model for the evolution of language, and

2. They evoke an image of innateness for human language that has consequences as to how one views both the ontogeny and phylogeny of language development.

Although the effect of this metaphor on how one views the phylogeny of language development is the major focus of this paper, a brief examination of how it affects the perception of the ontogeny of language development is warranted. By viewing language as the function of an imagined organ, one can postulate that humans are born with language. This view eliminates the need for intermediate stages of grammar and replaces the process of acquisition with an event. A child according to this model only has to be exposed to language in order to acquire language. Stokoe (1983) points out that there is no room in this view for the social interaction between the child and her linguistic environment, which is necessary for language acquisition outside of an idealized theoretical situation. The elimination of any pre-language and two-way social interaction in the development of the individual mirrors the punctuationalist view of language evolution.

By using the language organ metaphor simplistic models of evolution have been based on comparisons of two actual organs: the eye and the elephant's trunk. The eye analogy is often used to demonstrate how something as complex as language can evolve in a short period of time without an intermediate structure. It is often stressed that a partially developed eye would not be functionally the same and yet eyes have evolved as complex structures (Pinker 1994). This is then extrapolated to grammar that is hypothesized to have no functional intermediate (Bickerton 1995).

The elephant's trunk is used in conjunction with the eye to justify the obvious incongruity between this theory of glottogenesis and the concept of continuity inherent in evolutionary theory. Pinker (1994) points out that elephants have a unique organ in the trunk, yet there is no structure similar in their closest relatives. Both of these examples in reality illustrate the artificial nature of the analogy. The eye has intermediates in the photosensitive cells of organisms without eyes. The genetic difference between African and Indian elephants, both with fully functional trunks, is greater than that of humans and their closest living relatives the chimpanzees, whom both Pinker and Bickerton assert have no language capabilities (Fouts and Mills 1997).

This assertion is not based on observation, but rather a misunderstanding of the distinction of species. Darwin's conception of species was not based on static well-defined distinctions. Instead, Darwin saw the term *species* as one that is "arbitrarily given, for the sake of convenience, to a set of individuals closely resembling each other, and that it does not essentially differ from the term variety, which is given to less distinct and more fluctuating forms. The term *variety*, again, in comparison with mere individual differences, is also applied arbitrarily, for convenience's sake" (Darwin [1859] 1991, 40).

Richard Dawkins (1993) illustrates this definition of species in his article entitled "Gaps in the Mind" when he describes a "ring species." He uses the herring gull and the lesser black-backed gull as an example. He states that in Britain they are quite different in color and clearly distinct species. However, if you trace the herring gull population westward around the North Pole to North America and then through Alaska and across Siberia and back to Europe again something very strange happens. The herring gulls gradually become less and less like herring gulls and more and more like lesser black-backed gulls. It turns out that the lesser black-backed gulls are the other end of a ring that started out as herring gulls. At every stage along the way the gulls are similar enough to their neighbors so that they will interbreed with them. This is true until the continuum reaches Europe again, and here the herring gull and the lesser black-backed gull never interbreed regardless of the fact that they are linked by a continuous series of interbreeding colleagues right around the world. Dawkins points out that all pairs of related species are potentially ring species, but in the herring and black-backed gulls' case all the intermediates are still alive.

With regard to chimpanzees and humans, Dawkins (1993) asks us to imagine that we are holding our mother's hand. Now imagine that your mother takes her mother's hand, your grandmother, and she in turn takes her mother's hand until you are standing at the end of a line of grandmothers. If you allow one yard per person, twenty years for each generation, and six million years of separate evolution, in a surprisingly short distance of less than 170 miles your grandmother will take the hand of a chimpanzee's grandmother. This common grandmother would have at least two daughters, one your grandmother, and her sister, the chimpanzee's grandmother. The two sisters stand facing each other holding their mother's hand. If you imagine that the chimpanzee's grandmother has a daughter who stands facing her cousin, who in turn has a daughter and so on as this now double line of cousins winds its way back to the point where you are standing face to face with a chimpanzee. That is biological reality.

In contrast to biological reality, many of the Cartesian theories are dedicated to analogy and armchair theorizing with little effort put into the mechanisms by which language evolved. The explanation offered by Pinker (1994) in his appropriately titled chapter, "The Big Bang," is that a lucky mutation is responsible. This mutation becomes luckier yet when one realizes that one must not only develop the ability to produce language but someone must be around who has the mutation to understand it, and both of these mutations must remain in the gene pool until these two lucky individuals meet. When the complexities of language, which include "sequential and simultaneous development, coordination, reorganization, and elaboration of social, cognitive, symbolic, gestural and sound systems" (Parker 1985, 618), are set against this model it appears simplistic rather than parsimonious (Hewes 1973).

Gesture and the Foundation for Spoken Language

Rather than exclude nonhuman communication and social interaction from glottogenesis the proponents of a gradual gestural origin of language embrace them as a model for early stages of development (Parker 1985; Hewes 1973; Armstrong, Stokoe, and Wilcox 1994). Freed from the time constraint of spoken language, one can look for ultimate mechanisms that lie much deeper in evolutionary history. Gestural theories of the origin of language usually stem from the sociality of communication rather than the idealized disembodied language of the traditional linguists. Within the social framework of extant primates and extinct species in the human lineage, a number of possible situations that would facilitate complex communication can be found. Unlike those relying on mutations, these theories are testable via observations of social primates and artifacts from extinct ancestors.

Both Parker (1985) and Hewes (1973) suggest that iconic gestures could arise from pantomime and gestures used to transmit knowledge of material culture. This explanation serves as a far more parsimonious explanation since separate evolutionary pathways do not need to converge for both productive and receptive language. The sender would only need to modify a tool while the receiver observes. Contrasted to this passive observation mechanism, the active cultural transmission of teaching has been observed numerous times in extant apes (Russon 1997; Boesch 1991; Fouts, Fouts, and Van Cantfort 1989).

Cultural transmission in a captive chimpanzee was extensively studied when ten-month-old Loulis was adopted by Washoe and acquired signing and other skills from her and the other signing chimpanzees in his community. To ensure that Loulis would acquire his signs only from the chimpanzees, the humans in his presence restricted their signing to seven specific signs or used vocal English to communicate with him and the other chimpanzees. Washoe was observed to teach Loulis through modeling, molding, and signing on his body. Most of his signs appeared to be delayed imitations of signs he had seen Washoe and the other chimpanzees use in similar contexts. The development of social behavior, communication, and other skills were observed without human disruption and a comprehensive record of the cultural transmission of signing was obtained (Fouts, Hirsch, and Fouts 1982; Fouts and Fouts 1989; Fouts, Fouts, and Van Cantfort 1989).

The next stage in this process would require that the simple actor/observer relationship include gestures that are iconic or representational of the actions. Once again, observation from both wild and captive chimpanzees lends support to the hypothesis. For example, gestures that serve as invitations to groom have been observed that are not only consistent within chimpanzee populations but also evince dialectical variation between populations, suggesting the cultural transmission necessary for the evolution of a language (McGrew and Tutin 1978). It is also important to note that during grooming vocalization and lip movements accompany the hand movements (Goodall 1986). This highlights an often-overlooked aspect of a gestural stage in language evolution, that a gestural stage in not necessarily a completely silent stage (Armstrong, Stokoe, and Wilcox 1994).

Fouts, Haislip, Iwasazuk, Sanz, and Fouts (1997) have begun a long-term research project examining the use of gestural dialects and idiolects in wild and captive chimpanzees. The Fouts et al. (1997) study examined Washoe, Moja, Tatu, Dar, and Loulis's interactions for non-ASL sign gestures (nonverbal gestures) that were used during communicative interactions. The gestures were analyzed using the same methods as those used for the gestures of ASL in previous research. Each gesture was noted and analyzed for similarities and differences in place, configuration, and movement. They found eight gestures, both dialectical gestures and ideolectical gestures, among these five chimpanzees. For example a subtle "chin tip" (a quick raising of the head with a directional component) was observed in chase games, where the direction of tip (left or right) would indicate direction of the chase, and the active "chin tipper" would indicate the chaser.

Pantomime can explain the lexicon needed for language, however one still needs to explain syntax in order to catch up to the linguists' magical mutation. Armstrong, Stokoe, and Wilcox (1994) make the critical observation for all gestural theories that the arm and hand movements of gestures are inherently grammatical. These gestures contain the frame on which grammar is built. Since a gesture occurs in three-dimensional space, observation of directionality of a single sign can provide the syntax of an entire sentence. For example the sign for "catch" where the fist of one arm moves across the body and is caught by the other hand includes actor, action, and object within a single icon. Once again scientific studies on gestures in the great apes strengthen this argument. Most of the natural gestures observed in chimpanzees are representative of actions rather than objects (Tanner and Byrne 1996). A beautiful example of this theory in action was observed by

Rimpau, Gardner, and Gardner (1989) when the cross-fostered chimpanzee Dar places signs such as BRUSH on himself or on his friend to show who is to receive the action.

From Hand to Mouth

With the foundation of lexicon and syntax laid down in gesture, the final questions are how and why did a functional gestural language switch from a visual to an auditory modality? The why is often explained in very functional terms such as speech frees the hands and is possible in areas of poor visibility (Parker 1985; Hewes 1973). The how is slightly more complicated. It is helpful when trying to understand how such a transformation took place to rethink the definition of gesture and to realize that gesture and vocal communication are not separate but rather complementary.

If one expands the definition of gesture to include both mouth and hands the dichotomy disappears. This is not an obscure or new idea. In 1944, Paget suggested that speech consists of gestures of the vocal apparatus that are as iconic as manual gestures. Wilcox (1990) continues on this theme some forty-five years later. He suggests that a better understanding of speech can be gained by examining it in the same fashion as manual gestural communication, where the information is in the movement from segment to segment rather than in discrete units.

The continuity of speech and gesture is enhanced when the function of the two modes in relation to each other is examined. Gesture still accompanies speech and can help facilitate it when it breaks down. Beattie and Coughlan (1999) found that during induced tip-of-the-tongue incidents, gestures facilitated lexical search, especially for words of high imageability. Likewise during anxiety provoking situations when speech becomes hesitant, gestures telegraph and accompany vocal breakdown. Most often this "motor spill-over" includes hand movements (Ragsdale and Silvia 1982).

The natural connection between mouth and hand can also be observed in the deleterious effects speech can have on fine-motor activities. Activities as simple as tapping a dowel can be interfered with by linguistic speech, while the repetition of a single syllable has little effect (Ashton and McFarland 1991; Hiscock 1982). Likewise, patients with left-hemisphere brain injury consistent with movement and speech disorders can do a repetitive task or repeat syllables but have trouble sequencing movements of the mouth or hands (Kimura 1976). Psychophysical measurements of the tongue and hand suggest a connection outside the realm of communication. The curves generated by the perception of pressure and fatigue by the tongue and the hand produce similar results, although it is interesting to note that the tongue is most sensitive within the range of effort necessary to produce speech (Somodi, Robin, and Luschei 1995). Likewise the point at which a vibration on the hand and tongue is perceived as a single pulse is nearly identical (Petrosino and Fucci 1984), while the perception of the magnitude of the pulse and sensitivity create similar curves (Fucci, Harris, and Petrosino 1984).

The marriage of mouth to hand has enough support theoretically and empirically, as well as linguistically and neurologically, to suggest that a transformation along the evolutionary continuum was possible. However, much of this evidence is either correlational or concerns gestural spillover during linguistic tasks. In order to provide more direct evidence that the increasing complexity of gesture could produce vocal speech, one should examine transfer more closely from gesture or fine-motor movements of the hands to that of the tongue and mouth.

A couple of examples from fairly divergent sources suggest that such a transfer could be observable. Darwin ([1889] 1998) reported anecdotally that sympathetic mouth movements often accompany fine-motor tasks, while Fulwiler and Fouts (1976) found that spontaneous speech accompanied sign language instruction of a noncommunicative autistic child. When these examples are included with reports of vocal utterances by deaf signers that map to gestural language much like gesture maps spoken language (Kimura 1974), one can develop a clear picture of how gestures could precede glottogenesis. With more specific experimentation and observation, keeping the evolution of language in mind, one more gap in a robust and useful theory could be filled. A theory that is not only parsimonious but also follows the path of "least biological resistance" (Hewes 1973, 9).

Continuity and the "Language Organ"

Currently, the closest structure to a language organ that can be identified is a loose collection of areas within the brain that when damaged in adults result in similar language deficits. These structures have been synthesized into a neurological language processing model by Geschwind (1972) that includes Broca's area in the frontal lobe, Wernicke's area in the temporal lobe, and the angular gyrus, which acts as an intermediate between the visual cortex and Wernicke's area. Cartesian theories of language evolution would predict that these areas are the result of a mutation that either produced or transformed these areas from a previous nonlanguage function into a language organ. However, far from being neuro-anatomical adaptations exclusive to humans, the components of Geschwind's model have been found in nonhumans.

Gannon, Holloway, Broadfield, and Braun (1997) found asymmetries in the *planum temporale,* part of Wernicke's area, in the left hemisphere in 17 of 18 chimpanzee cadaver brains. These results and reports of asymmetries in the *angular gyrus* were later confirmed with the use of Magnetic Resonance Imaging (MRI) (Hopkins, Marino, Rilling, and MacGregor 1998). The comprehension of human speech by chimpanzees (Fouts, Chown, and Goodin 1976; Shaw 1989) suggests that these areas may also have a homologous function.

The presence of the cortical area homologous to Broca's area in nonhuman primates would not have been found if the importance of gesture to the evolution of language was not recognized. Rizzolatti and Arbib (1998) have reported that the rostral part of the ventral premotor cortex, area F5, in monkeys is active when they observe the motor behavior of another. Area F5 in monkeys is proposed to be homologous to Broca's area in humans. The neurons in area F5, mirror neurons, appear to map the motor neurons that are active when one produces similar actions. In other words, neural activity in the mirror system fires in a way that is sympathetic to the action observed. This system is a neurological bridge between the receiver's perceptions and the sender's actions.

What is remarkable about the mirror system is that different patterns of neural activity are observed for different actions. For example the pattern of neural discharge in a monkey observing another grasping a raisin will be different from when observing a larger item or grasping at nothing at all. Within this mirror system it is possible that we have a neural representation of not only lexicon, but when coupled with Armstrong, Stokoe, and Wilcox's (1994) observations, syntax. It may be the case that language is indeed the function of a language organ, but one based on the social interaction of an actor and an observer. A "language organ" that is not hardwired in humans alone for the purpose of a Universal Grammar, but rather in all social organisms for the adaptive purpose of understanding the actions of one another.

Continuity, Ethology, and Stokoe

The difference between the theories of the evolution of language is not simply whether or not a gestural stage is included. It suggests an approach to science and academics that transcends a single question or even a single discipline. It is what allowed William Stokoe to see language and culture in the signs of deaf people where others saw only a defective form of the "Ideal." It is the ability to be humble and take others on their own terms, whether the "other" in question is from a different culture or a different species. In the behavioral sciences we call this approach ethology and more than a common focus on sign language, it is what has linked the work of William Stokoe to those who have worked on Project Washoe.

Project Washoe began in 1966 and was an example of the ethological methodology referred to as *cross-fostering* (the process that occurs when members of one species raise a member of another). Washoe was cross-fostered by Allen and Beatrix Gardner and their students who only used ASL in her presence (Gardner and Gardner 1969, 1971, 1974, 1989). They raised Washoe in an environment similar to that of a deaf human child, in other words, in the context of a home rather than in an operant conditioning laboratory.

Washoe's upbringing approximated the upbringing of a deaf child in a household with parents who use ASL, and as Stokoe (1989) notes, in conditions that unfortunately are not even always available for deaf children. The choice of ASL for Washoe was also based on an ethological principle. Previous attempts to teach chimpanzees to speak had failed to produce results for the simple reason that chimpanzees do not have the capacity for voluntary speech. What chimpanzees do with proficiency in all situations is gesture. It is ironic that with deaf children similar errors are still in practice today when they are conditioned to use sounds they can't hear rather than use the gestures they can readily use to communicate.

While the ethological approach led to the success of Project Washoe and to Stokoe's identification of ASL as a fully functioning language the rest of the linguistic world has not embraced the practice. Stokoe (1989) recognized this when he stated that "the more practitioners of theoretical language science agree on their postulation of universal rules of language, the more other empirical investigators observing what is there, find differences in all kinds of circumstances surrounding the infant's [and chimpanzee's] acquisition of the system" (1989, 312).

Project Washoe led to a better understanding of chimpanzee culture and language as the work of William Stokoe led to a better understanding of Deaf culture and language. The two groups of researchers have crossed paths many times throughout this journey. Stokoe said in 1997 that the Gardners' "work as much as anything that has happened since 1960 has also helped validate as well as guide my own work with signed languages" (1997, 11). Likewise it is hard to imagine Project Washoe and the subsequent ape language projects being as successful without the insights of William Stokoe. While coming from such diverse disciplines both paths have led to the understanding that language and culture are not abstract concepts to be catalogued and unnaturally simplified, but rather aspects of the social interaction of social beings. When one observes and learns from this social dance by humble observation, differences of kind and images of defectives struggling towards an ideal disappear. What is left are not shadows on the walls of Plato's cave but rather understanding and compassion between organic beings.

References

Armstrong, David F., William C. Stokoe, and Sherman E. Wilcox. 1994. Signs of the origin of syntax. *Current Anthropology* 35: 349–66.

Ashton, Roderick, and Ken McFarland. 1991. A simple dual-task study of laterality, sex-differences and handedness. *Cortex* 27: 105–9.

Beattie, Geoffrey, and Jane Coughlan. 1999. An experimental investigation of the role of iconic gestures in lexical access using the tip-of-the-tongue phenomenon. *British Journal of Psychology* 90: 35–56.

Bickerton, Derek. 1996. *Language and human behavior.* Seattle: University of Washington Press.

Boesch, Christophe. 1991. Teaching among chimpanzees. *Animal Behaviour* 41: 530–32.

Cziko, Gary. 1995. *Without miracles: Universal selection theory and the second Darwinian revolution.* Cambridge: MIT Press.

Darwin, Charles. [1859] 1991. *The origin of species: By means of natural selection.* 6th ed. Reprint, Amherst, N.Y.: Prometheus Books.

———. [1889] 1998. *The expression of the emotions in man and animals.* Reprint, Oxford: Oxford University Press.

Dawkins, Richard. 1993. Gaps in the mind. In *The great ape project: Equality beyond humanity,* edited by Paola Cavalieri and Peter Singer, 80–87. New York: St. Martin's Press.

Fouts, Roger S., Bill Chown, and Larry Goodin. 1976. Transfer of signed responses in American Sign Language from vocal English stimuli to physical object stimuli by a chimpanzee (*Pan*). *Learning and Motivation* 7: 458–75.

Fouts, Roger S., and Deborah H. Fouts. 1989. Loulis in conversation with the cross-fostered chimpanzees. In *Teaching sign language to chimpanzees,* edited by R. Allen Gardner, Beatrix T. Gardner, and Thomas E. Van Cantfort. Albany, N.Y.: SUNY Press.

Fouts, Roger S., Deborah H. Fouts, and Thomas E. Van Cantfort. 1989. The infant Loulis learns signs from cross-fostered chimpanzees. In *Teaching sign language to chimpanzees,* edited by R. Allen Gardner, Beatrix T. Gardner, and Thomas E. Van Cantfort. Albany, N.Y.: SUNY Press.

Fouts, Roger S., Michelle Haislip, Wendy Iwaszuk, Crickette M. Sanz, and Deborah H. Fouts. 1997. *Chimpanzee communicative gestures: Idiolects and dialects*. Paper presented at the Rocky Mountain Psychological Association meeting in Reno, Nev., 17 April.

Fouts, Roger S., Alan D. Hirsch, and Deborah H. Fouts. 1982. Cultural transmission of a human language in a chimpanzee mother-infant relationship. In *Psychobiological perspectives*, edited by Hiram E. Fitzgerald, John A. Mullins, and Patricia Page, 159–93. Child Nurturance Series. New York: Plenum Press.

Fouts, Roger S., and Stephen T. Mills. 1997. *Next of kin: What chimpanzees have taught me about who we are*. New York: William Morrow and Company.

Freeman, Scott, and Jon C. Herron. 1998. *Evolutionary analysis*. Upper Saddle River, N.J.: Prentice Hall.

Fucci, Donald, Daniel Harris, and Linda Petrosino. 1984. Sensation magnitude scales for vibrotactile stimulation of the tongue and thenar eminence. *Perceptual and Motor Skills* 58: 843–48.

Fulwiler, Robert L., and Roger S. Fouts. 1976. Acquisition of American sign language by a noncommunicative autistic child. *Journal of Autism and Childhood Schizophrenia* 6: 43–51.

Gannon, Patrick J., Ralph L. Holloway, Douglas C. Broadfield, and Allen R. Braun. 1998. Asymmetry of chimpanzee planum temporale: Humanlike pattern of Wernicke's brain language area homolog. *Science* 279: 220–22.

Gardner, Beatrix T., and R. Allen Gardner. 1971. Two-way communication with an infant chimpanzee. In *Behavior of nonhuman primates*, edited by Allan Schrier and Fred Stollnitz, 117–84. New York: Academic Press.

———. 1974. Comparing the early utterances of child and chimpanzee. In *Minnesota symposium on child psychology*, edited by Allen Pick. Minneapolis: University of Minnesota Press.

Gardner, R. Allen, and Beatrix T. Gardner. 1969. Teaching sign language to a chimpanzee. *Science* 165: 664–72.

———. 1989. A cross-fostering laboratory. In *Teaching sign language to chimpanzees*, edited by R. Allen Gardner, Beatrix T. Gardner, and Thomas E. Van Cantfort. Albany, N.Y.: SUNY Press.

Gardner, R. Allen, Beatrix T. Gardner, and Patrick Drumm. 1989. Voiced and signed responses of cross-fostered chimpanzees. In *Teaching sign language to chimpanzees*, edited by R. Allen Gardner, Beatrix T. Gardner, and Thomas E. Van Cantfort, 29–54. Albany, N.Y.: SUNY Press.

Geschwind, Norman. 1970. Organization of language and the brain. *Science* 170: 940–4.

Goodall, Jane. 1986. *The chimpanzees of Gombe: Patterns of behavior.* Cambridge: Harvard University Press.

Hewes, Gordon W. 1973. Primate communication and the gestural origin of language. *Current Anthropology* 14: 5–24.

Hiscock, Merrill. 1982. Verbal-manual time sharing in children as a function of task priority. *Brain and Cognition* 1: 119–31.

Hopkins, William D., Lori Marino, James K. Rilling, and Leslie A. MacGregor. 1998. *Planum temporale* asymmetries in great apes as revealed by magnetic resonance imaging (MRI). *NeuroReport* 9: 2913–18.

Kimura, Doreen. 1974. The neural basis of language qua gesture. In *Studies in neurolinguistics,* edited by Haiganoosh Avakian-Whitaker and Harry A. Whitaker, 145–56. New York: Academic Press.

———. 1976. Neuromotor mechanisms in the evolution of human communication. In *Neurobiology of social communication in primates,* edited by Horst D. Steklis and Michael J. Raleigh, 197–219. New York: Academic Press.

McGrew, William C., and Caroline E. G. Tutin. 1978. Evidence for a social custom in wild chimpanzees? *Man* 13: 2234–51.

Paget, R. A. S. 1944. The origin of language. *Science* 99: 14–15.

Parker, Sue T. 1985. A social-technological model for the evolution of language. *Current Anthropology* 26: 417–639.

Petrosino, Linda, and Donald Fucci. 1984. Temporal resolution of successive brief stimuli for the tongue and hand. *Bulletin of Psychonomic Society* 22: 208–10.

Pinker, Steven. 1994. *The language instinct: How the mind creates language.* New York: Harper Collins.

Ragsdale, J. Donald, and Catherine F. Silvia. 1982. Distribution of kinesic hesitation phenomena in spontaneous speech. *Language and Speech* 25: 185–90.

Rimpau, James B., R. Allen Gardner, and Beatrix T. Gardner. 1989. Expression of person, place, and instrument in ASL utterances of children and chimpanzees. In *Teaching sign language to chimpanzees,* edited by R. Allen Gardner, Beatrix T. Gardner, and Thomas E. Van Cantfort, 240–68. Albany, N.Y.: SUNY Press.

Rizzolatti, Giacomo, and Michael A. Arbib. 1998. Language within our grasp. *Trends in Neuroscience* 21: 188–94.

Russon, Anne E. 1997. Exploiting the expertise of others. In *Machiavellian intelligence II*, edited by Andrew Whiten and Richard Byrne, 174–206. Cambridge: Cambridge University Press.

Seyfarth, Robert M., and Dorothy L. Cheney. 1997. Communication and the minds of monkeys. In *The origin and evolution of intelligence*, edited by Arnold B. Scheibel and J. William Schopf, 27–42. Boston: Jones and Bartlett.

Shaw, Heidi L. 1989. Comprehension of the spoken word and ASL translation by chimpanzees. Master's thesis, Central Washington University.

Somodi, Lori B., Donald A. Robin, and Eric S. Luschei. 1995. A model of "sense of effort" during maximal and submaximal contractions of the tongue. *Brain and Language* 51: 371–82.

Stokoe, William C. 1983. Apes who sign and critics who don't. In *Language in primates: Perspectives and implications*, edited by Judith de Luce and Hugh T. Wilder. New York: Springer-Verlag.

———. 1989. Comparative and developmental sign language studies: A review of recent advances. In *Teaching sign language to chimpanzees*, edited by R. Allen Gardner, Beatrix T. Gardner, and Thomas E. Van Cantfort, 308–16. Albany, N.Y.: SUNY Press.

———. 1997. *Understanding apes and men.* Paper presented at the Rocky Mountain Psychological Association meeting in Reno, Nev., 17 April.

Tanner, Joan E., and Richard W. Byrne. 1996. Representation of action through iconic gesture in a captive lowland gorilla. *Current Anthropology* 37: 162–73.

Wilcox, Sherman E. 1990. The structure of signed and spoken languages. *Sign Language Studies* 67: 141–51.

6

William C. Stokoe and the Gestural Theory of Language Origins

Sherman E. Wilcox

The American architect Frank Lloyd Wright was once asked how he could conceive and oversee so many projects. He answered, "I can't get them out fast enough." Wright was not talking about buildings; he was talking about ideas. He couldn't get his ideas out fast enough.

Bill Stokoe also was an architect of ideas. Like Wright's *Fallingwater*, Stokoe's ideas have a simple beauty that belies the radical way in which they have changed our intellectual landscape.

We are sometimes hesitant to mention beauty in the same breath as science. To many people, beauty seems to lie more in the realm of art. We tell ourselves that science is about objective facts, while art is about subjective qualities such as beauty. The history of science shows that the dichotomy between art and science is false. As David Gerlernter, professor of computer science at Yale University, reminds us, "We believe implicitly that the scientist is one type, the artist a radically different one. In fact, the scientific and artistic personalities overlap more than they differ, and the higher we shimmy into the leafy canopy of talent, the closer the two enterprises seem" (Gelernter 1998, 10).

We all know Bill Stokoe for his most famous idea: that the signs he saw his deaf students using at Gallaudet University were a language. We have heard a great deal about the impact of this idea in the decades since Stokoe first let it flutter down from the canopy. This chapter discusses another of Stokoe's grand ideas: the idea that language began as gesture.

Stokoe would be the first to point out that the gestural theory of language origins is not his unique creation. Centuries ago, philosophers such as Condillac, Herder, and Vico expounded gestural theories of language origins. Many of Stokoe's colleagues, including Adam Kendon, David Armstrong, and Frank Wilson, have contributed to modern gestural theory. But Stokoe's contribution is unique, and it is expressed most succinctly in a notion that unites his two grand ideas—the notion of semantic phonology.

I must admit that when I first began reading about and talking to Stokoe about the gestural theory of language origins, I was not convinced. It simply challenged too many of my basic assumptions about language. Once, while Stokoe, David Armstrong, and I were working on *Gesture and the Nature of Language,* I expressed my concern to Stokoe. "You know, Bill," I said, "I think some people are going to read our book and conclude that we're crazy." His response was, "Well, I've been there before!"

What finally opened my eyes to the gestural theory of language origins was the theory's beauty—a beauty that I only dimly perceived at first. The gestural theory of language origins, and Stokoe's unique notion of semantic phonology, possess a beauty that results from the "happy marriage of simplicity and power" (Gelernter 1998). This theoretical beauty is recognized by scientists as *elegance.*

Stokoe always strived for simplicity. When his idea that signs might be a language began to have an impact on linguists, the immediate reaction was to elaborate his idea, to add complications. Stokoe, on the other hand, thought he had already made the idea too complicated when he first proposed that a sign is composed of three parts: handshape, location, and movement. As others complicated, Stokoe simplified. He came to believe that a sign is more simply described as composed of only two parts: something that acts and its action.

In his seminal article on semantic phonology, Stokoe described his search for simplicity, as follows:

> What I propose is not complicated at all; it is dead simple to begin with. I call it semantic phonology. It invites one to look at a sign . . . as simply a marriage of a noun and a verb. . . . [O]ne needs only to think of a sign as something that acts together with its action; it's that simple: no features, no autosegments, no orientation, no contacting or contacted parts, no HOLDs, no MOVEs, no tiers, no tears—just something acting . . . along with its action. (Stokoe 1991, 111–12)

The second element that gives birth to elegance is power. The power of semantic phonology, and of gestural theory, is that it unites ideas and theories that were previously regarded as distinct. Gestural theory unites language and gesture, it unites perception and conception, and it unites the represented world of objects and events and the representing world of words and grammar. Semantic phonology is the means by which the unification takes place.

What exactly is semantic phonology? Although it is a simple idea, it is not a simple-minded idea. Stokoe described it this way:

> The usual way of conceiving of the structure of language is linear: First there are the sounds (phonology), these are put together to make the words and their classes (morphology), the words in turn, are found to be of various classes, and these are used to form phrase structures (syntax), and finally, the phrase structures, after lexical replacement of their symbols, yield meaning (semantics). A semantic phonology ties the last step to the first, making a seamless circuit of this progression. The metaphor for semantic phonology that jumps to mind is the Möbius strip: the input is the output, with a twist. (1991, 112)

It is not possible to understand the significance of semantic phonology if we begin by simply decomposing it into the two terms, *semantics* and *phonology*, and then attempt to understand the notion by somehow combining our knowledge of the two. The twist makes all the difference. The insight that Stokoe had was not just that phonology is somehow meaningful. Rather, semantic phonology suggests that language structures are built of components that are structurally identical to themselves: sentences are composed of words, but words are composed of semantic-phonological "sentences" or *noun–verb* constructions. I'll return to this recursive quality of semantic phonology in a moment.

I'd like to take a slightly different tack and approach the notion of semantic phonology from the linguistic framework that I work with, that of cognitive grammar (Langacker 1987, 1991). Cognitive grammar posits that the elements of language—not just words but also elements smaller than words such as morphemes and elements larger than words such as constructions—are symbolic structures. They are symbolic structures because they consist of a correspondence between two simpler structures: a semantic structure and a phonological structure. On one side of the symbolic unit are semantic structures that embody meaning. On the other side are phonological structures that, at their most concrete level, are the physical expression of language, the acoustic patterns of speech, and the optical arrays of signs.

A critical claim of cognitive grammar is that both semantic and phonological structures reside within semantic space. A linguistic symbol, which in cognitive linguistics is everything about language from lexicon to morphology and grammar, involves a correspondence, a mapping, between two structures in semantic space. Semantic space encompasses all of our thought and knowledge. It is, in the words of Ron Langacker, the primary architect of cognitive grammar, "the multifaceted field of conceptual potential within which thought and conceptualization unfold" (Langacker 1987, 76).

Semantic space is quite large, encompassing, literally, everything conceivable. And so it becomes necessary to talk about distances among notions that reside in semantic space. Notions reside close to each other in semantic space because they possess certain similarities. Dogs and cats are close to each other in our semantic space because they possess certain similar characteristics. Other notions reside far from each other in semantic space because they are quite distinct. Rocks and feathers reside in different regions of semantic space; chocolate cake and gravity occupy vastly different domains of semantic space.

Linguistic notions also occupy semantic space—notions ranging from fairly concrete (the way the word *dog* is pronounced and its meaning is contextualized) to fairly abstract (the way *verb* is pronounced and what it means—not a specific verb such as "throw" but the grammatical category *verb*).

Now comes the twist in the Möbius strip: remember, the phonological pole also resides in semantic space. The phonological and semantic poles of linguistic symbols reside in the same, broadly conceived semantic space. Because of this, it is possible to compare the regions in semantic space occupied by the semantic and phonological poles of symbolic structures.

The typical case for language is that the semantic pole and the phonological pole of a symbolic structure reside in vastly different regions of semantic space. For example, the sound of the spoken word *dog* has little in common with the meaning of the word. This vast distance in semantic space, and the resulting incommensurability of the semantic and phonological poles, is the basis for what linguists call the arbitrariness of the sign.

However, the semantic and phonological poles of linguistic symbols may occupy regions of semantic space that are not so distant. Sometimes the poles occupy regions that are quite close. When such cases occur we talk of onomatopoeic expressions, or iconicity. For example, the famous expression of Julius Caesar, "I came, I saw, I conquered," demonstrates how the semantic and phonological poles of an expression may occupy similar regions in semantic space: The temporal ordering of the events represented by the meaning of this expression is the same as the temporal ordering of the linguistic elements (I should point out that temporal order is an aspect of the phonological pole).

In fact, as a limiting case, the two poles of a linguistic symbol may occupy the same semantic space; they may be put into correspondence with each other and become self-symbolizing or self-referential. When the semantic and phonological poles of a symbol occupy similar, or the same, regions in semantic space, the resulting commensurability is the basis for what linguists call a motivated sign.

What does this have to do with semantic phonology? Semantic phonology suggests that visible gestures, whether the common everyday gestures we make when we speak or the conventionalized gestures that are the signs of natural signed languages, are primordial examples of self-symbolization. It is the twist in the Möbius strip. The phonological pole of gestures and signs consists of something that acts and its action. Hands are objects that move about and interact energetically with other objects. Hands are prototypical nouns and their actions are prototypical verbs. Hands and their actions manifest archetypal grammatical roles. A hand can act transitively on another hand, transmitting energy to the impacted object. Or, a hand can act intransitively, as when we trace the path of an object that has moved.

I like to think of this semantic-phonological quality of visible gesture as an example of recursion, because "recursive structures are built of components that are structurally identical to themselves" (Gelernter 1998, 59). Stokoe saw this connection as well. He wrote that semantic phonology reflected a Gödelian self-reference:

> An *s-p noun-verb* unit represents a word of sign language, it is both an agent-verb construct and in the lexicon a formal noun or verb or other part of speech of the language, and it can combine in the normal way with others like it to make a grammatical noun-verb structure. This structure in turn has meaning (actually it always had). (1991, 112)

Semantic phonology is elegant because it captures the simplicity and the power of visible gestures. Like the Roman god Janus, visible gestures simultaneously face in two directions: toward the perceived world of objects and events and toward the conceived world of grammar. Visible gestures are instrumental actions in the world that are recruited as communicative actions about the world. They are capable of serving as motivated signs for objects and events in the physical world, and in their internal structure they exhibit the properties of grammatical categories and relations. Visible gestures unite the represented world of objects and events and the representing world of language.

Semantic phonology thus answers the question of how gestures came to represent the world, but the answer also comes with a twist: they never didn't.

Semantic phonology is simple and powerful. It is elegant. And elegance in science is a clue that some significant, underlying truth may have been uncovered. But elegance isn't enough. Consider the case of what physicists call *superstring theory*. Some physicists believe that superstring theory must be correct because it is such an elegant theory. Others reply that, while undoubtedly elegant, superstring theory must offer testable predictions. These latter scientists express concern about whether superstring theory is, in fact, a *scientific* theory.

> Physicists working on superstring theory ... were no longer doing physics because their theories could never be validated by experiments, but only by subjective criteria, such as elegance and beauty. ... Previous theories of physics, however seemingly bizarre, won acceptance among physicists and even the public not because they made sense; rather, they offered predictions that were borne out—often in dramatic fashions—by observations. (Horgan 1996, 70)

In order to qualify as a scientific theory, the gestural theory of language origins—which is as bizarre to many scholars as superstring theory—must make testable predictions that will distinguish it from other, competing theories. And, in fact, it does. One set of predictions concerns the relation between gesture and language. The gestural theory of language evolution predicts a connection between gesture and language. Many linguists would predict precisely the opposite. Chomsky does. Comparing animal communication and human language, he offered the following prediction:

> The examples of animal communication that have been examined to date do share many of the properties of human gestural systems, and it might be reasonable to explore the possibility of direct connection in this case. But human language, it appears, is based on entirely different principles. (1972, 70)

Notice that while Chomsky is directly comparing human language and animal communication, and finds that they are based on entirely different principles, he asserts that human gestural systems do share many properties with animal communication; therefore, we must conclude (whether or not Chomsky did), human gestural systems and human language are also based on entirely different principles.

What is the evidence? Is human language based on entirely different principles than human gestural systems? The available evidence in fact supports a deep connection between language and gesture, as reported by scientists such as David McNeill (1992), Adam Kendon (1994, this volume), and Doreen Kimura (1993). McNeill, for example, on the basis of many years of psycholinguistic research on language and gesture, concludes that "gestures and speech should be viewed within a unified conceptual framework as aspects of a single underlying process" (1992, 23).

A second set of predictions may be made concerning the relation of spoken and signed languages. Gestural theory unites speech and sign: both are considered to be articulatory gesturing. The theory predicts that language will be acquired and created with ease in the signed modality. Once again, the evidence supports this prediction. The extensive research conducted by Susan Goldin-Meadow and her colleagues (Goldin-Meadow and Mylander 1998) on deaf children raised with little or no language input, as well as that conducted by Elissa Newport (Newport and Meier 1986) and others on deaf children acquiring signed languages as their native language impressively demonstrate that language is as easily acquired and even created in the visual-gestural modality as it is in the vocal modality. Many linguists interpret these findings to suggest that language is independent of modality. The gestural theory outlined here offers an alternative account with subtle but significant differences: Sign and speech are intrinsically bound in our evolutionary history to embodied perceptual, motor, and cognitive systems.

Is language intrinsically bound to speech? The legacy of Stokoe's first grand idea provides a clear answer: Certainly not. Is it intrinsically bound to sign? No, again. But, critically, gestural theory requires us to ask the complementary questions. Are speech and sign linked by common perceptual, motor, and cognitive systems? Yes. Are speech, sign, and gesture also intimately linked by these common systems? As we'll see below, the answer again is, yes.

Gestural theory predicts that gesture and language among hearing children will be tightly interwoven in development. This prediction is borne out in a growing number of studies examining children's gestural and linguistic development (Blake and Dolgoy 1993; Capirci et al. 1996), gesturing in mother-child interactions (Iverson et al. 1999), and even gesturing in congenitally blind children (Iverson 1999; Iverson and Goldin-Meadow 1997).

Finally, gestural theory makes predictions concerning the neural architecture of the perceptual, motor, and cognitive systems underlying gesture and language. It predicts, for example, that the neurological systems that implement the production and perception of symbolic gesturing, as well as language, will be deeply interconnected.

Frank Wilson calls this deep interconnection the "hand-thought-language nexus." In *The Hand: How Its Use Shapes the Brain, Language, and Human Culture* (1998), he suggests that the evolution of the hand, the brain, and language are interwoven in such a way that the brain required a redesign, or reallocation, of its circuitry to implement "a new way of registering and representing the behavior of objects moving and changing under the control of the hand." He also notes that "it is *precisely* such representational systems . . . that one finds at the deepest levels of the organization of human language" (Wilson 1998, 60).

Neuroscientists (Arbib and Rizzolatti 1996; Rizzolatti and Arbib 1998) have located the possible neural architecture of this nexus in so-called "mirror neurons." These are neurons in Broca's area of primates and humans that mediate visual perception and recognition of manual motor actions such as grasping, holding, and tearing. Rizzolatti and Arbib (1998, 190) suggest that the "precursor of Broca's area was endowed before speech appearance with a mechanism for recognizing actions made by others."

This finding supports gestural theory because it suggests that "language in humans . . . evolved from a basic mechanism originally not related to communication: the capacity to recognize actions" (Rizzolatti and Arbib 1998, 193). Thus, we arrive at the original Big Bang of the language universe: the point where language emerged from non-language. And at the heart of that event, we find gestures.

Many people are surprised at this conclusion. Some are even shocked and dismayed. How can it be that Bill Stokoe, the man who was so instrumental in convincing the world that signs are not just gestures but a real human language, sees gesture at the heart of human language? Isn't this a contradiction?

It is important to point out that the term *gesture* has many different meanings. For some researchers, speech is the product of gesture (Browman and Goldstein 1989). Others look at the everyday gestures that accompany speech (Kendon 1995; McNeill 1992). Liddell (this volume) offers the provocative proposal that some aspects of signed languages that we previously thought were linguistic may in fact be gestural. Given that (a) spoken language linguists confidently claim that speech is gestural and devise gestural phonologies for spoken language; (b) psycholinguists find that the same cognitive processes underlie language and gesture, and that gestural and linguistic development proceed apace in child development; and (c) neuroscientists discover that the same neurological substrate supports gesture and language and has been present in hominid brains at least since *Homo habilis;* isn't it odd that signed language linguists are still uncomfortable with research that links gesture with sign?

Perhaps it is time for sign linguists to take a lesson from another master of scientific elegance, Albert Einstein. Faced with the dilemma of explaining certain facts about the behavior of light, Einstein proposed to hold the speed of light constant. In doing so, our view of the universe was radically transformed. This one, apparently trivial, shift in conception of the universe rippled through and changed previously unchallenged facts about the physical world. We learned, for example, that time slows down and that mass increases as a moving object approaches the speed of light.

The lesson I take away from Bill Stokoe's view of the world is this: Signed languages are the light of the linguistic universe. *Signed languages are languages—this is a constant.* Nothing that we learn about signed languages can change this. In embracing this constant, however, we may well find that many cherished and unchallenged beliefs about the linguistic universe will be called into question.

One such belief is that there is a categorical difference between language and gesture, between the linguistic and the gestural. The Italian semiotician Umberto Eco (1983) makes a point that is worth repeating here: "There is unity in diversity, but also diversity in unity."

There is no contradiction in studying the important ways in which gesture differs from sign language or in seeking to discover the principles that unify gesture with language, both signed and spoken. While we do not want to deny the important differences between everyday gestures and language, we also must recognize the deeper unity that lies in action and movement—the basic mechanism that Rizzolatti and Arbib see as the evolutionary source of language.

There is also no contradiction in claiming that while signs are not gestures, they are, in fact, gestural. First, if speech is articulatory gesturing (a fairly uncontroversial claim), then signing is articulatory gesturing. Just as speakers move parts of their bodies to generate acoustic signals, so do signers move parts of their bodies to generate optical signals. In fact, we might even consider renaming "gestural theory"—if not for clarity then to assuage those who are still taken aback by the term *gestural*—to the MMM Theory: "Making Meaning with Movement."

More controversial is the claim that just as there is no categorical difference between language and gesture, there is also no cataclysmic break between gesture and sign (but see Singleton et al. [1995] for a dissenting view). Sign linguists can learn much in studying the cognitive and social processes by which manual and facial gestures become lexicalized and grammaticized into signed language lexical items and grammatical morphemes (Janzen and Shaffer 2000; Shaffer and Janzen 2000; Wilcox 2000).

Stokoe's idea that signed languages are true human languages is now well-accepted, so much so that it seems impossible that anyone could have thought otherwise. The same cannot be said for Stokoe's ideas about the gestural origins of language. The gestural theory of language origins is still controversial and not widely accepted. But if the history of Stokoe's ideas teaches us anything, it is this: their time will come!

Ralph Waldo Emerson's essay "Self-Reliance" could have been written to describe Bill Stokoe: "Insist on yourself; never imitate. Your own gift you can present every moment with the cumulative force of a whole life's cultivation . . . Whoso would be a man must be a nonconformist." This was Bill Stokoe, a man who allowed us to reap the harvest of his life's cultivation.

References

Arbib, Michael A., and Giacomo Rizzolatti. 1996. Neural expectations: A possible evolutionary path from manual skills to language. *Communication and Cognition* 29: 393–424.

Armstrong, David F., William C. Stokoe, and Sherman E. Wilcox. 1995. *Gesture and the nature of language.* Cambridge: Cambridge University Press.

Blake, Joanna, and Susan Dolgoy. 1993. Gestural development and its relation to cognition during the transition to language. *Journal of Nonverbal Behavior* 17: 87–102.

Browman, Catherine, and Louis Goldstein. 1989. Articulatory gestures as phonological units. *Phonology* 6: 201–51.

Capirci, Olga, Jana M. Iverson, Elena Pizzuto, and Virginia Volterra. 1996. Gestures and words during the transition to two-word speech. *Journal of Child Language* 23: 645–73.

Chomsky, Noam. 1972. *Language and mind.* New York: Harcourt Brace Jovanovich.

Eco, Umberto. 1983. *The name of the rose.* San Diego: Harcourt Brace Jovanovich.

Gelernter, David. 1998. *Machine beauty: Elegance and the heart of technology.* New York: Basic Books.

Goldin-Meadow, Susan, and Carolyn Mylander. 1998. Spontaneous sign systems created by deaf children in two cultures (Letter to Nature). *Nature* 391: 279.

Horgan, John. 1996. *The end of science: Facing the limits of knowledge in the twilight of the scientific age.* New York: Broadway Books.

Iverson, Jana M. 1999. How to get to the cafeteria: Gesture and speech in blind and sighted children's spatial descriptions. *Developmental Psychology* 35: 1132–42.

Iverson, Jana M., Olga Capirci, Elissa Longobardi, and M. Cristina Caselli. 1999. Gesturing in mother-child interactions. *Cognitive Development* 14: 57–75.

Iverson, Jana M., and Susan Goldin-Meadow. 1997. What's communication got to do with it? Gesture in children blind from birth. *Developmental Psychology* 33: 453–67.

Janzen, Terry, and Barbara Shaffer. 2000. Gesture as the substrate in the process of ASL grammaticization. Paper presented at the Texas Linguistics Society 2000 Conference "The Effects of Modality on Language and Linguistic Theory," University of Texas at Austin, 25–27 February.

Kendon, Adam. 1994. Do gestures communicate? A review. *Research on Language and Social Interaction* 27: 175–200.

Kimura, Doreen. 1993. *Neuromotor mechanisms in human communication.* Oxford: Oxford University Press.

Langacker, Ronald W. 1987. *Foundations of cognitive grammar, vol. 1: Theoretical prerequisites.* Stanford: Stanford University Press.

———. 1991. *Foundations of cognitive grammar, vol. 2: Descriptive application.* Stanford: Stanford University Press.

McNeill, David. 1992. *Hand and mind: What gestures reveal about thought.* Chicago: University of Chicago Press.

Newport, Elissa L., and Richard Meier. 1986. Acquisition of American Sign Language. In *The cross-linguistic study of language acquisition,* edited by D. Slobin. Hillsdale, N.J.: Lawrence Erlbaum Associates.

Rizzolatti, Giacomo, and Michael A. Arbib. 1998. Language within our grasp. *Trends in Neurosciences* 21(5): 188–94.

Shaffer, Barbara, and Terry Janzen. 2000. Gesture, lexical words, and grammar: Grammaticization processes in ASL. Paper presented at BLS 26, University of California, Berkeley, 18–21 February.

Singleton, J. L., Susan Goldin-Meadow, and David McNeill. 1995. The cataclysmic break between gesticulation and sign: Evidence against a unified continuum of gestural communication. In *Language, gesture, and space,* edited by Karen Emmorey and Judy S. Reilly. Hillsdale, N.J.: Lawrence Erlbaum Associates.

Stokoe, William C. 1991. Semantic phonology. *Sign Language Studies* 71: 99–106.

Wilcox, Sherman E. 2000. Gesture, icon, and symbol: The expression of modality in signed languages. Paper presented at BLS 26, University of California, Berkeley, 18–21 February.

Wilson, Frank R. 1998. *The hand: How its use shapes the brain, language, and human culture.* New York: Pantheon Books.

PART 3

Diverse Populations

INTRODUCTION

Michael A. Karchmer

The chapters in this section deal with varied issues and focus on diverse populations. The chapter by Ceil Lucas, Robert Bayley, Mary Rose, and Alyssa Wulf and the chapter by Glenn Anderson both consider the impact of sign language research on communities of users of American Sign Language (ASL). Britta Hansen describes the role of sign language research over the last thirty-five years in changing attitudes and practices in Denmark. John Bonvillian discusses how signing has been used to address communication issues faced by groups of disabled people who can hear but cannot speak. The chapter by the Italian research team of Olga Capirci, M. Cristina Caselli, Jana M. Iverson, Elena Pizzuto, and Virginia Volterra seeks to understand how gesture fits into the development of spoken language during a child's second year. Although the issues addressed by the chapters are varied, each chapter acknowledges a debt to Stokoe and his work. Indeed, this section, by its very diversity, illustrates the broad sweep of Stokoe's intellectual interests and the impact of his approach and his thinking.

The chapter by Lucas et al. on the impact of variation research on Deaf communities begins by recognizing the importance of the work of Stokoe and his colleagues. While variation has long been known to be a key feature of spoken languages, Lucas and her co-authors trace the interest in variation in American Sign Language to the original edition of *A Dictionary of American Sign Language on Linguistic Principles* (DASL) (Stokoe, Casterline, and Croneberg 1965). Specifically, two appendices by Croneberg in the DASL deal with cultural and social aspects of the Deaf community and with the issue of sociolinguistic variation in relation to the preparation of a dictionary. According to Lucas et al., the inclusion of information about variation in the DASL reinforced the status of ASL as a genuine language. Moreover, the fact that variation was cast as an integral part of ASL meant that it had to be considered if the language was to be understood fully. Lucas et al. maintain that the publication of the DASL, complete with its appendices, legitimized sign language research in all its aspects as well as the formal teaching of ASL. In doing so, the DASL had a major impact on the Deaf community by opening up opportunities for Deaf people in these areas.

Lucas et al. also report findings from the large program of research on sign language variation undertaken in the mid- to late-1990s. The purpose of the research was to assemble a large videotaped corpus representative of the use of ASL. Drawn from a large number of individuals at seven sites across the United States, the corpus allowed for a wide range of questions to be asked about constraints on sign language variation. To give a taste of this project, the chapter focuses on findings about location signs (signs produced in citation form around the forehead or temple). The chapter describes how phonological features as well as grammatical categories are important determiners of variation. Social and economic factors, such as age, ethnicity, and social class are also found to be important. However, Lucas et al. report that some of these social and economic factors relate to variation in ASL differently from the patterns normally seen for spoken languages. The findings in relation to Black Deaf signers are particularly puzzling and Lucas et al. offer possible explanations.

The interest in ethnic variation in Lucas et al. reverberates in Anderson's chapter, which he devotes specifically to issues concerning Black Deaf communities in the United States. After describing the role these communities play as distinct cultural and linguistic entities within the larger American Deaf Community, Anderson acknowledges Stokoe's pioneering efforts and wonders what the impact of sign language research has been on that particular community. Like Lucas et al., Anderson credits Croneberg's appendix to the 1965 DASL as the starting point for his interest. Croneberg suggested that "a study of

ASL dialects of the Negro deaf will constitute an important part of the full-scale sign language dialect study." After determining that the amount of sign language research on Black Deaf people in the ensuing years has not been great, Anderson reports on an informal canvas of colleagues that he did to gauge the impact of sign language research on the Black Deaf community. Anderson concludes that the impact has been modest to date, but he expresses the hope that the situation may change as more Black Deaf people become directly involved in sign language research.

Hansen's chapter provides an interesting counterpoint to Anderson's chapter. Whereas Anderson maintains sign language research has had limited influence on Black Deaf Americans, Hansen concludes precisely the opposite in relation to Europe: that sign language research has played a major role on changing thinking and practices about Deaf people. Focusing on her own country of Denmark, Hansen attributes the change in attitudes toward sign languages and Deaf people to the influence of Stokoe and his associates at the Linguistics Research Laboratory. She acknowledges how Danish researchers and educators relied heavily on Stokoe's approach and used his research as a starting point for their own. From the initial goal of showing that Danish Sign Language was a language equal in function to Danish and other spoken languages, Danish researchers expanded to other research. Without this research, introducing the teaching of sign language into the Danish curriculum would not have been possible. Overall, Hansen concludes that the concept of Deaf bilingualism engendered by sign language research has "opened up new perspectives on the language situation of deaf people." Moreover, Deaf people's participation and leadership in research and teaching have become important features of the Danish situation. And it is here that Hansen's chapter strikes a note in common with Anderson's: both stress the importance of the meaningful involvement of and leadership by the members of the Deaf community in sign language research and education. Hansen forcefully concludes, "academic research on sign language will almost always have an impact on deaf education and the cultural and social situation of deaf people, but only if the results are made available and used pragmatically in cooperation with deaf people, parents, and educators."

Bonvillian's chapter considers the use of signing with children who can hear but cannot speak. In doing so, he provides evidence of the reach of Stokoe's ideas about sign language. The chapter begins by reviewing the rapid rise that took place during the 1970s of educational and training programs in which signing was used. These programs were established with groups of people as diverse as those with mental retardation, with autism, with specific neuromotor deficits, and with aphasia. Bonvillian states that one of the principal reasons for the increase in these programs was the recognition—largely due to Stokoe—that sign languages used by Deaf persons were genuine languages. Because language was no longer equated to speech, sign languages began to be viewed as alternatives for facilitating communication with nonspeaking, hearing people. As Bonvillian makes clear in the chapter, trying to develop and adapt signs and sign systems to the specific needs of these children has proved to be complex and challenging. To date the results of the use of signs with these hearing, nonspeaking children have been mixed—ranging from unqualified success to complete failure. But through the process of implementing the programs, Bonvillian notes how efforts to teach the children to sign have helped uncover unexpected findings and have led to highly beneficial insights.

Finally, the section ends with the chapter by Capirci et al. on language development, specifically on the role of gesture as a transitional device as children begin to engage in two-word speech. Again, this group of Italian researchers acknowledge Stokoe, who devoted much of his last decade to bridging the gulf between gesture and language. The chapter focuses on hearing children exposed only to spoken language, but almost as if tipping a hat to Stokoe, the research includes as a subject a hearing child of deaf parents who was exposed to both spoken and signed input.

Reference

Stokoe, William C., Dorothy C. Casterline, and Carl G. Croneberg, eds. 1965. *A dictionary of American sign language.* Washington, D.C.: Gallaudet College Press.

7

The Impact of Variation Research on Deaf Communities

Ceil Lucas, Robert Bayley,
Mary Rose, and Alyssa Wulf

Both spoken languages and sign languages exhibit variation. That is, users of spoken languages and sign languages have alternate ways of saying the same thing. Variation is found at all levels of a language. For example, we often see variation in the lexicon of a language, such that in spoken English, some speakers use the word *couch* while others say *sofa* or even *davenport*. In American Sign Language (ASL), we know that there are numerous signs for the concepts glossed by BIRTHDAY, PICNIC, or HALLOWEEN. Variation is often seen in the phonology of a language, in the individual segments that make up words or signs or in the parts of those segments. For example, in English words that end in clusters of consonants, as in *test, round,* or *past,* speakers often delete the final

---

The collaborators on the data collection for this chapter were Clayton Valli, Susan Schatz, Leslie Saline, and Ruth Reed. For the analysis, the co-authors of this chapter were joined by Paul Dudis. We are grateful to Robert Walker for the drawings, to MJ Bienvenu for serving as the artist's model, and to Jayne McKenzie for the preparation of this manuscript.

consonant of the cluster when it is followed by another consonant, the result being *tes' students, roun' midnight, pas' glory*. An example of phonological variation in ASL can be seen in signs such as BORED or DEAF, usually signed with a 1 handshape (index finger extended, all other fingers and thumb closed) but sometimes produced with the pinky finger extended.

Variation is also seen in the morphological and syntactic components of a language. For example, in African American Vernacular English (AAVE), the copula *be* is variably deleted, such that the sentences *He is my brother* and *He my brother* both occur. The example of consonant cluster reduction given earlier also concerns morphological variation, in that the final consonant deleted is sometimes a past tense morpheme (that is, a meaningful unit). An example of syntactic variation in ASL is the variable realization of subjects. For example, the verb THINK can be produced with an overt noun phrase subject, as in the sentence J-O-H-N THINK, or with an overt pronoun subject, as in the sentence PRO.1 THINK ("I think"). However, ASL is what is known as a pro-drop language and verbs that have overt subjects are sometimes produced without them, such that the above sentence might be produced simply as THINK (Wulf et al. in press).

Furthermore, studies of spoken languages and sign languages over the past 40 years have shown that variation frequently correlates in a patterned way with social factors such as region, age, gender, ethnicity, and socioeconomic status. This is known as sociolinguistic variation. That is, older people may use more of a certain variant than younger people; women may use a given variant less than men; a given variant may be used more by working-class people than by middle-class people.

Variation in the DASL

The original edition of *A Dictionary of American Sign Language on Linguistic Principles* (DASL) written by William Stokoe, Dorothy Casterline, and Carl Croneberg (1965), includes two appendices written by Croneberg. Appendix C, "The Linguistic Community," describes the cultural and social aspects of the Deaf community and discusses the issues of economic status, patterns of social contact, and the factors that contribute to group cohesion. These factors include the extensive networks of both a personal and organizational nature that ensure frequent contact even among people who live on opposite sides of the country. Croneberg states that "there are close ties also between deaf individuals or groups of individuals as far apart as California and New York. Deaf people from New York on vacation in California stop and visit deaf friends there or at least make it a practice to visit the club for the deaf in San Francisco or Los Angeles. . . . The deaf as a group have social ties with each other that extend farther across the nation than similar ties of perhaps any other American minority group" (310). These ties of a personal nature are reinforced by membership in national organizations such as the National Association of the Deaf (NAD), the National Fraternal Society of the Deaf (NFSD), and the National Congress of Jewish Deaf (NCJD). These personal and organizational patterns of interaction are central to understanding patterns of language use and variation in ASL. Specifically, while variation can definitely be observed in ASL, there is at the same time the reality and the recognition of a cohesive community of ASL users that extends across the United States.

In Appendix D, "Sign Language Dialects," Croneberg deals with the issue of sociolinguistic variation as it pertains to the preparation of a dictionary. As he states, "One of the problems that early confronts the lexicographers of a language is dialect, and this problem is particularly acute when the language has never before been written. They must try to determine whether an item in the language is *standard*, that is, used by the majority of a given population, or *dialect*, that is, used by a particular section of the population" (Stokoe, Casterline, and Croneberg 1965, 313). He outlines the difference between what he terms *horizontal* variation (regional variation) and *vertical* variation (variation that occurs in the language of groups separated by social stratification) and states that ASL exhibits both. He then describes the results of a study of lexical variation based on a 134-item sign vocabulary list that he undertook in North Carolina and Virginia and in Maine, New Hampshire, and Vermont. He finds that for ASL, the state boundaries between North Carolina and Virginia also constitute dialect boundaries, in that North Carolina signs are not found in Virginia and vice versa. He finds the three New England states to be less internally standardized (that is, people within each of the three states exhibit a wide range of variants for each item) and the state boundaries in New England to be much less important, with a lot of overlap in lexical choice observed between the three states. He points out the key role of the residential schools in the dissemination of dialects, stating, "At such a school, the young deaf learn ASL in the particular variety characteristic of the local region. The school is also a source of local innovations, for each school generation comes up with some new signs or modifications of old ones" (314).

In the discussion of vertical variation, Croneberg mentions age, ethnicity, gender, religion, and status as factors in variation. Status is related to economic level, occupation, relative leadership within the deaf community, and educational background. Individuals in professional-level jobs who are financially prosperous graduates of Gallaudet College (now Gallaudet University) "tend to seek each other out and form a group. Frequently they use certain signs that are considered superior to the signs used locally for the same thing. Examples of such signs are Gallaudet signs, transmitted by one or more graduates of Gallaudet who are now teaching at a school for the deaf, and who are members of the local elite. The sign may or may not later be incorporated in the sign language of the local or regional community" (Stokoe, Casterline, Croneberg 1965, 318).

Finally, Croneberg comments on what a standard sign language might be and states that "few have paid any attention to the term *standard* in the sense of 'statistically most frequent.' The tendency has been to divide sign language into good and bad" (Stokoe, Casterline, Croneberg 1965, 318), with older signers and educators of the deaf maintaining the superiority of their respective signs for various reasons. He neatly captures the essence of the difference between prescriptive and descriptive perspectives on language when he states, "What signs the deaf population actually uses and what certain individuals consider good signs are thus very often two completely different things" (319).

The Significance of Including Variation in the DASL

Stokoe (1994) addresses the issue of why the publication of any new dictionary makes headline news. In the following passage he explains that a serious dictionary is a lot more than a word book:

> By defining hundreds of thousands of English words in phrases and sentences in English, [the *Oxford English Dictionary*] describes this language more completely than any other single book can do. By quoting the passage in which a word was first used and by quoting other examples of its use as the meaning has changed, [it] also presents a rich history of the language and a history of users' thought. That is why publication of a serious dictionary makes news. Between the covers of a serious dictionary we find, all ready for us, the tools of thought. (331)

Stokoe extends the importance of spoken language dictionaries to sign language dictionaries because, beyond describing and arranging the tools of thought that sign language users need, sign language dictionaries can "show the world that deaf signers can think in their sign languages, with logic and precision and even elegance. [They] can wipe out, as nothing else can so well, the false ideas that ignorant people have about deaf people and deaf society and sign languages" (Stokoe 1994, 332).

In discussing what guided him in the preparation of the DASL as early as 1957, Stokoe cites the thinking of George Trager and Henry Lee Smith: "They insisted that language could not be studied by itself, in isolation, but must be looked at in direct connection to the people who used it, the things they used it to talk about, and the view of the world that using it imposed on them" (Stokoe 1994, 333). This perspective clearly guided the inclusion of Croneberg's appendices in the DASL, appendices that showed "how language and culture as well as deafness formed a special community" (334). By 1989 (the year of the Deaf Way conference), public attitudes toward deafness and deaf people and their sign language had changed, in part because of the publication of the DASL and the inclusion of Croneberg's appendices. Stokoe also attributed the success of the Deaf President Now movement at Gallaudet University to the DASL:

> I would like to think anyway—when the student leaders stood in front of TV cameras in March of 1988 and said that the University needed a deaf president now because the language and culture of deaf people must be respected—that the germ of that idea was presented in the dictionary twenty-three years earlier. (334)

This observation by Stokoe is reiterated by a number of his colleagues and associates. George Detmold (in Maher 1996, 90) stated that he thought that the significance of the DASL "was that their [deaf people's] language was treated here like any other language." Mervin Garretson, former president of the National Association of the Deaf, wrote that "to know, once and for all, that our 'primitive' and 'ideographic gestures' are really a formal language on a par with all other languages of the world is a step towards pride and liberation" (Baker and Battison 1980, vi).

The inclusion of information about variation in the DASL has had an impact on the Deaf community in three important ways.

1. By simply recognizing that ASL exhibits variation like other entities we recognize as languages, it reinforces that status of ASL as a real language. Since it is known that variation is often the precursor to change (Milroy 1992), the study of variation in ASL, as in other languages, leads us to an understanding of how ASL, like other languages, changes.

2. Including information about variation in the DASL—a volume that by definition aims to represent the structure of the language and is accepted by the community as a reliable representation—reinforces the position that rather than being just a curiosity or an anomaly, variation is an integral part of the structure of a language; in order to truly understand the nature of a language, variation must be

considered. In this regard, Weinreich, Labov, and Herzog (1968) introduced the idea of structured heterogeneity as the most useful metaphor for understanding the nature of language:

> If a language has to be structured in order to function efficiently, how do people continue to talk while the language changes, that is, while it passes through periods of lessened systematicity? Alternatively, if overriding pressures do force a language to change, and communication is less efficient in the interim . . . why have such inefficiencies not been observed in practice?
>
> This, it seems to us, is the fundamental question with which a theory of language change must cope. The solution, we will argue, lies in the direction of breaking down the identification of structuredness with homogeneity. The key to a rational conception of language change—indeed, of language itself—is the possibility of describing orderly differentiation in a language serving a community. We will argue that nativelike command of heterogeneous structures is not a matter of multidialectalism or "mere" performance, but is part of unilingual linguistic competence. One of the corollaries of our approach is that in a language serving a complex (i.e., real) community, it is the *absence* of structured heterogeneity that would be dysfunctional. (Weinreich, Labov, and Herzog 1968, 99–100)

Simply, the inclusion of information about variation in the DASL provides a much wider perspective on the fundamental nature of ASL structure.

3. Publishing the DASL with its sociolinguistic appendices represented a huge step toward legitimizing (a) sign language research in all of its numerous aspects, from phonology, morphology, and syntax to sociolinguistics, discourse analysis, language policy and planning, and language attitudes; and (b) the formal teaching of sign languages. It had a powerful impact on the Deaf community by opening up research and sign language teaching as areas accessible to Deaf people.

It is also useful to consider Croneberg's appendices within the context of other variation research being undertaken at the same time. The years between 1958 (the year Fischer's pioneering study of sociolinguistic variation was published) and 1977 were very busy for spoken languages and sign languages alike. Labov's study of vowel centralization on Martha's Vineyard was published in 1963 and his pivotal study of New York City speech followed in 1966. Both studies explored a new area, the correlation of linguistic variables with social factors. Shuy, Wolfram, and Riley completed their urban language study of Detroit in 1968 and Wolfram's dissertation on what is now known as African American Vernacular English (AAVE) appeared in 1969. Georgetown University's doctoral program in sociolinguistics was established in 1971, and James Woodward was one of the first students in that program. His 1973 dissertation was the first one to explore variation in a sign language. In short, the years immediately preceding and following the publication of the DASL saw a growing awareness about sociolinguistics in general and variation in particular. All of this occurred at a time, of course, when the whole field of linguistics itself was in the midst of a paradigm shift, following the publication of Noam Chomsky's *Syntactic Structures* (1957) and *Aspects of the Theory of Syntax* (1965).

The years following the publication of the DASL witnessed a number of studies of variation in ASL. In addition to Woodward's dissertation, phonological variation in the form of thumb extension (for example, FUNNY, BLACK) was explored by Battison, Markowicz, and Woodward (1975). Woodward, Erting, and Oliver (1976) looked at signs that are produced variably on the face or the hands (for example, MOVIE, PEACH), and Woodward and DeSantis (1977) examined signs that are variably one-handed or two-handed. DeSantis (1977) looked at location variation, in signs variably signed at the elbow or on the hands (for example PUNISH, HELP), and while called a historical study, Frishberg (1975) looked at processes such as centralization still witnessed in ASL today. Morphological and syntactic variation have also been explored, as well as lexical variation. (For a full review of variation research in ASL, see Lucas 1995; Lucas et al. 2001).

Recent Study of Sociolinguistic Variation in ASL

Thirty years after the publication of the DASL, a study of sociolinguistic variation in ASL began based in the Department of ASL, Linguistics, and Interpretation of Gallaudet University and funded by the National Science Foundation. The goal of the project, which lasted from June 1994 through July 2000, was to create a large videotaped corpus representative of the use of ASL, in order to investigate two theoretical questions: Can internal linguistic constraints on variation such as those identified and described in spoken languages be identified and described for variation in ASL? and Can external constraints on variation such as those identified and described in spoken languages be identified and described for variation in ASL?

Following Guy's dictum that "to shed light at the same time on both linguistic structure and social structure we are necessarily required to amass large amounts of data from many individuals" (1993, 223), we chose seven sites across the United States for the creation of a representative corpus: Staunton, Virginia; Frederick, Maryland; Boston, Massachusetts; Kansas City, Missouri, and Olathe, Kansas; Fremont, California; and Bellingham, Washington (see figure 7.1). All of these sites have thriving communities of ASL users. In addition, Staunton, Frederick, Boston, Fremont, and Olathe are the sites of residential schools for deaf children. Following demographic studies of the Deaf community (see, for example, Schein 1987 and Schein and Delk 1974), working-class participants were defined as individuals whose educational careers did not extend past high school (in some cases in our corpus, not past elementary school or eighth grade), and who were working in blue-collar, vocational jobs. In most cases, they had also lived all of their lives in the same place where they grew up and went to school. Middle-class participants were individuals who had completed a college education (and in many cases, had graduate degrees), were working in professional positions, and often may have left the area to go to college and graduate school but have since returned and settled there.

The division into age groups was motivated by changes in language policies in deaf education. The early 1970s witnessed changes from

A six-year project funded by the National Science Foundation, on sociolinguistic varation in ASL. (June 1, 1994–July 31, 2000)

OVERVIEW OF DATA COLLECTION:

Visited seven sites:

1. Staunton, Virginia
2. Frederick, Maryland
3. Boston, Massachusetts
4. New Orleans, Louisiana
5. Fremont, California
6. Kansas City, Missouri/Olathe, Kansas
7. Bellingham, Washington

Twelve groups at each site, except for Virginia, Maryland, and Bellingham, Washington (only Caucasian groups).

African American Groups:		Caucasian Groups:	
Middle Class:	Working Class:	Middle Class:	Working Class:
15–25	15–25	15–25	15–25
26–54	26–54	26–54	26–54
(55–up)	55–up	55–up	55–up

A total of 207 American Sign Language signers. (Each group consisted of 2–6 signers; no participants were recruited in the middle-class African American 55–up age group.)

OVERALL GOAL OF THE PROJECT:

A description of phonological, morphosyntactic, and lexical variation in ASL, and the correlation of variation with external factors such as age, region, gender, ethnicity, and socioeconomic status.

Figure 7.1 The project at a glance.

purely oral education in residential schools (with ASL used by students outside the classroom and in some vocational training classes) to the use of Total Communication, which usually entails talking and signing at the same time, in residential schools and mainstreaming programs. More recently, students in some programs are being educated through ASL, with English as a language for reading and writing. Participants in the study who were 25 at the time of data collection would just have been entering school when the changes were beginning to take place, while those 55 and up would have been educated by and large in residential schools with oral-only policies. Most of the participants in the 15–25 age range were in programs that use ASL as the medium of instruction.

The approach to the participants was informed by the work of Labov (1972) and Milroy (1987). Participants came together in groups of two to six and the groups were assembled in each area by a contact person, a deaf individual living in the area with good knowledge of the community. These contact persons were similar to the "brokers" described by Milroy (1987, 70). Participants first engaged in approximately one hour of free conversation without the researchers present. Two participants from each group were then selected and interviewed by the deaf researchers in depth about their backgrounds, their social networks, and their patterns of language use. In the four sites with African American participants (Boston, New Orleans, Kansas City, Fremont), the African American participants were interviewed by an African American researcher. The session concluded with the interviewees being shown the same set of 34 pictures to elicit their signs for the objects or actions represented in the pictures. Table 7.1 shows the distribution of the participants in the study. As can be seen in table 7.2, "target" variables were identified in the data. Target variables are ones that exhibit variation and that occur frequently enough to allow for a statistical analysis. The target variables include: (1) signs with a 1 handshape (index finger extended, all other fingers and thumb closed). 1 handshape signs exhibit a wide range of variation, from extended thumb to all fingers open. Many kinds of signs have a 1 handshape and the focus of this study was on pronouns and lexical signs. 1 handshape classifier predicates and indexic signs were not included

TABLE 7.1. Signer Social and Demographic Characteristics

Site	AGE 15–25	26–54	55+	SOCIAL CLASS Working	Middle	GENDER M	F	ETHNICITY AA	C	LANGUAGE BACKGROUND ASL	Other
Boston, Mass. (n = 30)	9	12	9	17	13	15	15	11	19	5	25
Frederick, Md. (n = 21)	7	6	8	11	10	11	10	—	21	6	15
Staunton, Va. (n = 26)	5	11	10	15	11	12	14	—	26	5	21
New Orleans, La. (n = 34)	7	15	12	20	14	17	17	13	21	8	26
Olathe, Kans./Kansas City, Mo. (n = 42)	12	16	14	26	16	20	22	14	28	7	35
Fremont, Calif. (n = 34)	6	16	12	18	16	16	18	15	19	11	23
Bellingham, Wash. (n = 20)	6	7	7	9	11	12	8	—	20	3	17
Totals (n = 207)	52	83	72	116	91	103	104	53	154	45	162

Introduction: A total of 207 signers from seven locations throughout the United States.

I. FOUR TARGET VARIABLES

A. 1 Handshape Signs	B. Location	C. DEAF signs	D. Pronoun Drop
• 25 signs × 207 signers = 5,175 tokens • Most frequent occurrence variable • THINK; PRO-1,2,3; TELL; BLACK	• 13 signs × 207 signers = 2,862 tokens • Decentralization • KNOW, THINK, FOR, SUPPOSE	• Record all possible occurrences for each signer • Follow-up Lucas' study • ear to chin; chin to ear; contact chin w/no movement	• 463 tokens • Pattern of subject presence and subject absence?

II. LEXICAL VARIATION:

A. Elicited   B. Observed

- 33 pictures used in all of sites
- To determine any patterns throughout the U.S.A.
- Record all possible signs that differ from citation form
- To determine a regional pattern and to make a note of it

III. GENERAL VARIATION: NONTARGET VARIABLES

A. Any sign that differs from its citation form, any interesting observations related to discourse, syntax, verbs and semantics. These observations may not occur often enough to be analyzed by the VARBRUL program, e.g., non 1 handshape target signs such as BUTTER, CUTE

IV. BACKGROUND INFORMATION ON SIGNERS

a. Questionnaire paper
b. Interviews: social networks and language use (Milroy)

Figure 7.2. What does variable data look like?

in the analysis; (2) the sign DEAF, which in citation form (the form of the sign that typically appears in dictionaries and is taught in sign language classes) is produced from just below the ear to just above the chin. However, it can also be produced from chin to ear or simply as a contact on the cheek; (3) a class of signs that we refer to as location signs, signs such as KNOW and SUPPOSE, which in citation form are produced at forehead or temple but which also occur at points on the cheek and even in the space in front of the signer; (4) subject pronouns. With some ASL verbs, the subject occurs variably. This happens with pronouns, which is why ASL is known as a "pro-drop" language, similar to Chinese, Italian, or Spanish, but full noun phrases may also be omitted. These are the four target variables being investigated in the study. In addition, lexical variation was examined, based on the 34-picture elicitation task, and note was being made of instances of variation that are not numerous enough for statistical analysis.

Location Variation in ASL

This chapter focuses on the location signs. (For a full account of the results of the project, see Lucas, Bayley, and Valli 2001) As mentioned above, what we are calling location signs are produced in citation form at the forehead or temple. In addition to KNOW, signs in this class include verbs of thinking and perception (for example, BELIEVE, DECIDE, FORGET, REMEMBER, SUPPOSE, SUSPECT, SEE, THINK), as well as a variety of adjectives (for example, DIZZY, FEDERAL, REASONABLE), nouns (for example, DEER, HORSE), prepositions (for example, FOR), and interrogatives (for example, WHY). Figure 7.3 illustrates KNOW and FOR in their citation forms.

It is well recognized by ASL signers and linguists that signs like KNOW can "move down" (Frishberg 1975). Variants of these signs are produced at locations that are lower than the forehead or temple. Liddell and Johnson state that

> many signs which are produced with contact at the SFH [side forehead] location in formal signing may be produced in casual signing at the CK [cheek] location. Similarly, signs produced at the CK location

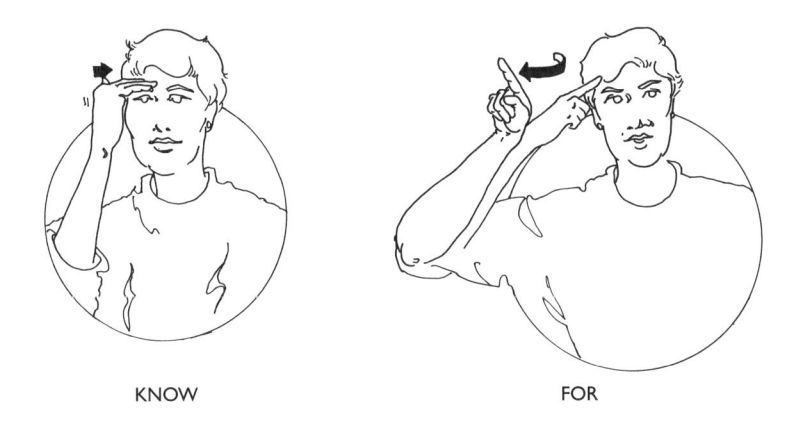

The Impact of Variation Research on Deaf Communities 151

KNOW   FOR

Figure 7.3. Citation forms for KNOW and FOR

(including those moved from the SFH location) may be produced at the JW [jaw] location. These same signs also appear at times without contact in the area immediately in front of the iNK [ipsilateral neck] location. (1989, 253)

Figure 7.4 illustrates KNOW and FOR in their noncitation forms.

KNOW   FOR

Figure 7.4. Noncitation forms for KNOW and FOR

The question to be taken up, then, is just what causes signs produced as high as the signer's temple or forehead to be produced lower on the head or face or indeed, in the space in front of the signer? Liddell and Johnson state that, ". . . the phonological processes that originally must have moved them are still active in contemporary ASL. The rules which account for [these signs] appear to be variably selected by casual signing, and like vowel reduction rules in spoken languages, have the effect of neutralizing contrasts of location" (1989, 253). This suggests a phonological process of assimilation, whereby the location of the sign preceding or following the target sign might contribute to the lowering of the target sign.

To investigate the variation that we observed with these signs, we collected approximately 13 tokens of these signs from each signer, for a total of 2,862 tokens. We coded each token for linguistic and social factors. Linguistic factors included the location of the preceding and following sign and whether or not the preceding or following sign involved contact with the body or head. And since the grammatical category of the target sign has proven to be the most significant factor in accounting for the variation seen with two of the other target variables, 1 handshape signs and DEAF, we coded for grammatical category of the location signs (see Bayley, Lucas, and Rose 2000; Rose, Lucas, Bayley, and Wulf 1999). Finally, we coded each token for the kind of discourse it occurred in—conversation or narrative. The 268 tokens in which the signer's arm or elbow was resting on a table or on the signer's knee were excluded, as we reasoned that this would automatically raise the location of the target sign. After exclusions, the total number of tokens available for analysis was 2,594. The tokens were also coded for social factors, including region, age, gender, ethnicity, socioeconomic status, and language background. The latter refers to whether the signer is from a deaf ASL-using family or from "other," such as a hearing non-signing family.

We analyzed the coded tokens using Rand and Sankoff's (1990) version of VARBRUL, a specialized application of logistic regression (Sankoff 1988). The VARBRUL program is designed specifically for the analysis of sociolinguistic variation. It assigns weights to each of the factors identified and the weight is essentially a measure of the influence of a given factor on the occurrence of variation. A weight of .50 is considered to be neutral, a weight above .50 is considered to be an indication that the factor favors the occurrence of whichever value of the dependent variable has been chosen, and a weight below .50 is considered to be an indication that the factor disfavors the occurrence of the chosen dependent variable. Our analysis showed that the variation that we see with the location signs is systematic and constrained by both linguistic and social factors. Table 7.2 shows the results for the linguistic factors. We see here that phonological factors—preceding location and following contact—do indeed play a role. The application value is the value of the dependent variable that counts as an application of the 'rule' being investigated. The application value here is the noncitation lowered form, and preceding signs produced at head level disfavor this form, while a preceding pause or a preceding sign produced below the head forms the neutral reference point. In line with Liddell and Johnson, this suggests that assimilation may be at work —that is, preceding signs produced at head level prefer citation for

TABLE 7.2. VARBRUL Analysis of Location: Linguistic Factors (Application Value: -cf)

Factor Group	Factor	VARBRUL Weight	Percentage	N
Grammatical function	Preposition, interrogative	.581	59	485
	Noun, verb	.486	52	2,052
	Adjective	.316	35	57
Preceding location	Body	.514	53	1,648
	Head	.463	48	614
Following contact	No contact	.525	55	1,323
	Contact	.466	48	991
Input (p_o)	TOTAL	.518	53	2,594

Note: χ^2/cell = 1.1702; all factor groups significant at $p < .05$; results for preceding location and following contact do not include pauses, which were tested in separate factor groups that proved not to be significant.

location signs. As for contact, a following sign that involves contact with the head or body slightly disfavors noncitation forms, while noncontact signs are close to neutral.

However, the analysis revealed that the most important factor in the variation is the grammatical category of the target sign. As we can see, prepositions and interrogative signs favor noncitation forms, adjectives strongly disfavor them, while nouns and verbs, which comprise the great majority of tokens, are the nearly neutral reference point. That is, grammatical function signs are more likely to be produced in noncitation form, while content signs are more likely to be produced in citation form. The finding that grammatical function is the most important factor in accounting for the variation parallels what we have found in our analysis of 1 handshape signs and of DEAF. This consistent result with all three of the phonological variables clearly suggests that we cannot assume that phonological variation in ASL is fully accounted for by phonological factors alone.

The analysis of the social factors reveals both similarities to and differences from results reported for hearing communities. As seen in table 7.3, women tend to prefer the more standard, or citation, form. This result parallels results for spoken languages, at least with respect to socially stigmatized forms (see, for example, Trudgill 1974; Labov 1990). In addition, as in spoken language communities, younger signers favor the innovative form, while older signers tend to be linguistically conservative. The results for social class and ethnicity, however, differ from results reported for most English-speaking communities. As table 7.3 shows, there is no significant difference between white middle- and working-class signers. Both favor noncitation forms. In contrast, the results for African Americans illustrate class differences as well as the generally more conservative nature of African American ASL (Aramburo 1989). Middle-class African Americans disfavor noncitation forms, although not strongly. Working-class African Americans are more linguistically conservative and strongly disfavor noncitation forms. That is, in contrast to studies of African American Vernacular English (for example, Wolfram 1969; Labov 1972; Rickford 1999), working-class African American signers adhere much more closely to the standard, or dictionary, form than do their middle-class African American counterparts or white signers.

TABLE 7.3. VARBRUL Analysis of Location: Social Factors (Application Value: -cf)

Factor Group	Factor	Weight	Percentage	N
Age	15–25	.602	61	554
	26–54	.517	54	1,133
	55+	.416	46	907
Gender	Male	.544	56	1,376
	Female	.451	49	1,218
Region	CA, LA, MD, MA, KS/MO	.529	54	2,055
	Washington St.	.461	56	259
	Virginia	.334	40	280
Language background	Hearing parents	.519	53	1,940
	Deaf parents	.444	52	654
Ethnicity, SES	Caucasian, middle and working class	.555	56	1,882
	African Am., middle class	.445	55	257
	African Am., working class	.314	40	455
Input	TOTAL	.518	53	2,594

Note: χ^2/cell = 1.1702; all factor groups significant at $p < .05$.; no African Americans participated in Virginia and Washington State. African American middle-class signers include persons aged 15–54.

The more conservative nature of African American ASL, at least with respect to the variable discussed here, may be attributable to the fact that the effects of the Observer's Paradox (Labov 1984) are intensified in studies of sociolinguistic variation of sign languages. Speakers who participate in studies of variation in spoken languages can remain relatively secure in their anonymity because such studies have usually relied upon audiotape rather than videotape. Moreover, spoken language communities are typically much larger than sign language communities. Preserving anonymity is much more difficult in sociolinguistic studies of sign languages. We suggest that the African American signers in this study may have felt the effects of the Observer's Paradox particularly acutely. These signers, as African American deaf people, belong to at least two groups that are stigmatized by the dominant society. Given this situation, as well as the generally conservative nature of African American ASL, it is possible that the African Americans whose data are included here felt considerable pressure to produce a more standard form of ASL.

The regional patterns are a focus of our current work. The transmission of ASL across the United States and much of Canada did not necessarily follow the settlement routes that account for some of the broad patterns that we see in studies of spoken English dialects. Rather, ASL was more often transmitted through the institution of state schools for the deaf. Of particular relevance to the results by region shown in table 7.3 is the fact that the Washington State School for the Deaf employed a teacher from the Virginia school at Staunton (Brelje and Tibbs 1986). The more innovative nature of ASL in these widely separated regions may be a reflection of the historical connections between the schools for the deaf in the two states.

The results for age also suggest that we may be seeing change in progress with this variable. As explained earlier, grammatical function signs like interrogatives and prepositions are likely to be produced in noncitation form, while content signs are more likely to be produced in citation form. When the data are broken down by age and grammatical function, we find that not only are grammatical function signs more likely than content signs to be produced in noncitation form, but that, where we have large numbers of tokens, the numbers of noncitation forms within each of the broad grammatical categories increase as the age of the signers decreases. We hypothesize that grammatical function signs favor the gradual change from citation to noncitation forms begins with the grammatical function signs, perhaps because they are typically unstressed. This is not to suggest, of course, that the citation forms will disappear any time soon. The citation forms are clearly the ones taught in sign language classes and the ones that appear in sign language dictionaries and in formal signing, and all of these factors reinforce their standing.

We will recall that in his appendices in the DASL, Croneberg outlined the existence of what he called horizontal (regional) and vertical (social) variation, and that is exactly what we see in our results. He remarks that his observations on the subject of ASL dialects are "in anticipation of future study" (Stokoe, Casterline, and Croneberg 1965, 313). It would seem that our study is at least one part of that future study, part of a lively and ongoing tradition of research on variation in sign languages, a tradition which Croneberg initiated with his appendices.

The Impact of Variation Research on Deaf Communities

Earlier, we outlined the three-fold impact of variation research on Deaf communities: (1) the recognition of ASL as a language, (2) the understanding of the true nature of ASL structure, and (3) the direct impact on the lives of deaf people in terms of educational and employment opportunities. Indeed, it seems fair to say that this impact has been very tangible. Research on sign language structure has led to the recognition of sign languages as real languages and has had the effect of legitimizing them. This legitimization has allowed for the discussion of what the medium of instruction should be in deaf education and to the question as to why it should not be sign language. This discussion has led to the improvement of deaf education at all levels and to, as Johnson, Liddell, and Erting said in 1989, the unlocking of the curriculum, at least for some deaf students. It has led to the improvement of services for deaf people such as interpreting, and has opened up new career paths for deaf people as teachers both of deaf children and adolescents and as teachers of sign language. The research on sign language structure which William Stokoe initiated and to which Croneberg contributed his appendices on variation has ultimately contributed to the continuing of the empowerment of deaf people all over the world.

References

Aramburo, Anthony. 1989. Sociolinguistic aspects of the Black Deaf community. In *The sociolinguistics of the deaf community,* edited by Ceil Lucas, 103–19. San Diego: Academic Press.

Battison, Robbin, Harry Markowicz, and James C. Woodward. 1975. A good rule of thumb: Variable phonology in American Sign Language. In *Analyzing variation in language,* edited by R. Fasold and Roger Shuy, 291–302. Washington, D.C.: Georgetown University Press.

Bayley, Robert, Ceil Lucas, and Mary Rose. 2000. Variation in American Sign Language: The case of DEAF. *Journal of Sociolinguistics* 4: 81–107.

Brelje, H. W., and V. Tibbs. 1986. *The Washington State School for the Deaf: The first hundred years, 1886–1986.* Vancouver: Washington State School for the Deaf.

Chomsky, Noam. 1957. *Syntactic structures.* The Hague: Mouton.

———. 1965. *Aspects of the theory of syntax.* Cambridge, Mass.: MIT Press.

DeSantis, Susan. 1977. Elbow to hand shift in French and American Sign Language. Paper presented at NWAVE conference, Georgetown University, Washington, D.C., October.

Frishberg, Nancy. 1975. Arbitrariness and iconicity: historical change in American Sign Language. *Language,* 51 (3): 696–719.

Garretson, Mervin. 1980. Foreword. In *Sign language and the deaf community: Essays in honor of William C. Stokoe,* edited by Charlotte Baker and Robbin Battison, v–vi. Silver Spring, Md.: National Association of the Deaf.

Guy, Gregory. 1993. The quantitative analysis of linguistic variation. In *American dialect research,* edited by D. Preston, 223–49. Philadelphia: John Benjamins.

Johnson, Robert E., Scott Liddell, and Carol J. Erting. 1989. Unlocking the curriculum: Principles for achieving access in deaf education. Working Paper 89–3. Washington, D.C.: Gallaudet University Research Institute.

Labov, William. 1963. The social motivation of a sound change. *Word* 19: 273–309.

———. 1966. *The social stratification of English in New York City.* Washington, D.C.: Center for Applied Linguistics.

———. 1972. *Language in the inner city.* Philadelphia: University of Pennsylvania Press.

———. 1984. Field methods of the Project on Language Change and Variation. In *Language in Use: Readings in Sociolinguistics,* edited by John Baugh and Joel Scherzer, 28–53. Englewood Cliffs, N.J.: Prentice Hall.

———. 1990. The interaction of sex and social class in the course of linguistic change. *Language Variation and Change* 2: 205–54.

Liddell, Scott, and Robert E. Johnson. 1989. American Sign Language: The phonological base. *Sign Language Studies* 64: 195–277.

Lucas, Ceil. 1995. Sociolinguistic variation in ASL: The case of DEAF. In *Sociolinguistics in Deaf communities,* vol. 1, edited by Ceil Lucas, 3–25. Washington, D.C.: Gallaudet University Press.

Lucas, Ceil, Robert Bayley, Clayton Valli, Mary Rose, and Alyssa Wulf. 2001. Sociolinguistic variation. In *The sociolinguistics of sign languages,* edited by Ceil Lucas, 61–111. Cambridge: Cambridge University Press.

Lucas, Ceil, Robert Bayley, and Clayton Valli. 2001. *Sociolinguistic variation in ASL.* Sociolinguistics in Deaf Communities, vol. 7. Washington, D.C.: Gallaudet University Press.

Maher, Jane. 1996. *Seeing language in sign: The work of William C. Stokoe.* Washington, D.C.: Gallaudet University Press.

Milroy, James. 1992. *Linguistic variation and change.* Oxford: Blackwell.

Milroy, Leslie. 1987. *Observing and analysing natural language.* Oxford: Blackwell.

Rand, David, and David Sankoff. 1990. GoldVarb: A variable rule application for the Macintosh (version 2.0). Montréal: Centre de recherches mathematiques, Université de Montréal.

Rickford, John R. 1999. *African American vernacular English.* Oxford: Blackwell.

Rose, Mary, Ceil Lucas, Robert Bayley, and Alyssa Wulf. 1999. Sociolinguistic variation in American Sign Language: The 1 handshape variable. Paper presented at the annual meeting of the American Dialect Society, Los Angeles, Calif., January.

Sankoff, David. 1988. Variables rules. In *Sociolinguistics: An international handbook of the science of language and society,* vol. 2, edited by Ulrich Ammon, Norbert Dittmar, and K. Mattheier, 984–97. Berlin: Walter de Gruyter.

Schein, Jerry. 1987. The demography of deafness. In *Understanding deafness socially,* edited by Paul C. Higgins and Jeffrey E. Nash, 3–28. Springfield, Ill.: Charles C. Thomas.

Schein, Jerry, and Marcus Delk. 1974. *The Deaf population in the United States*. Silver Spring, Md.: National Association of the Deaf.

Shuy, Roger, Walt Wolfram, and William Riley. 1967. *Linguistics correlates of social stratification in Detroit speech*. Final Report, Project 6-1347, Washington, D.C.: Office of Education.

Stokoe, William C. 1994. A sign language dictionary. In *The Deaf Way*, edited by Carol Erting, Robert C. Johnson, Dorothy L. Smith, and Bruce D. Snider, 331–34. Washington, D.C.: Gallaudet University Press.

Stokoe, William C., Dorothy C. Casterline, and Carl G. Croneberg. 1965. *A dictionary of American Sign Language*. Silver Spring, Md.: Linstok Press.

Trudgill, Peter. 1974. *The social differentiation of English in Norwich*. Cambridge: Cambridge University Press.

Weinreich, Uriel, William Labov, and Martin Herzog. 1968. Empirical foundations for a theory of language change. In *Directions for Historical Linguistics*, edited by Winfred Lehmann and Yakov Malkiel, 99–100l. Austin: University of Texas Press.

Wolfram, Walt. 1969. *A linguistic description of Detroit Negro speech*. Washington, D.C.: Center for Applied Linguistics.

Woodward, James C. 1973. Implicational lects on the deaf diglossic continuum. Ph.D. diss., Georgetown University.

Woodward, James C., Carol J. Erting, and Susan Oliver. 1976. Facing and hand(l)ing variation in American Sign Language. *Sign Language Studies* 10: 43–52.

Woodward, James C., and Susan DeSantis. 1977. Two to one it happens: Dynamic phonology in two sign languages. *Sign Language Studies* 17: 329–46.

Wulf, Alyssa, Paul Dudis, Robert Bayley, and Ceil Lucas. In press. Variable subject presence in ASL narratives. *Sign Language Studies*.

8

The Impact of Sign Language Research on Black Deaf Communities in America

Glenn B. Anderson

The American Deaf community is undergoing a demographic revolution. It is becoming more dynamic, diverse, and multicultural. This is especially true among the young people who will be tomorrow's leaders—the students who are currently attending elementary and secondary schools. As a group, deaf students are probably more diverse and multicultural than the general school-aged population (Sass-Lehrer, Gerner de Garcia, and Rovins, 1995). During the 1993–1994 school year, approximately 40 percent of school-aged deaf students attending K-12 programs in the United States were students of color or from diverse non-White racial, ethnic, and linguistic backgrounds. Within the larger Deaf community, Black Deaf people make up the largest racial or ethnic group (Schildroth and Hotto 1995).[1]

---

1. In this chapter, I use the term *Black* to refer to people of African descent who may trace their heritage to America, Africa, Canada, the Caribbean, South America, or other parts of the world.

Deaf persons of color maintain boundaries and interact in multiple cultures—their hearing racial or ethnic culture, their Deaf racial or ethnic culture, the mainstream Deaf culture, and the mainstream, predominantly White, hearing culture (Sass-Lehrer, Gerner de Garcia, and Rovins 1995; Janesick and Moores 1992). Furthermore, it is also important to be aware of and give attention to the internal diversity (for example, variations due to historical origins, shared experiences and identity, language variation or dialects, etc.) that exists within each of these cultural groups (Anderson 1997).

Black Deaf communities in the United States possess the three basic ingredients suggested by Padden and Humphries (1988) that are helpful for researchers who wish to collect data and make generalizations about a cultural group. These ingredients are as follows:

A Common Language. Black Deaf communities share a common language with the larger Deaf mainstream community. Also, unique sign language varieties or dialects common among some Black Deaf communities in the South emerged and were transmitted from one generation to another (Woodward 1976). This occurred, at least in part, because as many as fifteen southern states maintained separate schools for Black Deaf students. The first school opened in 1867 in North Carolina, and the last school integrated in 1978 in Louisiana.

Unique Patterns for Transmitting Culture. Like members of the mainstream Deaf community, most Black Deaf individuals are born to hearing parents and acquire knowledge about Deaf culture outside of the home from Deaf peers—in schools where they interact with other Deaf classmates and through social networks within the Deaf community. Through formal structures such as the family and the church, as well as informal structures such as social networks in their home communities, Black cultural knowledge is transmitted to Black Deaf individuals. Additionally, the Black Deaf community is well-organized. There are two national organizations, National Black Deaf Advocates (NBDA), which has approximately twenty-seven local chapters; and the National Alliance of Black Interpreters (NAOBI), which sponsors annual training programs and has a membership of close to one hundred individuals with national and state-level credentials as sign language interpreters.

A Large Population. As mentioned earlier, Black Deaf people comprise the largest racial/ethnic group within the Deaf community (Schildroth and Hotto 1995). Black Deaf students represent 60 percent of the students enrolled in educational programs serving deaf students in the South.

The Impact of Sign Language Research on Black Deaf Communities

Sign language research has had a major impact on the larger, mainstream Deaf community. This is evident in the many books and journal articles that have been published and in the way that we talk about Deaf culture and American Sign Language (ASL). Within the context of the growing diversity of the American Deaf community, it is important to examine the impact of sign language research on Black Deaf communities. Thanks to the pioneering efforts of Bill Stokoe forty years ago, examining the impact of sign language research on the American Black Deaf community can also contribute to the greater understanding and appreciation of the cultural and linguistic richness of the culture of all Deaf people.

Bill Stokoe's colleague, Carl Croneberg was probably the first researcher to publish research on ethnic variation among ASL signers (Croneberg 1965). Through his research in North Carolina, at a time when the state maintained separate schools for deaf students, he noted differences in the signs used by the Black and White informants even though they lived in the same city. His observations led him to say, "a study of ASL dialects of the Negro deaf will constitute an important part of the full-scale sign language dialect study" (1965, 315). Despite Croneberg's call for more research, little has been published in the intervening years about sign language use in the Black Deaf community. In fact, I have found only five articles: Woodward 1976; Maxwell and

Smith-Todd 1986; Aramburo 1989; Valli, Reed, Ingram, and Lucas 1990; and Lewis 1997.

Given this lack of research, it is difficult to make an informed judgment about the impact of sign language research on Black Deaf communities. Therefore, I decided to ask members of NBDA and the NAOBI their perception of this issue. I posed the following questions:

1. How has sign language research contributed to knowledge about the culture and language of Black Deaf people?

2. How has sign language research fostered research collaboration with the Black Deaf community?

3. How has sign language research encouraged Black Deaf and hearing scholars to conduct and publish research?

4. What types of sign language research would you like to see conducted that would be relevant and beneficial for the Black Deaf community?

5. Overall, how would you describe or summarize the impact of sign language research on the Black Deaf community?

The questions were distributed through the web site of the NAOBI and a listserv maintained by a group of Black Deaf leaders associated with NBDA. It was designed as an informal inquiry to obtain feedback on whether these key groups perceived that sign language research had made an impact on the lives of Black Deaf people. This informal inquiry has limitations since the responses represent only a small sample of individuals who were motivated and interested in the e-mail questions. However, this small sample appears quite representative of the thinking of many Black interpreters as well as Black Deaf individuals who are active in NBDA. The responses to each question are briefly summarized below.

How Has Sign Language Research Contributed to Knowledge about the Culture and Language of Black Deaf People?

Some of the respondents indicated that sign language research has had a positive impact on the culture and language of Black Deaf people. The research on the signs used by Black Deaf people who attended segregated schools for Deaf students, as well as on the history of these schools, has resulted in greater understanding of the rich cultural legacy of Black Deaf communities, particularly in the South. One individual reported,

> A lot of the knowledge taken with us when performing our day-to-day work as interpreters or professionals has its roots in sign language research in the Black Deaf community, as well as in the mainstream Deaf community. The information we use to help understand and interpret the signs used by both young and older Black Deaf people and understand the relationship African American culture plays in African American Deaf culture are products of the research pioneered by individuals such as Bill Stokoe, Ceil Lucas, Ernest Hairston, Linwood Smith, and Sam and Ted Supalla, to name a few.

Other respondents could not easily specify how or in what ways sign language research has had any impact on them. Several reasons may explain why it was difficult to respond to this question. One could be that a body of knowledge with extensive literature regarding sign language research and the Black Deaf community is not readily available. Another is that very little information is disseminated about sign language research to the Black Deaf community through workshops, lectures, or other appropriate dissemination channels.

One respondent stated that it appeared the Black Deaf community had been underrepresented or overlooked in much of the sign language research that has been published in the literature. Another mentioned, "I learned what I know about African American Deaf culture and signs used by African American Deaf just by being involved in the community. While I was attending an ITP (Interpreter Training Program) there was not much mentioned about ANY other cultures." Someone else mentioned that the few known studies that focused on the Black Deaf community were "better than none at all."

How Has Sign Language Research Fostered Research Collaboration with the American Black Deaf Community?

The general consensus was that over the past forty years little collaborative research between sign language researchers and the Black Deaf community has occurred. Some are aware of the work Ceil Lucas has done on sign language variation through her collaboration with individuals who are active in NBDA and NAOBI (for example, Ruth Reed, Anthony Aramburo, and John Lewis). Others knew that between 1993 and 1996, James Woodward, through a grant from the National Endowment for the Humanities, conducted collaborative research with Black Deaf communities in several southern states including Alabama, Arkansas, Florida, Georgia, Louisiana, Mississippi, North Carolina, and South Carolina.

From these few examples it seems evident that the Black Deaf community has been supportive of collaborating with sign language researchers whenever the opportunity occurred. Most of the respondents indicated that much more collaboration is needed to build a body of knowledge about the language and culture of Black Deaf people. Once that happens, the research will have a significant impact on both the Black Deaf community and the mainstream Deaf community.

How Has Sign Language Research Encouraged Black Deaf and Hearing Scholars to Conduct and Publish Research?

Some respondents recognized the Gallaudet University Department of ASL, Linguistics, and Interpretation for encouraging several Black Deaf and hearing individuals to conduct and disseminate research on sign language through a publication called "Gallaudet University Communication Forum" and through Ceil Lucas's book, *The Sociolinguistics of the Deaf Community* (1989). The consensus, however, was that much more needs to be done to recruit Black Deaf and hearing scholars to provide them with the knowledge and tools to conduct and disseminate research on sign language. Some respondents suggest that recruitment begin at the undergraduate level. Others encourage the establishment of American Sign Language and interpreting programs at historically Black colleges and universities (HBCUs). At present, I believe the only HBCU with an undergraduate program in ASL and Interpreting is Bishop State Community College in Mobile, Alabama. The head of that program is a former Gallaudet student whose research was published in the *Gallaudet University Communication Forum*.

Another person suggested that undergraduate programs in Deaf Studies can play an important role in encouraging students to conduct research related to sign language and the Black Deaf community. She stated,

> this makes me think of Carolyn Emerson's course about Black Deaf people that she is teaching at Gallaudet. One of the assignments for students is doing independent research on topics related to the Black Deaf community. I am sure some of the students have focused on sign language research. I don't think it is the sign language research community that has done the job of encouraging Black Deaf and hearing scholars to conduct research about the language and culture of Black Deaf people. I think it is Deaf Studies Professors like Ms. Emerson who encourage it.

Some of the respondents indicated they were unaware of a Black Deaf or hearing scholar who has earned a doctorate in the area of linguistics or a related field and is actively engaged in sign language research. Of course, that will change once Laurene Gallimore and Nathie Marbury complete their doctoral studies in the near future. Perhaps, they will become the torchbearers and pave the way for more Black Deaf and hearing individuals to conduct research on sign language.

What Types of Sign Language Research Would You Like to See Conducted That Would Be Relevant and Beneficial for the Black Deaf Community?

For some of the same reasons identified under question no. 1, the respondents could not easily specify the kinds of research they wanted to see conducted. In theory, it is easier to offer suggestions for research when one has prior knowledge, awareness, and experience with research. Nevertheless, the following general areas of research interest were mentioned:

1. The historical origins of Black sign dialects. How did they emerge? What were the key influences? How were they transmitted from one generation to another?

2. Sign language acquisition among young Black Deaf children. Many are aware that the number of Black Deaf children who grow up in Deaf families is much smaller than for Deaf children in White Deaf families.

3. The impact of the popular language styles of Black urban culture (primarily rap and hip-hop music and culture) on sign language variation in Black and White Deaf youth, especially those who reside and attend school in urban communities.

4. The impact of Black hearing culture on Black Deaf culture.

Overall, How Would You Describe or Summarize the Impact of Sign Language Research on the Black Deaf Community?

Many of the respondents found this question quite easy to answer. A sampling of their comments follows.

- "Research serves no benefit if it is not put to use. I have no knowledge of the impact of sign language research other than its discussion at national conferences and institutions of higher learning."

- "I don't know the extent of the impact of sign language research on the Black Deaf community. Right now, I think it's marginal."

- "I would summarize by saying there is not much of an impact. Most Black Deaf communities are not exposed to such information. I would like to see more of this type of information [sign language research] disseminated among the Black Deaf community in the form of workshops, discussion groups, or just word of the mouth. It just needs to start somewhere!"

Concluding Remarks

If Carl Croneberg were to take stock of how much progress has been made since he published his observations some forty years ago about the need for research on ethnic variation in ASL, he would be quite disappointed. While sign language research clearly has had a significant impact on the larger, mainstream Deaf community, it apparently has not had as much impact on the Black Deaf community. Have we made a wrong turn somewhere? Maybe we have.

A few years ago I examined some of the literature in the area of research dissemination and utilization in hopes that I might offer some guidance and direction for the future (National Center for the Dissemination of Disability Research 1996). One question often asked is, Why, after years of effort and substantial literature regarding dissemination and utilization, do gaps remain between research and its use? The most frequently cited reason is the lack of communication and collaboration between researchers and their intended audiences (National Center for the Dissemination of Disability Research 1999). As indicated in the responses to my informal inquiry, many of the respondents had little if any opportunity to collaborate and engage in direct communication with individuals involved in sign language research. Evidently, more attention needs to be given to ways to collaborate with members of the Black Deaf community to facilitate sign language research dissemination and utilization.

One of the factors crucial to successful dissemination is personal contact. In other words, simply disseminating research information through a book, journal article, or web posting may not be sufficient. Often it is necessary for researchers to "rub elbows" and "be visible" with the potential users of their research. The responses to the informal survey indicate that one of the main reasons sign language research has not had much impact is because sign language researchers have little direct personal contact with members of Black Deaf communities.

Another contributing factor is that potential users of research tend to accept research information and ideas better from people they know and trust. The implication is that it is important to build relationships with potential users of research. It also helps to work with intermediaries who have established ties with a particular group or community.

These suggestions clearly reinforce the value of engaging in collaborative research with the Black Deaf community. They also add credence to the need for recruiting and encouraging Black Deaf and hearing scholars to acquire the knowledge and tools needed to engage in sign language research. If these suggestions are acted upon we will be able to say much more affirmatively in the future that sign language research is making an impact on all the diverse groups that are part of the American Deaf community.

References

Anderson, Glenn B. 1997. In their own words: Researching stories about the lives of multicultural deaf people. In *Deaf studies V: Toward 2000—Unity and diversity*, edited by Cathryn Carroll, 1–16. Washington, D.C.: Gallaudet University.

Anderson, Glenn B., and Grace, Cynthia A. 1991. Black Deaf adolescents: A diverse and underserved population. *Volta Review* 93 (5): 73–86.

Aramburo, Anthony. 1989. Sociolinguistic aspects of the Black Deaf community. In *The sociolinguistics of the Deaf community*, edited by Ceil Lucas, 103–19. San Diego: Academic Press.

Croneberg, Carl G. 1965. Sign language dialects. In *A dictionary of American sign language*, edited by William C. Stokoe, Dorothy C. Casterline, and Carl G. Croneberg, 313–19. Washington, D.C.: Gallaudet College Press.

Janesick, Valerie J., and Donald F. Moores. 1992. Ethnic and cultural considerations. In *Toward effective public school programs for deaf students*, edited by

Thomas Kluwin, Donald Moores, and Martha Gaustad, 45–65. New York: Teachers College Press.

Lucas, Ceil, ed. 1989. *The sociolinguistics of the deaf community.* San Diego: Academic Press.

Maxwell, Madeline, and Sybil Smith-Todd. 1986. Black Sign Language and school integration in Texas. *Language in Society* 15 (March): 81–93.

National Center for the Dissemination of Disability Research. 1996. *A review of the literature on dissemination and knowledge utilization.* Austin, Texas: Author.

Padden, Carol A., and Tom Humphries, 1988. *Deaf in America: Voices from a culture.* Cambridge: Harvard University Press.

Sass-Lehrer, Marilyn, Barbara Gerner de Garcia, and Michele Rovins. 1995. Creating a multicultural school climate for deaf children and their families. *Perspectives in Education and Deafness* 14(1): 2–4.

Schildroth, Arthur N., and Sue A. Hotto. 1995. Race and ethnic background in the annual survey of deaf and hard of hearing children and youth. *American Annals of the Deaf* 140(2): 96–9.

Westbrook, John. 1999. A word from the director. *Research Exchange* 4(1): 2–3.

Woodward, James C. 1976. Black southern signing. *Language and Society* 5: 211–18.

9

Bilingualism and the Impact of Sign Language Research on Deaf Education

Britta Hansen

In Denmark there are about 4,000 people who are either deaf or severely hard of hearing. Because of their hearing loss, they do not acquire and use spoken and written language in the same way as hearing people. By necessity, most deaf adults have had to become bilingual to greater or lesser degrees. In order to function as members of the majority society, they have to learn as much Danish as possible. In order to function as members of the deaf linguistic and social community, however, they have to acquire sign language.

This view of deaf people as bilingual is fairly new. Traditionally, deafness was thought of as something that would eventually be cured by medical treatment and speech training or at least alleviated by electronic devices such as hearing aids. Articles on issues related to deafness could be found under headings such as handicap, disability, special education, and rehabilitation. It is of great importance that we so-called experts clarify, at least for ourselves, our basic attitudes toward deafness because they will inevitably influence any course of action we recommend.

Over the last thirty years sign language research in the United States, Sweden, Great Britain, and Denmark has led to a radical change in attitudes toward sign languages and the deaf people who use them (Stokoe 1960, 1965, 1970; Engberg-Pedersen, Hansen, and Kjaer Sørensen 1981; Bergman 1979; Klima and Bellugi 1979; Brennan 1990). In 1970 sign language was not considered a language in its own right, and it was not used in the education of deaf children in Denmark. In 1973 a teacher of the deaf in Copenhagen, Ruth Kjaer Sørensen, initiated the first research project to study deaf children's sign language communication. I joined the project to set up what was then called the Center for Total Communication (now the Center for Sign Language and Sign-Supported Communication), in Copenhagen. Ruth Kjaer Sørensen was an experienced teacher and her husband was deaf, so she was skilled in sign language. She had long felt that the oral approach and sign-supported communication were not effective with the majority of deaf children. Giving a deaf child full access to spoken language (that is, the spoken language used in the child's environment) had rarely been accomplished. Deaf children's reading abilities also had proven to be far below their hearing peers' average levels. Although many dedicated teachers struggled, they had not been successful in teaching deaf children spoken Danish by means of the oral approach; as a result deaf people did not acquire the social, cognitive, and academic skills necessary to become fully integrated members of society. They were excluded, low-status citizens, and their potential was overlooked because the educational system focused on the weaknesses caused by their lack of hearing. They were often stigmatized as individuals and as a group.

Sign Language Research

The inspiration for our early research projects on deaf children's sign language use (1973–1976), came from William Stokoe and the work of his staff at the Gallaudet University Linguistics Research Laboratory. We adopted their attitude toward sign language and bilingualism, and their support was of great importance in our struggle against the prejudices and criticism we met during our first ten years of work. One project concentrated on the analysis of spontaneous storytelling by five children who ranged in age from seven to twelve years. In another study we investigated how well children actually understood each other's sign language communication, and how they expressed certain grammatical features (for example, nominal phrases, cause and effect, sign order, and the use of space). We videotaped forty-four deaf children solving specific linguistic tasks, and the results can be summarized as follows:

- The children understood each other's sign language; 70 percent of all the tasks were solved correctly.

- The children generally used the same sign language—the same signs and the same grammatical features—as deaf adults.

- The younger children used more pantomime, except for those who had deaf parents.

- Deaf children with deaf parents used sign language more fluently and with more confidence than those with hearing parents. They were also able to adjust their signing to the person they were talking to.

One of our goals was to prove that sign language was a language equal in function to Danish and other spoken languages, which at that time was an important issue in sign language research. We started a new research project on the use of sign language by deaf adults, focusing on grammatical features like simultaneity, iconicity and arbitrariness, expression of time, pronouns, the use of space, sign order, marking of sentence boundaries, noun-verb pairs and signs derived from fingerspelling, and the Mouth Hand System. Elisabeth Engberg-Pedersen joined our team for this project. Our discussions included deaf professionals employed at the center. The first book on the grammar of Danish Sign Language (Engberg-Pedersen, Hansen, and Kjaer Sørensen) was published in 1981 and a more substantial grammar book appeared in 1991.

The teaching of sign language as a subject in the curriculum would not have been possible without our early research. Teachers must be familiar with linguistic, psycholinguistic, and sociolinguistic rules of a particular language in order to be able to teach that language. I still remember when we discovered and analyzed proforms (classifiers), and the teachers started to discuss and play with this distinct but very productive feature of sign language in their sign language teaching. This had a great impact and supported the step away from a word-for-word Danish/sign translation type of thinking among the deaf teachers.

During the 1980s awareness grew among teachers, parents, and public authorities that sign languages, just like spoken languages, are structured according to rules that can be identified through linguistic analysis, though again, as with spoken languages, there are exceptions to those rules. Another similarity is that young children acquire sign language as their first language without systematic instruction.

The Implementation of Research Results

In order to transform our research findings into practical application, we set up intensive one-week courses for parents and teachers of the deaf in 1975. We used the videotapes from our research that showed deaf children communicating with each other. The parents and teachers were amazed when they learned that most of the children (sometimes their own child or pupil) had a rich and very appropriate sign language —a language they did not understand; the feelings aroused during this experience included anger, frustration, resistance, and hope. We also videotaped the teachers while they communicated by simultaneously using signs and speech (this was a popular method in the late 1970s). When we presented their own communication to them several months later without sound and asked them to translate it into Danish, most failed. At that point the teachers began to realize the importance of using one language at a time instead of trying to convey one language through a combination of two.

Bilingualism

The concept of deaf bilingualism has opened up new perspectives on the language situation of deaf people. This is due to the lack of understanding of (a) the function of sign language as deaf people's primary language, (b) the characteristics of sign language as a language in its own right, and (c) the ability of sign language to fulfill the same needs of communication as other languages. Thus sign language was formerly regarded as a poor substitute for deaf people's often inadequate communication in the majority language.

In contrast to other minority languages that tend to disappear after two or three generations, sign language has maintained its position for centuries as the heart of deaf culture. This is all the more remarkable considering the fact that only about 5 percent of deaf children have deaf parents. Most deaf children grow up in hearing families surrounded by a spoken language that they cannot automatically acquire.

All sign languages that have so far been described have certain features in common. These features, combined with the unusual visual sensitivity and linguistic creativeness that deaf people develop, enable them to communicate and understand each other across national barriers, even though their own national sign languages are quite different (Battison and Jordan 1976). Deaf refugees and immigrants who come to Denmark already knowing Polish or Hungarian Sign Language, for instance, are quickly able to learn Danish Sign Language. It is also true that many deaf immigrants have been more successful in learning written or spoken Danish when the Danish words are translated and explained in Danish Sign Language by a deaf person. Similarly the meaning of a word is more easily understood when the spoken word is accompanied by the corresponding sign. This simultaneous production and perception of two linguistic symbols is quite unique and is only made possible because one of the languages involved is a visual language.

Two Languages, One Family

> Deaf woman: My sister Jette thinks I am stupid, I can feel that. Jette does not know any other deaf persons so she does not know what deaf people are like. My father also thinks I am a bit stupid—but my brother Jens doesn't think I am stupid. I am sure of that. Sometimes I myself used to feel a little stupid, but I don't feel that any more. The important point here is that one's own family thinks that one is stupid. (Hansen 1980)

Deaf woman: Sometimes it is difficult for me to understand what Bente (the hearing daughter) says. I can read her lips sometimes but right now Bente is changing her teeth and in the upper part of her mouth there are no teeth at all so it is difficult for me to understand all she is trying to tell me. Then she tends to lose her patience with me.

When I was Bente's age I hardly knew any words. Strange that she already has several thousand words. My parents didn't know sign language. They only know the signs for FATHER, MOTHER, COME HERE, FOOD, LOOK, HOUSE, ROAD; this kind of simple words. Apart from that, nothing. But maybe there weren't any proper sign language courses at that time?

My childhood always was like that. Never any explanation. I just had to put up with everything they did to me.

I don't quite remember when I realized that I was deaf. Well, we were having coffee with some people. And they sat talking and laughing. And their mouths moved and I just sat there looking from one person to another. And their mouths moved. Then I realized that I wasn't able to hear. I must have been about five. (Hansen 1980)

Hearing parents and their deaf child do not automatically share a common language. To compound the problem, most hearing families with a deaf child have almost never before been in contact with deaf people or sign language. Thus most deaf children grow up in hearing families where the child is "different" and where the language spoken on television and radio; in film, theater, and music; at family gatherings; and among friends forms the natural basis for communication for everyone but the deaf child. This gives rise to frustrations for all family members. These frustrations can be overcome only if parents and child develop a common language that enables them to communicate fluently. Through natural interaction and family experiences the child will develop language in much the same way as a hearing child does.

Inger Ahlgren, a Swedish Sign Language researcher, once said that every time a deaf child is born a need for special education is born at the same time. What she had in mind was not so much the needs of the child, but the needs of the parents for sign language courses so that they can give their child the possibility of normal language development through the visual sense, through sign language.

Today most deaf children in Denmark grow up in families that accept and use signs or even sign language in their daily communication with their child. Approximately 90 percent of all parents take courses in sign language almost from the moment their child is diagnosed as deaf or severely hard of hearing. At the Center for Sign Language and Sign Supported Communication we teach 600 parents each year, offering intensive one-week courses on a progressive scale of difficulty amounting to a total of 540 hours. Specially designed courses are offered to parents from different language backgrounds and to parents with deaf children who have additional handicaps. Although the fluency and general mastery of signs vary a lot within individual families, almost all deaf children start their schooling at the age of five or six with language competence and an understanding of their surroundings.

Sign language is just as hard to learn as other languages, so many parents will only be able to pick up certain elements from that language. Some parents use a combination of signs and grammatical rules from sign language along with spoken Danish. Even if the parents' signing is neither very grammatical nor very rich in vocabulary, and even if it is very different from the sign language of deaf adults, the deaf child will nevertheless learn from the parents and, in that way, will learn the basic principles of a visual language system (Ahlgren 1980; Schlesinger and Meadow 1972). It is also important for the child to interact socially with other deaf children and deaf adults who can function as linguistic role models for the child.

When deaf children are able to interact socially with other deaf children their sign language usually develops at a much quicker rate than their parents will be able to follow. At the same time it is quite evident that children adjust to the linguistic competence of their parents. Most deaf children who communicate with older deaf children or deaf adults on a regular basis will thus develop at least two linguistic codes—sign language, for use with other deaf people, and signed Danish, for use with hearing family members and professionals. Signed Danish is a variable code that combines elements from Danish and sign language.

This process of code switching was very evident in a group of Swedish deaf children who were studied from the age of two until they started school. The children would have animated conversations with their hearing parents and unconsciously adapted their signing to their parents' level of proficiency by using a variety of signed Swedish. Sometimes the children would teach their parents new signs or grammatical structures, and sometimes the parents would teach the children new concepts by means of signs. The children were together as a group with deaf adults once every two weeks. When the children started school the teachers evaluated their communicative competence and found that the children had appropriate cognitive and linguistic skills in sign language. The children were able to code switch between signed Swedish and sign language. Another interesting conclusion from the Swedish project was that the children were very eager to learn more Swedish. They wanted to learn new words, how to pronounce them, and try to pronounce them themselves. They showed an unexpected interest in and curiosity for the strange sounds issuing from the mouths of their parents and other hearing people because they could see that they meant something (Ahlgren 1979, 1980). As far as I can see this spontaneous interest in spoken language is the best possible inducement for spoken language learning.

Deaf children are no different from other children when it comes to elementary curiosity, and they are stimulated by communication even if sometimes (or even often) communication fails. Attention and questions will increase only if there is some understanding. If no understanding or very limited understanding takes place, children will not be linguistically stimulated. In fact they might well become linguistically backward, at least to a certain degree. At the same time, they will lose interest in the linguistic communication taking place in their environment. This is evident in a child's averted gaze and lack of interest in the communication among the grown-ups. If children constantly avert their gaze, they will miss a lot of what is going on and will turn elsewhere for stimulation and excitement. Often children will react with aggression because they do not understand what is going on and cannot make themselves understood. Conversely, children who are used to linguistic communication will focus hard on the people trying to communicate with them.

When deaf children are used to being unable to understand and do not bother to look at people unless they are more or less forced to do so, then something is wrong. But it is important to bear in mind that there is nothing the matter with the child. The sense of sight as the primary source of linguistic information must be stimulated through repeated success. If children do not have success they will lose patience and use their natural potential for survival and appetite for experience to seek other, more interesting challenges. In our sign language courses for deaf and hard of hearing mainstreamed young people, we have observed that the students do not often spontaneously try to follow other people's conversation, whether in sign or spoken language. They must be told to look or they will only look at the teacher, expecting her to tell them what the others are talking about. They have more or less given up trying to understand linguistic communication when it is not directly addressed to them. Quite clearly this makes their world more restricted and deprives them of information that people exchange in different contexts. In this respect in our courses we try to give them new and positive experiences. We tell them to "look at the other children, look at hearing and deaf adults when they talk together. You can understand more than you expect because they are using sign language, which you can also pick up at a distance, as well as when they are partly turned away, stand in the shade, etc." For many orally educated deaf and hard of hearing children it is a great linguistic and emotional experience when, at the age of sixteen, they go to the continuation school in Nyborg with other deaf students because they can then listen in on other people's communication and pick up information without actually being part of the conversation.

Sign Language and Danish: A Bilingual Model

Deaf people differ in their mastery of Danish. Very few deaf people think they know enough Danish to be competent users of that language in various situations—most of them understand and use Danish only to a limited extent, which is a clear handicap in relation to the majority of the hearing population. A small group of deaf people has a very restricted vocabulary that they are able to combine only in simple sentences. Many surveys have found that there is a clear relationship between the degree of hearing loss, the age of the onset of deafness and deaf and hard of hearing people's mastery of spoken and written language (Quigley and Kretschmer 1982). Thus it is the degree of the hearing loss that is the primary cause of deaf people's severe difficulties in acquiring the majority language, Danish.

Whatever the degree of mastery of Danish we find that most deaf people have completely mastered sign language. This shows that it is not the deaf people's ability to learn a language that is the problem, and consequently it should be possible for most deaf people to use this natural gift for foreign language learning. In fact this is the only viable argument in any discussion of giving deaf children normal language development by means of signs or sign language from the moment deafness is diagnosed and the possibility of bilingual teaching based on the two languages: sign language and Danish (Ahlgren 1979).

In 1982 the first bilingual experiment started in the Copenhagen School for the Deaf with Ruth Kjaer Sørensen as the head teacher. The students' parents had wanted the bilingual approach, and the experiment covered the whole group of deaf children starting that year. Sign language was defined as the language of instruction—as the children's primary language—with Danish as their second language to be taught as a foreign language and with English as their possible third language. A deaf teacher was involved on equal terms with the hearing teachers to act as the sign language model in the classroom. Our center was involved in the experiment in several ways. We set up courses in sign language for the parents and the teachers; we evaluated the children's sign language usage and development; and we helped produce instructional tapes in sign language.

This experiment attracted a lot of positive interest, especially as all the children involved reached higher academic standards in the same subjects as their hearing peers. This was proven by their results in the final exams after ten years of schooling, exams equivalent to the graduation exams of hearing children. But what was equally important, apart from the improvement in academic skills, was and is their ability to control their daily lives through purely linguistic means. They can argue and sometimes provoke the hearing adults in their environment into new areas of explanation and thinking. They are not ashamed of using sign language openly, and neither are their parents. They know sign language and Danish as two different languages, and they are aware of the importance of both languages in their lives (Kjaer Sørensen et al. 1983, 1985; Lewis 1995; Mahshie 1995).

In 1992 the Danish Ministry of Education and Research published the *Guiding Proposals Concerning the Teaching of Sign Language in the Folkeskole (Danish Municipal Primary and Lower Secondary School)*. The guidelines state that each pupil should continually develop his or her mastery of sign language so that all pupils can understand and express themselves in sign language at a level that corresponds to their general development. The instruction in sign language will include not only conversation and discussion in sign language, but also grammatical identification and analysis of the elements of sign language. The guidelines also state that sign language should be used as the language of instruction in the classroom, which implies that teachers of deaf students must be proficient in sign language. These guidelines represent official recognition by all public authorities that deaf children should be brought up as bilingual with sign language as their primary language and Danish as their second, and that all teachers at deaf schools are accordingly offered a training program in sign language amounting to 550 lessons.

Teaching Written Danish: The Monolingual and Bilingual Approach

> Deaf woman: I do not read a lot, but that is because it is a completely new world to me. I have never heard the word so it is like a dead language. But I can read okay. I prefer books with pictures in them. That helps to keep your attention on the words. Deaf people will easily get tired from reading, but I can do it all right. I can write too, but I have some trouble with word order. Maybe because I write down the words the same way as when I use sign language. (Hansen 1980)

For deaf and hard of hearing people, written Danish is different than it is for hearing people, who derive their reading experience from their general experience with sound and spoken language. Research shows that most deaf people have had great problems attaining a level of reading proficiency comparable to that of hearing people (Vestberg 1994; Rasmussen 1980; Lundin and Hansen 1979). Therefore it is a central problem in deaf education to find generally applicable methods for teaching deaf children to read. Oral education (that is the instructional method based on spoken language) has turned out to be of no avail for most deaf people. This was irrefutably documented by a study of British deaf students that found out of 359 students, less than 10 were able to read at a level appropriate to their age, while more than one-third were unable to read at all (Conrad 1979).

Instruction in Danish, as well as in other subjects such as history and math, has so far been by the monolingual approach in spoken Danish. Even if many teachers have used some form of sign-supported communication with children, it is only very recently that the above-mentioned bilingual approach has been adopted in deaf education. In the bilingual approach sign language is used for the classroom teaching of, for instance, Danish, and preliminary results seem to indicate that this approach might give far more deaf children skills in reading and spontaneous writing appropriate to their ages than the monolingual approach. If the teacher knows both sign language and Danish she will be in a position to help the children find out what is difficult in Danish—and maybe even why.

Some typical errors in deaf children's written Danish are omission of the copula ("is," "was," etc.), incorrect conjugation of verbs for tense or no conjugation at all, omission of pronouns, incorrect use of prepositions, and incorrect word order. All these errors are probably due to the difference in grammatical structures between the two languages. In bilingual teaching the teacher will be able to explain the differences between the two languages and teach the children to watch out for the pitfalls. It is of course essential to concentrate on types of errors that may interfere with successful communication in relation to the hearing surroundings instead of insisting on correctness for correctness' sake.

A Different Form of Bilingualism: Integration with Whom?

Bilingualism in deaf children is actually no different in nature from the bilingualism that hearing children who grow up surrounded by two languages develop. However, a number of features are quite specific to deaf bilingualism.

1. Sign language and Danish are languages within one national culture. One might say that the two languages belong to the same monocultural setting.

2. Sign language is the only language deaf children will acquire spontaneously through social interaction with other sign language users. The children are dependent on instruction based on foreign-language-learning principles for the acquisition of functional Danish (in its spoken and written form).

3. Sign language and Danish are used for different purposes and with different people. Sign language is the language of the deaf community and the language for acquisition of knowledge and social interaction with others. Danish is the language of the majority society and the language for gaining access to information from that society—chiefly in the form of written information, but also through direct personal communication with hearing individuals.

Deaf people will never be bilingual in the sense that they will achieve equal fluency in their two languages. Deaf people's hearing loss will always be an obstacle to complete mastery of spoken Danish —and therefore deaf people will never be able to engage in profound conversation with new acquaintances or in linguistic and social interactions with hearing friends anywhere the majority language is the dominant language. In all these contexts the deaf student will be isolated or at best accepted but without any real influence on what is going on.

This difficult and often painful experience of being deaf in a hearing world naturally has the effect that most deaf people will prefer each other's company. Most deaf people marry a deaf spouse. Deaf adults have rich social lives as members of the deaf community—a cultural group with its own events, such as Scandinavian and international Deaf cultural festivals, political conferences, sports events, theater, sign language video productions, social gatherings, and evening classes, all based on Deaf people's primary language, sign language. Deaf people who have not been brought up with sign language and who do not acquire fluency in their teens (at the very latest) run the risk of not being accepted in either the hearing or the deaf world.

At our center we have been in contact with fifteen young mainstreamed deaf or hard of hearing individuals, and we have experienced their risk of becoming very isolated or developing disintegrated personalities. Some have been employed at the center with the aim of learning sign language and "learning to be deaf," in part so they can later continue their education by means of a sign language interpreter and in part to overcome their extreme social isolation. Some have expressed great bitterness at being reduced to poor and lonely replicas of hearing persons, while others have felt that they had appropriate and relevant schooling in a hearing school. Almost all of them have chosen to belong to the deaf community in their leisure time. The words of one of these young people exemplifies the experience of all: "I have tried to belong to both worlds, the deaf and the hearing world, but even if I can speak rather well and am good at reading people's lips I am most deaf and much prefer to be with other deaf people. In fact I have almost no hearing friends left—I always felt left out when we were several people together. Those of my friends who are hearing impaired all know sign language" (Rasmussen 1980).

In 1979 psychologist Kirsten Nielsen carried out an investigation into deaf children's leisure activities. The investigation covered children who were mainstreamed individually or were in classes where they were orally educated and children who attended schools for the deaf. Nielsen found that not only did the children who attended schools for the deaf have more deaf and thus equal friends, but they also had more hearing friends than the mainstreamed deaf children who were not sign language users. It appears as if most mainstreamed deaf children, that is to say monolingual deaf children, have difficulty in establishing friendships in their leisure time—which highlights an important social aspect in deaf people's language situation.

Deaf and Hearing Professionals

An important consequence of the acceptance of deaf bilingualism has been a growing awareness of deaf people's roles in working with deaf children and adults and in teaching sign language. Whereas no deaf people were trained in 1973, today more than forty are trained teachers and work on equal terms with their hearing colleagues in schools and educational centers.

This positive change also creates new problems and discussions. It has given deaf people status and influence in the daily work with children and parents, but it takes time to fully accept and integrate deaf professionals, sign language, and Deaf cultural ways in a profession long dominated by hearing professionals. The 120-year history of oppressors and oppressed in deaf education will take time to change, but there is a growing awareness among deaf people—especially the younger generation—and among hearing teachers and school principals that these problems will have to be overcome through honest and open dialogue, confrontation, and cooperation. One school, for example, has started a program for all employees with the aim of setting up ten rules for how to create an equal working environment for deaf and hearing professionals. I have cooperated closely with deaf employees at the Centre for Sign Language and Sign-Supported Communication for twenty-six years. We have a teaching staff of fifty-two people, twenty-two of whom are deaf, and I have found that equality is not something one decides to have but is something one has to work for continuously.

The Bilingual Challenge in the Future

It may sound as if the bilingual approach has opened the door to paradise for deaf education. However, although there has been improvement in the academic, social, and cognitive skills of deaf children, we still have to face the fact that their reading and writing skills are generally below those of hearing children. One might argue that parents and teachers still are not fluent enough in sign language and that there are not enough bilingual teaching materials. These arguments are valid, but I believe that the bilingualism in the deaf community will always differ from bilingualism found among hearing people because of deaf people's inability to hear, speechread, or even speak the language of the majority culture fluently. No matter how idealistic we might be when setting up goals for the bilingual education of deaf children, we have to modify our expectations and teaching methods when it comes to teaching them a second language that was developed for a sense they do not have. We must do this in order to respect Deaf identity and culture.

I sometimes fear that a new wave of oralism will start. I see examples of this in discussions of the "advantages" of cochlear implants for deaf children who still do not read, write, and speak like hearing children. As long as their skills in their second language are the main (and sometimes only) measure of deaf educational success, we might lose what the bilingual approach and the acceptance of sign language have meant for the development of deaf people's potentials as equal and fully integrated individuals in our society—individuals with high degrees of self-esteem and independence.

In Scandinavia and other countries where the bilingual approach is becoming accepted, we need more sign language research, especially research in the sign language development of deaf children with deaf as well as hearing parents. This research must be used to develop tests of deaf children's linguistic competencies at different ages. In the past, I never believed in language tests because they usually show only a test-defined area of a child's ability to communicate, but right now I see a necessity for tests to help parents and teachers who feel they cannot evaluate the linguistic progress and proficiency of their children because sign language is foreign to them. I think that academic research on sign language will almost always have an impact on deaf education and the cultural and social situation of deaf people, but only if the results are made available and used pragmatically in cooperation with deaf people, parents, and educators. The responsibility for the interchange between researchers and practitioners lies with researchers and educators alike.

References

Ahlgren, Inger. 1979. *Döva barn och vuxna döva*. Stockholm: Stockholm University, Institute for Linguistics.

———. 1980. *Döva barns teckenspråk*, FOT VII. Stockholm: Stockholm University, Institute for Linguistics.

Battison, Robbin M. and I. King Jordan. 1976. Communication with foreign signers: "Fact and fancy." *Sign Language Studies* 10: 53–68.

Bergman, Brita. 1979. *Dövas teckenspråk* FOT VII. Stockholm: Stockholm University, Institute for Linguistics.

Bergmann, Asger, and Ritva Bergmann. 1985. Tegnsprogets plads i døveskolen. In *Tegnsprogsforskning og tegnsprogsbrug*, edited by Britta Hansen. Copenhagen: Døves Center for Total Communication.

Brennan, Mary. 1990. Word formation in British Sign Language. Stockholm: University of Stockholm.

Conrad, Reuben. 1979. *The deaf schoolchild : Language and cognitive function*. New York: Harper and Row.

Engberg-Pedersen, Elisabeth. 1985. Proformer i dansk tegnsprog. In *Tegnsprogsforskning og tegnsprogsbrug*, edited by Britta Hansen. Copenhagen: Døves Center for Total Communication.

———. 1993. *Space in Danish Sign Language*. Hamburg: Signum-Verlag.

Engberg-Pedersen, Elisabeth, Britta Hansen, and Ruth Kjaer Sørensen. 1981. *Døves tegnsprog*. Århus, Denmark: Arkona.

Hansen, Britta. 1980. Interview by author. Doves Tosprogethed. Danish Broadcasting Corporation, 31 July.

Hansen, Britta, ed. 1985. *Tegnsprogsforskning og tegnsprogsbrug*. Copenhagen: Døves Center for Total Communication.

———. 1986. Døves Tosprogethed. *Skolepsykologi* 4: 396–409.

Klima, Edward S., and Ursula Bellugi. 1979. *The signs of language*. Cambridge, Mass.: Harvard University Press.

Lewis, Wendy, and Ruth Kjaer Sørensen. 1985. Tegnsprogsundervisning i en førsteklasse. In *Tegnsprogsforskning og tegnsprogsbrug*, edited by Britta Hansen. Copenhagen: Døves Center for Total Communication.

Lewis, Wendy, ed. 1995. *Bilingual teaching of deaf children in Denmark*. Døveskolernes Materialecenter. Aalborg, Denmark: Aalborgskolen.

Lundin, Karen, and Sven E. Hansen 1979. *Døve unges læsning.* Unpublished report, Nyborgskolen.

Mahshie, Shawn Neal. 1995. *Educating deaf children bilingually.* Washington D.C.: Gallaudet University, Pre-College Programs.

Nielsen, Kirsten. 1979. *Unge hørehaemmedes samvaer med jaunaldrende.* Damarks Laererhøjskole.

Quigley, Stephen P., and Robert E. Kretschmer. 1982. *The education of deaf children: Issues, theory, and practice.* Baltimore, Md.: University Park Press.

Rasmussen, Alida. 1980. Jeg har lært at tale, men alligevel. In *Døve børn-sprog, kultur, identitet,* edited by Britta Hansen. Copenhagen: Døves Center for Total Communication.

Schlesinger, Hilde S., and Kathryn P. Meadow. 1972. *Sound and sign.* Berkeley: University of California Press.

Sørensen, R. Kjær, Wendy Lewis, Hanne Lutz, and Jørgen Sønnichsen. 1983. *Tosproget døveundervisning.* Copenhagen: Københavns Kommunale Skolevaeseb.

Stokoe, William C. 1960. *Sign language structure: An outline of the visual communication systems of the American Deaf.* Studies in Linguistics no. 8. Buffalo, N.Y.: State University of New York at Buffalo.

Stokoe, William C. 1970. *The study of sign language.* Washington D.C.: Center for Applied Linguistics.

Stokoe, William C., Dorothy C. Casterline, and Carl G. Croneberg. 1965. *A dictionary of American Sign Language on linguistic principles.* Washington D.C.: Gallaudet College Press.

Undervisningsvejledning for Folkeskolen. 1991. *Undervisningsvejledning for Folkeskolen.* Copenhagen: Undervisningsministeriei.

Vestberg, Palle. 1994. *Undervisning af døve og hørehæmmede børn.* Aalborg, Denmark: Døveskolernes Materialecenter.

10

Sign Communication Training and Motor Functioning in Children with Autistic Disorder and in Other Populations

John D. Bonvillian

During the 1970s there was a dramatic increase in the use of sign language systems with children and adults who did not speak. Whereas sign communication programs for such individuals were virtually nonexistent when the decade began, by the time Goodman, Wilson, and Bornstein (1978) conducted their national survey later that decade, there were over 10,000 students in sign-training programs. The participants in these programs constituted a very diverse population. Some had relatively intact cognitive abilities; their failure to learn to speak was often attributed to specific neuromotor deficits. Many more of the participants, however, were low-functioning children with autistic disorder or individuals with severe mental retardation. There were also occasional reports of successful sign learning by aphasic adults who had lost their ability to speak after a stroke or serious accident (Christopoulou and Bonvillian 1985).

What led to this dramatic increase in the number of hearing, but nonspeaking, persons being taught to communicate through signs? Clearly, one of the principal factors contributing to this remarkable increase was the recognition that the sign languages used by deaf persons constituted full and genuine languages. This was an important conceptual breakthrough: language no longer was equated with speech. Soon after this breakthrough, sign languages began to be viewed as viable alternatives to speech by teachers and language therapists working to foster communication development in nonspeaking, severely impaired, hearing persons.

The person most responsible for the recognition of sign languages as full and genuine languages was William C. Stokoe. The focus of Stokoe's pioneering sign language investigations was the structure of American Sign Language (ASL) signs. In his investigations, Stokoe (1960; Stokoe, Casterline, and Croneberg 1965) showed that ASL signs had a distinct linguistic structure. More specifically, he identified three formational aspects that differentiated one ASL sign from another. These three aspects were the place where the sign was made, the shape and orientation of the hand or hands making the sign, and the action or movement of the hand or hands in forming the sign. Each of the three aspects (usually referred to as location, handshape, and movement) consisted of a limited set of formational elements that functioned in a manner analogous to that of phonemes in spoken languages. In the years following the publication of Stokoe's initial discoveries, additional investigations showed that ASL has an extensive lexicon and that it operates according to rule-governed phonological, morphological, and syntactic processes (Klima and Bellugi 1979; Wilbur 1987). An outgrowth of these investigations was the acceptance of ASL (and other sign languages used by deaf persons) as genuine languages. With this acceptance of sign languages as genuine languages, investigators began examining whether hearing individuals who had never learned to speak or who had lost the ability to speak could learn to communicate through signs.

I begin this chapter by reviewing the findings of a number of studies of sign language training in nonspeaking, yet hearing, individuals. From this review, it becomes evident that many autistic and mentally retarded children and individuals with aphasia benefited from sign communication training programs. The range in training program outcomes, however, was quite wide. Some participants made substantial gains in their ability to communicate. Other participants made little or no progress despite years of sign training. In addition, it was found that certain types of signs typically were learned more readily than others. In the latter half of this chapter, I examine a series of investigations of language and motor functioning in children with autistic disorder. These studies not only underlined the wide range in communication training program outcomes found in these children, but showed that the children's motor functioning abilities were associated with their language learning. Efforts to teach these children to sign, moreover, helped reveal that many children with autistic disorder have serious motor disturbances. Finally, I suggest that these observations of motor disturbances in children with autistic disorder may lead to a reconsideration of the principal characteristics of the syndrome of childhood autism.

Review of Sign Communication Training Program Outcomes

In the last thirty years, there have been many dozens of reports of the use of sign training in nonspeaking, but hearing, individuals. These programs, to a considerable extent, were quite successful. Many persons learned a sign vocabulary and were able to convey basic needs and wants. Some participants acquired extensive sign lexicons and were able to generate multi-sign utterances. Yet it should also be acknowledged that, except in a few instances, the participants did not approach fluency in sign language usage. Participants often made errors in sign formation, frequently did not spontaneously use the signs they had learned to communicate with others, and the complexity of their utterances typically was quite limited. (Signs were not considered "spontaneous" if they were either imitations of others' immediately prior sign productions or were parts of familiar interactive routines.) It was also observed that individual participants varied widely in how they responded to sign language and other augmentative training programs.

At the same time, it should be noted that investigators frequently reported that the use of sign communication not only did not preclude or prevent participants from learning to speak, but may have served to facilitate speech.

Many of the studies of sign communication training in severely mentally retarded individuals and children with autistic disorder also reported improvements in adaptive behaviors (see Bryen and Joyce 1985 and Silverman 1995). Interestingly, these improvements in adaptive behaviors were not typically the product of direct training, but often were associated with the participants' increased communication abilities. These improvements in adaptive behaviors included, among others, increased bladder control, increased attention span, decline in the incidence of tantrums and bizarre and stereotypic behaviors, increased willingness to participate in group activities, and better self-help skills. In some instances, investigators noted that the introduction of sign communication programs had positive effects on caretakers as well as the low-functioning participants.

Despite the large number of sign language intervention programs with severely mentally retarded persons and children with autistic disorder, there were very few instances where investigators determined whether the participants in their programs had sufficient motor skills to produce recognizable signs (Bryen and Joyce 1985). This appears to be the case particularly for studies involving children with autistic disorder. One reason for this failure to test these children's motor abilities was a widely shared view that these children had nearly intact motor abilities. Two quotations from an article published in 1988 attest to this belief that motor disturbances were not a characteristic of children with autistic disorder: "The combination of severe social-cognitive limitations and relatively well-developed motor skills that is so typical of the autistic syndrome" (Mirenda and Schuler 1988, 25) and "Autism thus presents a profile that is almost diametrically opposed to that of individuals with primary physical and motor limitations" (Mirenda and Schuler 1988, 25). This assumption of relatively normal motor functioning, as I suggest below, was fundamentally incorrect.

Childhood Autistic Disorder

The syndrome known as childhood autistic disorder was first described by Kanner in 1943; interest in this disorder has been growing ever since. The principal identifying characteristics of childhood autism are a failure to interact socially, repetitive production of stereotyped behaviors, and marked difficulties or deficiencies in language and communication (American Psychiatric Association 1994; Lord, Rutter, and LeCouteur 1994; World Health Organization 1993). Difficulties in language production and comprehension often are particularly striking, with about one half of all children with autism failing to acquire useful speech (Konstantareas 1985; Rutter 1966; Schuler and Prizant 1987). The prognosis for those children who fail to acquire useful speech by the age of five years historically has been quite bleak (Eisenberg 1956), with their most probable outcome lifelong institutionalization (Lotter 1974). It should also be noted that about three-quarters of those children with autistic disorder score in the mentally retarded range on tests of intelligence (Fombonne 1998; Rutter 1978).

In light of the profound difficulties that many children with autistic disorder experience in acquiring spoken language, a number of investigators have examined whether these children have the ability to acquire a sign communication system. By the early 1980s, the results of more than twenty-five studies had underlined the potential effectiveness of sign training with mute or severely speech-limited children with autistic disorder (Bonvillian, Nelson, and Rhyne 1981). Many of the children in these studies learned to communicate effectively for the first time through signs. Concomitant improvements in their personal and social skills typically were reported.

Although sign communication training enabled many nonspeaking children to communicate effectively, wide variability in the outcome of sign training also was reported. Whereas some children with autism acquired hundreds of signs, others made only very modest gains despite years of training (Layton 1987). Similarly, while some children learned to generate complex, multi-sign utterances, others produced only single-sign utterances. This very wide range in sign communication training outcomes led investigators to ask whether certain children with autism would be more likely to benefit from sign training while others would be more likely to benefit from other approaches.

Some evidence to support this view that individual children with autistic disorder derive varying amounts of benefit from different forms or types of communication training has emerged in recent years. For example, Layton (1988) examined whether children with moderate or severe autism acquired and retained more signs or words depending on whether they were taught with signs alone, speech alone, simultaneous sign and speech input, or alternating sign and speech input. For high-verbal imitators, Layton found that the type of communication training did not have an effect; the children did equally well in all four conditions. In contrast, those children who were low-verbal imitators did the most poorly in the speech-alone condition. Hurd (1996) also reported that individual autistic children responded differentially depending on the form of input. One child responded better to sign input, whereas a second child did better when the input was in the form of printed words. Neither child preferred the spoken word. In light of these findings and those of other investigators, it has become apparent that teachers and investigators in the future will need to examine more carefully the individual characteristics of each child with autism before selecting a particular intervention strategy for that child.

Mentally Retarded Individuals

Even after years of speech training and therapy, some mentally retarded children and adults fail to acquire minimal spoken language skills. Many of those who fail to acquire speech have the lowest IQs (Sheehan, Martyn, and Kilburn 1968) and multiple handicaps. Because the absence of useful communication skills is such a debilitating problem, teachers and researchers began several decades ago to explore the use of signs as a communication alternative for those mentally retarded persons who failed to learn to speak. An important impetus behind this sign communication training initiative was the recognition accorded sign languages in the 1960s.

Early reports and reviews of the efficacy of sign communication training for nonspeaking mentally retarded persons tended to accentuate the positive (for example, Hall and Talkington 1970; Kiernan 1977). That is, investigators often concluded that many severely and profoundly mentally retarded persons made considerable progress in learning to sign. Many of these early studies (for example, Cornforth, Johnston, and Walker 1974; Richardson 1975; Wilson 1974) revealed very wide individual differences in the level of sign communication mastery demonstrated by the participants. Indeed, in one study (Richardson, 1975) the range in training program outcomes after one year extended from one participant who had learned only a small receptive sign vocabulary to another participant who had acquired an expressive sign lexicon of 400 signs. Clearly, the benefits of sign communication training were not being shared equally by all participants.

In these early studies, teachers and investigators typically selected signs according to their perceptions of their students' functional communication needs. It was observed in some of these studies, however, that certain signs appeared to be learned more easily and rapidly than others. This observation helped spur investigators to examine the characteristics of those signs that were associated with more rapid sign acquisition. Signs that were rated as more iconic (Griffith and Robinson 1980; Snyder-McLean 1978) or higher in translucency (Luftig 1983) were found to be more readily acquired. Signs with symmetrical movements and those that involved touch or contact with the signer's other hand or part of the body also were shown to be learned more quickly (Kohl 1981). As a result of these studies, investigators and teachers began to focus more intently on the particular characteristics of the signs they selected for vocabulary training. Consideration also was given to making signs easier for the participants to produce.

Although some severely and profoundly mentally retarded persons acquired communication skills through manual sign training, the results of more recent studies have underlined that many others failed to do so or made only quite limited progress. The results of two longitudinal investigations that traced the language development of severely and profoundly mentally retarded students underscored this conclusion. In one study (Bryen, Goldman, and Quinlisk-Gill 1988), the sign language learning of severely and profoundly mentally retarded students was assessed after a mean training duration of 2.9 years. These students imitated an average of only 9.2 signs and spontaneously produced an average of only 4.2 signs. A similar outcome was reported in the second study. In this study (Kahn 1995), 34 severely and profoundly mentally retarded children were taught manual signs over a four-year period. Of these 34 children, 20 failed to use a single sign independently and only 6 formed two-sign combinations. The results of these two studies, as well as those of other investigations, indicate that many severely and profoundly mentally retarded students do not acquire functional communication skills despite extensive sign training. Some of these students might possibly benefit from other alternative or augmentative communication systems such as the use of picture boards. This use of other alternative communication systems besides signs appears to be a particularly helpful strategy for those mentally retarded individuals who have serious motor functioning difficulties or disturbances.

Aphasic Individuals

In the past several decades, there have been a number of studies designed to determine whether nonspeaking aphasic persons could learn manual signs. Unlike children with autistic disorder and mentally retarded individuals taught to sign, sign-learning aphasic persons typically had been fluent users of a spoken language for many years prior to their loss of language. For most aphasic individuals, their language loss was the outcome of cerebrovascular accidents or strokes, although tumors, abscesses, and traumas may also have caused their language loss. Depending on the location and magnitude of the lesions causing their language loss, aphasic individuals often differed in the severity of their impairments and in the types of language skills lost. The extent and type of loss, in turn, may have affected how successful aphasic participants were in learning manual signs.

Most of the early studies of manual sign learning by aphasic individuals asked whether or not aphasic individuals could acquire some form of manual communication system that would enable them to communicate more effectively than they could with their impaired speech skills. For many aphasic individuals, the answer to this inquiry was yes, as they were able to acquire aspects of a manual communication system. Although the aphasic participants in these studies (for example, Bonvillian and Friedman 1978; Eagleson, Vaughn, and Knudson 1969; Holmes 1975; Skelly 1979) appeared to be less impaired in their visuomotor processing than in their auditory-vocal processing, it should be recognized that their sign-learning abilities often were relatively limited as well.

In more recent studies, investigators have tried both to identify those aphasic individuals who would be more likely to be successful in acquiring manual signs and to determine what types of signs would be learned more readily. Severity of aphasic impairment was found to be an important factor in predicting successful sign learning (Coelho 1990; Coelho and Duffy 1987). The number of signs an aphasic participant learned and whether that individual learned to combine signs was shown to be strongly related to severity of impairment; less-impaired individuals typically made much more progress. Indeed, Coelho and Duffy (1987) advanced the view that there may be a threshold level of severity of aphasia below which sign acquisition is extremely limited or negligible. Another approach to determining who would benefit more from sign communication training has involved the use of neuroanatomical analysis of magnetic resonance images. In one such study (Anderson et al. 1992), the two patients with lesions in the left posterior temporal and parietal regions were much more successful in learning signs and combining them than a patient with damage to nearly all her left temporal cortices. In the future, such use of neuro-imaging techniques may enable clinicians to make highly informed judgments as to which aphasic individuals are the best candidates for intensive sign-language communication programs.

Progress also has been made in determining those characteristics of signs that are associated with more successful learning by aphasic individuals. Movement complexity was examined as a potentially important factor in predicting whether a sign was learned or not. Signs in ASL can have up to three movements; these movements can be produced simultaneously or sequentially (Stokoe, Casterline, and Croneberg 1965). In general, signs with a low or medium level of motor complexity were more often acquired than those with greater complexity

(Coelho and Duffy 1986). Iconic or pantomimic signs—signs with clearly transparent meanings—also tended to be learned more readily by aphasic participants. Finally, investigators have examined whether ASL signs or Amer-Ind signs (signs used by American Indians) were easier for aphasic individuals to imitate and recognize. Amer-Ind signs were found to be significantly easier for aphasic individuals both to imitate and to recognize (Daniloff et al. 1986). Daniloff et al. attributed this finding to the greater motoric coordination involved in the production of ASL signs than in the production of Amer-Ind signs. At the same time, it should be recognized that ASL has certain advantages over Amer-Ind and other nonvocal systems; among the advantages of ASL are its much more extensive vocabulary and its large number of users. In the future, it will be important to develop a sign system for aphasic individuals that has an extensive lexicon of signs with clearly transparent meanings and that are motorically easy to produce.

Motor Impairments and Language in Children with Autistic Disorder

In 1983, Deborah Webb Blackburn and I embarked on a study to determine what factors were associated with sign learning in children with autistic disorder (Bonvillian and Blackburn 1991). To accomplish this task, we collected background information and language data on 22 autistic children from two different programs for children with developmental disabilities. These children ranged in age from 3.5 to 17 years of age. To obtain this information on the children's development, we observed the children in their classrooms and on the playground, interviewed their teachers, and reviewed the children's educational records.

The outcome of this investigation was a set of findings that was fully expected in some ways and in other ways was totally unanticipated. In light of previous findings, we had expected that there would be a wide range in the number of signs that the teachers would report that the children had learned. This, indeed, was the case. At one end of the distribution were several children who had been both credited by their teachers with knowing hundreds of signs and who used their extensive vocabularies spontaneously in diverse settings. At the other end of the distribution were about half the children in the study. Despite being credited by their teachers with learning dozens of different signs, these children produced only several different signs on a spontaneous basis. This discrepancy between the number of signs the children were credited by their teachers as learning and the number of signs that many children used on their own had not been anticipated. In between these two extremes were a handful of children who spontaneously used a substantial portion of their class-taught sign lexicons. This pattern of findings underlined the importance of examining the spontaneous production of signs in diverse settings in conducting an evaluation of the success of sign communication training programs.

With regard to predicting which children would be more successful sign learners, several pretreatment background measures of the children's abilities that we had hypothesized would be positively related to their sign language development were, in fact, found to be significantly associated. These three background measures were the children's performance on tests of social skills, mental ability, and receptive language ability. The children's performance in these three domains was highly correlated with both the number of different signs the children used spontaneously and the length of their longest sign utterance. This finding is in accord with the results of numerous previous studies that reported that autistic children's successful development was related to their social skills, mental abilities, and level of language understanding. The children's scores on these three measures—social skills, mental age, and receptive language—also were highly intercorrelated with each other; together they constituted a single factor in the regression analyses conducted on the sign language outcome measures.

The regression analyses, however, revealed the presence of another factor from the children's pretreatment background measures that also predicted the children's sign language development. That second factor was the children's fine-motor ability scores. The children's fine-motor ability scores were highly correlated with both their sign vocabulary size ($r = .63$, $p < .005$) and length of longest sign combination ($r = .71$, $p < .001$). Furthermore, all of the children's scores on the tests of fine-motor ability were well below age-appropriate levels. Clearly, these children did not have intact motor skills, but had distinct deficits in this domain.

In retrospect, it seems quite logical that the children's fine-motor ability scores would be strongly associated with their success in learning a visual-motor language. Yet at the time of the study we were quite surprised, as motor functioning difficulties were not viewed as a characteristic of children with autistic disorder. Additional discussions with the children's teachers after we had completed our study, moreover, underscored for us that this finding of an important role of motor ability in sign learning was not the result of some statistical anomaly. Rather, many of the children's teachers stressed that motor disturbances adversely affected the children's sign production. In addition, the director of one of the two programs involved in the study urged us to consider modifying how many signs were formed to make them easier for children with autism to produce.

The first study to systematically examine the interrelationships between autistic children's sign production and their motor functioning was conducted by Brenda Seal for her doctoral dissertation (Seal 1993; Seal and Bonvillian 1997). In this study, 14 nonspeaking autistic children and adolescents at a school for students with serious developmental disorders were videotaped while interacting in sign with their principal language teachers. The signs on these videotapes were then transcribed using the sign notation system developed by Stokoe (1960; Stokoe, Casterline, and Croneberg 1965). At the time of this study, these students ranged in age from 9 to 20 years. The length of their sign communication training also varied widely, extending from a low of 6 months to a high of more than 15 years. The mean duration of their sign training was 6 years and 5 months. The duration of the students' sign language training, however, was not significantly correlated with the size of their sign vocabularies.

Eleven of these students also were given an apraxia test battery to assess their ability to perform purposeful motor movements. Apraxia is a neuromotor disorder that precludes or constrains an individual's ability to produce planned, voluntary, and purposeful motor movements in the absence of muscle weakness, paralysis, or serious cognitive decline (Wertz, LaPointe, and Rosenbek 1984). Most of the students made a large number of errors on the apraxia test battery. Such a high incidence of errors would be consistent with an assessment of dyspraxia or apraxia in these autistic students.

When the autistic students' sign production was compared with that of their teachers, it was evident that the students made formational errors in many of their signs. Although all 14 students made sign formational errors, the error rate across students varied widely. Those students who produced the largest number of signs had much lower error rates than those students who had smaller vocabularies. Furthermore, the students' sign formational errors were not evenly distributed across the three sign formational aspects identified by Stokoe or within each formational category. Of the students' formational errors, handshape and movement errors were much more common than location errors. Moreover, certain handshapes and movements were produced either quite rarely or had high error rates (Seal and Bonvillian 1997).

The movement aspect of signs proved to be a source of particular difficulty in the sign formation of many of the autistic students. In addition to making errors in carrying out the required movements of their signs, the students often added extraneous movements to some signs and deleted movements from signs when sequential movements were required. Finally, a significant negative correlation was found between the percentage of movement errors present in the students' signs and the students' apraxia scores ($r = -.70$, $p < .02$), but not between the students' apraxia scores and their percentages of location or handshape errors (Seal and Bonvillian 1997). These findings were interpreted as suggesting that motor or movement functioning difficulties played an important role in the signing of students with autistic disorder.

Another way in which these sign-learning students with autism differed from their teachers was in their signing hand preference (Bonvillian, Gershoff, Seal, and Richards 2001). Whereas the teachers made the large majority of their one-handed signs with their right hands, a similar right-hand preference was not evident in their autistic students. More specifically, 4 of the 14 students demonstrated a distinct right-hand preference in their signing, 4 showed a distinct left-hand preference, and 6 did not significantly favor either hand in their signing. In contrast with this finding of relatively few right-handed signs among the students with autism, children of deaf parents and young, sign-learning deaf children of hearing parents typically show a very strong right-hand preference in their sign production (Bonvillian, Richards, and Dooley 1997; Seal and Bonvillian 1996). The present finding of an elevated level of non-right-handedness among the students with autistic disorder provides additional support for the view that neuromotor dysfunction underlies some of their difficulties. Furthermore, the failure of most of the students with autism to develop a distinct right-hand preference was particularly evident because their use of a visuomotor or sign language was the focus of the inquiry.

Motor impairments in children with autistic disorder also were examined in a recent study conducted by Page and Boucher (1998). Nearly 80 percent of the 33 children they examined showed marked impairments in some form of motor functioning. These impairments included oromotor skills (for example, tongue and lip movements, chewing), manual skills (for example, forming correct handshapes, sequencing handshapes, object manipulation), and gross-motor skills (for example, running, hopping). Although deficits were observed in all three skill areas, oromotor and manual skill deficits were the most prevalent across the children. These findings led the investigators to suggest that oral and manual dyspraxia may play an important role in the impaired speech and signing of many children with autism.

Finally, Georgina Slavoff and I have continued this exploration of the interrelationships between motor functioning deficits and language production in children with autistic disorder over the past few years (Slavoff 1998; Slavoff and Bonvillian n.d.). In our study, we collected information about the motor and language abilities of 13 children with autism. Seven of these children communicated mostly through speech, 6 primarily through signs. The mean age of these children was 9 years and 3 months, with their ages extending from a low of 33 months to a high of 17 years. Participation in the study was limited to children who did not have a clearly discernible visual or physical disability (for example, blindness, cerebral palsy) other than autistic disorder.

We obtained information on the children's motor abilities through two different approaches. One way was by administering the Peabody

Developmental Motor Scales (PDMS) (Folio and Fewell 1983). The PDMS is a comprehensive motor development assessment instrument that has been shown to provide reliable and valid measures of the fine- and gross-motor abilities of normally developing children and children who are developmentally delayed.

The scores of the children on the gross- and fine-motor scales of the PDMS were far below those of normally developing children. When the children's raw scores on the PDMS were converted to z-scores, their mean gross-motor z-score was -9.59 and their mean fine motor z-score was -6.20. Both these means are far below those of normally developing children of the same chronological ages from normative studies of motor development. Moreover, the children's z-scores on the gross-motor scale were significantly lower than their z-scores on the fine-motor scale. These findings indicate that children with autistic disorder evidence pronounced deficits in motor functioning, with gross-motor ability impaired to a greater extent than fine-motor ability. A recent study by Teitelbaum et al. (1998) also found substantial and individually quite variable disturbances in movement in very young children with autism. Thus, many children with autistic disorder appear to have severe motor impairments, and these impairments appear to emerge early in development.

The second way we (Slavoff 1988; Bonvillian and Slavoff n.d.) obtained information about the children's motor processing abilities was through a series of gesture imitation and sequencing tests. Two of the tests, the apraxia section of the Boston Diagnostic Aphasia Examination (BDAE) (Goodglass and Kaplan 1983) and the Motor Imitation test of the SBGI (Slavoff 1998), involved items that required a participant to produce only a single movement and no change in hand configuration. Two additional tests, the Movement Copying Test (MCT) (Kimura 1986) and the Action Sequencing test of the SBGI (Slavoff 1998), contained items that required up to three movements as well as changes in hand configuration. These tests were included in order to probe more systematically whether the autistic children had an apraxia-like deficit and to determine how their performance on these measures would interrelate with their language abilities.

The children's scores on this series of gestural imitation and sequencing tests were highly intercorrelated. This outcome probably indicates that the different tests are measuring the same, or a highly similar, process or mechanism. It should also be noted that individual children varied quite widely in their scores. Some of the children successfully produced only a few of the gestures on the tests, whereas other children accurately produced the large majority of the test items. As a group though, the autistic children experienced considerable difficulty in their imitation of both single gestures and gestural sequences. The children also showed deficits in buccofacial or oromotor skills as well as limb or manual skills.

The relationships between the children's performance on the various tests of motor abilities and their language production were examined in two ways. The first approach was to analyze the data separately by language modality. That is, the 7 children who communicated primarily by speech were analyzed as a distinct group as were the 6 children who communicated primarily through signs. In the second approach, the modality of the children's language production was ignored and vocabulary size was determined by the number of items in each of the 13 children's lexicons regardless of language modality.

As it turned out, the separate analyses proved largely unnecessary. The pattern of interrelationships between the children's language production measures and their scores on the various motor tests was quite consistent across the different approaches used. The children's vocabulary size, regardless of whether it was calculated on the basis of spoken words, signs, or independent of language modality, was highly correlated with the children's scores on the different tests of gestural imitation and sequencing. More specifically, these correlations ranged in magnitude from .76 to .94 (Slavoff and Bonvillian n.d.). In contrast, the children's scores on the gross- and fine-motor scales of the PDMS were not significantly correlated with the children's vocabulary size. Thus, whereas children with autistic disorder now appear to have distinct deficits in their overall gross- and fine-motor functioning, it is likely that their language difficulties are more closely tied to particular deficits in praxis.

Childhood Autism: A Changing Perspective

An unintended consequence of training children with autistic disorder to communicate with signs is that it helped investigators to focus on the motor skills and disabilities of these children. If children have difficulty forming a particular sign handshape or generating certain sign movements, then such sign formational errors underscore for the teacher and investigator those children's motor-functioning problems. Similarly, if children with autistic disorder fail to imitate accurately their teachers' sign productions, then such failures underline the children's problems with motor imitation. By highlighting autistic children's difficulties learning a visuomotor language, investigators teaching these children to sign helped lead to a reconsideration of the basic characteristics of the disorder.

Although the perspective that children with autism typically are relatively well-coordinated and skilled in manual tasks has begun to change in recent years, a number of contemporary scholars in the field of autism continue to dismiss the notion that autism often involves a movement disorder or disturbance. There are probably a host of reasons why motor or movement difficulties in children with autistic disorder did not receive special attention from parents, therapists, or researchers in the past and continue not to do so today. One reason is that children with autistic disorder originally were thought to have intact fine-motor skills (Kanner 1943). Because the initial description of the syndrome of childhood autism did not indicate motor disturbances, then that description helped frame the syndrome for future investigators.

A second likely reason why motor functioning difficulties in autistic children were not closely examined until recently is that such difficulties may not be as striking or seem as important as other areas of developmental difficulty. When a child fails to acquire speech, does not respond emotionally to others in a normal way, or lags far behind peers cognitively, then such deficiencies are both highly conspicuous and disturbing to all concerned. But when a child lags behind motorically after achieving the gross-motor milestones of sitting, standing, and walking, then other motor development difficulties may not be either particularly evident or appear to be especially important. A third reason for the limited focus historically on the motor aspects of autism is that autistic children often have been found to do relatively well on certain perceptual-motor tasks. For example, autistic children tend to do well on such perceptual-motor tasks as form board completion (DeMyer, Barton, and Norton 1972; Geddes 1977), at least in comparison with their performance in other domains. Unfortunately, form board completion and other puzzle-like tasks do not appear to be good indicators of autistic children's more general motor abilities. Finally, another likely reason why motor functioning in children with autism received little attention from investigators and therapists is that many of these specialists apparently did not receive much training on motor development in their scientific education.

In addition to helping change investigators' views about the nature of childhood autism, the studies of sign language production in autistic children have had a very practical consequence. That practical consequence is reflected in efforts to modify signs to make them easier to form. Those handshapes that were the source of many children's sign formation errors are being replaced by those handshapes that typically were produced frequently and accurately. Similarly, the movement aspects of many signs are being modified to make them easier to produce. Because many autistic children have difficulty producing multi-movement signs, these signs are being transformed into single movement signs. Finally, the observation that certain types of sign movement result in a high percentage of formational errors means that these movements probably will need to be replaced by movements that are easier for children with autism to produce.

Concluding Remarks

In conclusion, it appears that sign language research has contributed in three important ways to programs for hearing, but nonspeaking, individuals. One contribution is that the sign language research that led to the recognition of sign languages as full and genuine languages helped spark a major change in communication training for autistic, aphasic, and mentally retarded individuals. With language no longer equated with speech, investigators initiated a number of non-oral communication programs for nonspeaking persons. A second contribution is that studies of nonspeaking individuals' difficulties in sign formation are helping to guide investigators in their efforts to modify signs to make them easier to produce. Finally, the focus on autistic children's difficulties in forming signs is helping to lead investigators towards a reconsideration of the syndrome to include an emphasis on motor disturbance.

References

American Psychiatric Association. 1994. *Diagnostic and statistical manual of mental disorders*. 4th ed. Washington, D.C.: American Psychiatric Association.

Anderson, Steven W., Hanna Damasio, Antonio R. Damasio, Edward S. Klima, Ursula Bellugi, and Joan P. Brandt. 1992. Acquisition of signs from American Sign Language in hearing individuals following left hemisphere damage and aphasia. *Neuropsychologia* 30: 329–40.

Bonvillian, John D., and Deborah W. Blackburn. 1991. Manual communication and autism: Factors relating to sign language acquisition. In *Theoretical issues in sign language research*. Vol. 2. *Psychology,* edited by Patricia Siple and Susan Fischer. Chicago: University of Chicago Press.

Bonvillian, John D., and Robert J. Friedman. 1978. Language development in another mode: The acquisition of signs by a brain damaged adult. *Sign Language Studies* 19: 111—20.

Bonvillian, John D., Elizabeth T. Gershoff, Brenda C. Seal, and Herbert C. Richards. 2001. Hand preferences in sign-learning students with autistic disorder. *Laterality* 6: 261–81.

Bonvillian, John D., Keith E. Nelson, and Jane M. Rhyne. 1981. Sign language and autism. *Journal of Autism and Developmental Disorders* 11: 125–37.

Bonvillian, John D., Herbert C. Richards, and Tracy T. Dooley. 1997. Early sign language acquisition and the development of hand preference in young children. *Brain and Language* 58: 1–22.

Bryen, Diane N., Amy S. Goldman, and Susan Quinlisk-Gill. 1988. Sign language with students with severe/profound mental retardation: How effective is it? *Education and Training in Mental Retardation* 23: 129–37.

Bryen, Diane N., and Dennis G. Joyce. 1985. Language intervention with the severely handicapped: A decade of research. *Journal of Special Education* 19: 7–39.

Christopoulou, Christina, and John D. Bonvillian. 1985. Sign language, pantomime, and gestural processing in aphasic persons: A review. *Journal of Communication Disorders* 18: 1–20.

Coelho, Carl A. 1990. Acquisition and generalization of simple manual sign grammars by aphasic subjects. *Journal of Communication Disorders* 23: 383–400.

Coelho, Carl A., and Robert J. Duffy. 1986. Effects of iconicity, motoric complexity, and linguistic function on sign acquisition in severe aphasia. *Perceptual and Motor Skills* 63: 519–30.

———. 1987. The relationship of the acquisition of manual signs to severity of aphasia: A training study. *Brain and Language* 31: 328–45.

Cornforth, A. R. T., K. Johnston, and M. Walker. 1974. Teaching sign language to the deaf mentally retarded. *Apex* 2: 23–25.

Daniloff, Joanne K., Giovanna Fritelli, Hugh W. Buckingham, Paul R. Hoffman, and Raymond G. Daniloff. 1986. Amer-Ind versus ASL: Recognition and imitation in aphasic subjects. *Brain and Language* 28: 95–113.

DeMyer, Marian K., Sandra Barton, and James A. Norton. 1972. A comparison of adaptive, verbal, and motor profiles of psychotic and non-psychotic subnormal children. *Journal of Autism and Childhood Schizophrenia* 2: 359–77.

Eagleson, Hodge M., Gwenyth R. Vaughn, and Alvin B. Knudsen. 1970. Hand signals for dysphasia. *Archives of Physical Medicine and Rehabilitation* 51: 111–13.

Eisenberg, Leon. 1956. The autistic child in adolescence. *American Journal of Psychiatry* 112: 607–12.

Folio, M. Rhonda, and Rebecca R. Fewell. 1983. *Peabody developmental motor scales and activity cards.* Chicago: Riverside Publishing.

Fombonne, Eric. 1998. Epidemiological surveys of autism. In *Autism and pervasive developmental disorders,* edited by Fred R. Volkmar. Cambridge: Cambridge University Press.

Geddes, Dolores. 1977. Motor development of autistic monozygotic twins: A case study. *Perceptual and Motor Skills* 45: 179–86.

Goodglass, Harold, and Edith Kaplan. 1983. *The assessment of aphasia and related disorders.* 2d ed. Philadelphia: Lea and Febinger.

Goodman, Linda, Paula S. Wilson, and Harry Bornstein. 1978. Results of a national survey of sign language programs in special education. *Mental Retardation* 16: 104–6.

Griffith, Penny L., and Jacques H. Robinson. 1980. Influence of iconicity and phonological similarity on sign learning by mentally retarded children. *American Journal of Mental Deficiency* 85: 291–8.

Hall, Sylvia M., and Larry W. Talkington. 1970. Evaluation of a manual approach to programming for deaf retarded. *American Journal of Mental Deficiency* 75: 378–80.

Holmes, Jane M. 1975. Manual signing with an aphasic patient. Paper presented at the 13th Academy of Aphasia meeting, Victoria, B.C., Canada.

Hurd, Angela. 1996. A developmental cognitive neuropsychological approach to the assessment of information processing in autism. *Child Language Teaching and Therapy* 12: 288–99.

Kahn, James V. 1996. Cognitive skills and sign language knowledge of children with severe and profound mental retardation. *Education and Training in Mental Retardation and Developmental Disabilities* 31: 162–8.

Kanner, Leo. 1943. Autistic disturbances of affective contact. *The Nervous Child* 2: 217–50.

Kiernan, Chris. 1977. Alternatives to speech: A review of research on manual and other forms of communication with the mentally handicapped and other non-communicating populations. *British Journal of Mental Subnormality* 23: 6–28.

Kimura, Doreen. 1986. *Neuropsychology test procedures.* Rev. ed. London, Ont.: dk Consultants.

Klima, Edward S., and Ursula Bellugi. 1979. *The signs of language.* Cambridge: Harvard University Press.

Kohl, Frances L. 1981. Effects of motoric requirements on the acquisition of manual sign responses by severely handicapped students. *American Journal of Mental Deficiency* 85: 396–403.

Konstantareas, M. Mary. 1985. Review of evidence on the relevance of sign language in the early communication training of autistic children. *Australian Journal of Human Communication Disorders* 13: 77–97.

Layton, Thomas L. 1987. Manual communication. In *Language and treatment of autistic and developmentally disordered children*, edited by Thomas L. Layton. Springfield, Ill.: Charles C. Thomas.

———. 1988. Language training with autistic children using four different modes of presentation. *Journal of Communication Disorders* 21: 333–50.

Lord, Catherine, Michael Rutter, and Ann LeCouteur. 1994. Autism Diagnostic Interview Revised: A revised version of a diagnostic interview for caregivers of individuals with pervasive developmental disorders. *Journal of Autism and Developmental Disorders* 24: 659–85.

Lotter, Victor. 1974. Factors related to outcome in autistic children. *Journal of Autism and Childhood Schizophrenia* 4: 263–77.

Luftig, Richard L. 1983. Translucency of sign and concreteness of gloss in the manual sign learning of moderately/severely mentally retarded students. *American Journal of Mental Deficiency* 88: 279–86.

Mirenda, Pat, and Adriana L. Schuler. 1988. Augmenting communication for persons with autism: Issues and strategies. *Topics in Language Disorders* 9: 24–43.

Page, Jenny, and Jill Boucher. 1998. Motor impairments in children with autistic disorder. *Child Language Teaching and Therapy* 14: 233–59.

Richardson, Toni. 1975. Sign language for the SMR and PMR. *Mental Retardation* 13: 17.

Rutter, Michael. 1966. Psychosis: Psychotic children in adolescence and early adult life. In *Early childhood autism*, edited by J. K. Wing. London: Pergamon Press.

———. 1978. Diagnosis and definition. In *Autism: A reappraisal of concepts and treatment*, edited by Michael Rutter and Eric Schopler. New York: Plenum Press.

Schuler, Adriana, and Barry Prizant. 1987. Facilitating communication: Prelanguage approaches. In *Handbook of autism and pervasive developmental disorders*, edited by Donald Cohen, Anne Donnellan, and Rhea Paul. Silver Spring, Md.: V. H. Winston and Sons.

Seal, Brenda C. 1993. Autism and sign language: Analysis of the signs used by autistic children. Ph.D. diss., University of Virginia, Charlottesville.

Seal, Brenda C., and John D. Bonvillian. 1996. Hand preference in young deaf children of hearing parents. *Sign Language Studies* 93: 301–26.

———. 1997. Sign language and motor functioning in students with autistic disorder. *Journal of Autism and Developmental Disorders* 27: 437–66.

Sheehan, Joseph, Margaret M. Martyn, and Kent L. Kilburn. 1968. Speech disorders in retardation. *American Journal of Mental Deficiency* 73: 251–6.

Silverman, Franklin H. 1995. *Communication for the speechless.* 3d ed. Englewood Cliffs, N.J.: Prentice Hall.

Skelly, Madge. 1979. *Amer-Ind gestural code based on Universal American Indian Hand Talk.* New York: Elsevier Press.

Slavoff, Georgina R. 1998. *Motor development in children with autism.* Ph.D. diss., University of Virginia, Charlottesville.

Slavoff, Georgina R., and John D. Bonvillian. n.d. Exploring motor functioning in children with autistic disorder. Forthcoming.

Snyder-McLean, L. 1978. Functional stimulus and response variables in sign training with retarded subjects. Paper presented at the annual convention of the American Speech and Hearing Association, San Francisco, California.

Stokoe, William C. 1960. *Sign language structure: An outline of the visual communication system of the American deaf.* Studies in Linguistics, Occasional Papers 8. Buffalo, N.Y.: University of Buffalo.

Stokoe, William C., Dorothy C. Casterline, and Carl G. Croneberg. 1965. *A dictionary of American Sign Language on linguistic principles.* Washington, D.C.: Gallaudet College Press.

Teitelbaum, Philip, Osnat Teitelbaum, Jennifer Nye, Joshua Nye, Joshua Fryman, and Ralph G. Maurer. 1998. Movement analysis in infancy may be useful for early diagnosis of autism. *Proceedings of the National Academy of Sciences* 95: 13982–87.

Wertz, Robert T., Leonord L. LaPointe, and John Rosenbek. 1984. *Apraxia of speech in adults: The disorder and its management.* Orlando, Fla.: Grune and Stratton.

Wilbur, Ronnie B. 1987. *American Sign Language: Linguistic and applied dimensions.* 2d ed. Boston: College Hill.

Wilson, Paula S. 1974. Sign language as a means of communication for the mentally retarded. Paper presented at the annual meeting of the Eastern Psychological Association, Philadelphia, Pa.

World Health Organization. 1993. *The ICD-10 classification of mental and behavioural disorders: Diagnostic criteria for research.* Geneva, Switzerland: World Health Organization.

11

Gesture and the Nature of Language in Infancy: The Role of Gesture as a Transitional Device En Route to Two-Word Speech

Olga Capirci, M. Cristina Caselli,
Jana M. Iverson, Elena Pizzuto,
and Virginia Volterra

> *"It is common knowledge that persons who share no language can communicate by using gestures; all infants communicate gesturally before they use a language; moreover, there exist many languages that use visible but not vocal symbols. Nevertheless, the general public and many scientific observers seem to perceive an impassable gulf between gesture (or what they call 'nonverbal communication') and language." (Stokoe 1999, 1)*

Too few people, even scientists, are able to think of language apart from speech, and so it has been difficult to get a perspective on language acquisition and development that includes gestures. If spoken linguistic communication develops from gestural communication then the human species may not be as special as many wish to believe.

A number of studies conducted in the past twenty years have pointed out that, in the early stages of development, children's communicative repertoires are not limited solely to the vocal symbols of spoken languages (for reviews see the collection of papers in Volterra and Erting [1990] 1994; more recently Abrahamsen 2000). One body of work (Bates et al. 1979; Bates, Camaioni, and Volterra 1975; Lock et al. [1990] 1994; Masur [1990] 1994) has indicated that the onset of intentional communication between the ages of 9 and 13 months is marked by the emergence of a series of gestures—RITUALIZED REQUEST, SHOWING, and POINTING[1] that precede the appearance of first words.

These gestures, characterized as "performatives" in earlier studies or as deictic gestures in later studies, are used to refer to external objects or events and express only communicative intent on the part of the child. The precise referent of these gestures is only interpretable by referring to the extralinguistic context in which communication occurs. Some authors have attributed a special role to pointing, which Bruner (1975) describes as an important way of establishing the joint attention situations within which language will eventually emerge (see also Lock 1980; Lock et al. [1990] 1994).

A second line of work (Bates et al. 1979; Nicolich 1977; Piaget 1945; Shore et al. [1990] 1994; Volterra et al. 1981), looking at children in approximately the same age range, has reported striking parallels between early vocal productions and gestural productions which have been characterized with different terms such as schemes of symbolic play, referential gestures, and more recently representational gestures. Many of the referential meanings expressed by these representational gestures (for example, bringing hand to mouth for EAT or FOOD) were equivalent to those conveyed by first words (for example, *pappa* [lunch]; Volterra et al. 1981; Volterra et al. 1993). In addition, both first words and representational gestures have been shown to undergo a similar process of progressive decontextualization. Children's first gestures and words are initially found as parts of routines from which they are progressively detached until they are used in a referential manner to name

---

1. Throughout this chapter gestures are denoted in small capitals and Italian words are italicized.

new objects or events independent of a specific context (Caselli [1990] 1994; Folven and Bonvillian 1991).

The data led Volterra and Erting ([1990] 1994, 303) to propose that around one year of age "there is a basic equipotentiality between the gestural and vocal channels, the final result depending on the modality in which the linguistic input is offered to the child."

At this point in development, the only difference between the two domains seems to be in the modality of expression. A 13-month-old child does not appear to be in any way biased toward the development of vocal language as compared to gestural language. Using Kendon's words (1995): "This would mean that using speech for language or using gesture for language are not so radically different as might be supposed." Abrahamsen (2000) has also suggested that during what she calls the "bimodal period": "words are not as distinct from gestures and gestures are not as distinct from words as they first appear."

However, only a few studies have examined the role that gestures play in the transition to two-word speech (Caselli 1983; Caselli and Volterra [1990] 1994; Morford and Goldin-Meadow 1992; Butcher and Goldin-Meadow 1993). This issue is fundamental for exploring whether there is any continuity between an earlier preverbal and a later, functionally equivalent linguistic form, or more specifically, between the structuring of gestures and crossmodal combinations and later word combinations. Is the transition largely one of modality of expression? Do two-word combinations emerge relatively late in speaking children because they require coordination of two elements in the vocal modality? Or does the constraint lie in the fact that they require production of two linguistic elements in the same modality in succession?

In this chapter, we address the following questions:

1. When children move to two-word speech, is the use of gesture and gesture-speech combinations a robust developmental phenomenon, exhibiting similar features across different children and cultures, or are there significant individual differences?

2. Is the information content of children's crossmodal, gesture-word utterances, which are apparently used at both the one-word and the

two-word stage, comparable to that conveyed by two-word utterances?

3. What is the role of linguistic input in the structuring and information conveyed by two element combinations?

In order to address these questions we reconsider data collected by our Italian team at the Institute of Psychology of the National Research Council (CNR) and already partially published (see following section). The data will be discussed taking into account some fascinating theoretical speculations advanced in the book *Gesture and the Nature of Language* by Armstrong, Stokoe, and Wilcox (1995) and in more recent work by Lock (1997), Deacon (1997), and Iverson and Thelen (1999).

The Data

The data presented are drawn from the following studies:

- Two related studies on the spontaneous communication of twelve Italian children, observed at the ages of 16 months, when the children's vocal communication consisted largely of one-word utterances, and 20 months, when two-word utterances were produced in appreciable numbers (Iverson, Capirci, and Caselli 1994; Capirci et al. 1996).
- A third study conducted on the same group of children but focused on maternal use of gesture during mother-toddler interactions in the same set of participants and data (Iverson et al. 1999).
- A study of the spontaneous communication of a bilingual hearing child of deaf parents in the first two years of life, focusing on his manual (gestures and signs) and vocal production. (Capirci et al. forthcoming).

The monolingual children (six boys and six girls) were from upper-middle-class hearing families living in the Rome area. They were native speakers of Italian and had no exposure to sign language (for further details and description of this group of children, see Capirci et al. 1996; Iverson et al. 1994). The hearing child of deaf parents (here called Marco), was observed at monthly intervals between the ages of 10 and 30 months. Both of Marco's parents are deaf but they use Italian Sign Language (LIS), spoken Italian and simultaneous speech-sign communication when interacting with their child. While Marco's father preferred to use only LIS, his mother made use of all three modes of communication. Marco was thus exposed from the beginning of his life to LIS and simultaneous communication at home, and to spoken Italian at the nursery.

Videotaped observations for Marco and the monolingual children took place in their homes and lasted approximately 45 minutes. During this time, the mothers were instructed to interact and play with their children as they normally would. The observations were divided equally into three 15-minute segments, so that the children were filmed in three different contexts: playing with familiar objects, playing with new examples of familiar objects, and while eating a meal or snack.

The age range studied, from 16 to 20 months, is particularly interesting because around this period several major changes in the child's linguistic abilities occur: vocabulary grows at a very fast rate, the ability to combine two linguistic symbols usually develops, two- and multi-word utterances become progressively more frequent and articulated in their meaning and structure, and the acquisition of grammar begins.

Production of Words and Gestures

The different types of gestures and words produced by the children were classified according to the coding scheme shown in table 11.1.

Three deictic gestures (DG) types were identified in the children's production: REQUEST, SHOW, and POINTING, as previously noted. The class of deictic words (dw) consisted of demonstrative and locative expressions and personal and possessive pronouns.

The class of representational gestures (RG) included some gestures iconically related to salient aspects of a referent or an action (for example, opening and closing the mouth for FISH; flapping the arms for BIRD; a stylized grabbing gesture for OPEN). The remaining RGs

TABLE 11.1. Coding Scheme and Notational Conventions with Illustrative Examples of the Children's Vocal and Gestural Productions

DEICTIC		REPRESENTATIONAL	
Gestures (DG)	Words (dw)	Gestures (BG)	Words (rw)
REQUEST, SHOW, POINTING	*qua* (here) *là* (there) *questo* (this) *eccolo* (here it is) *io* (I) *tu* (you) *mio* (mine) *tuo* (yours)	FISH, BIRD, OPEN, GOOD, BYE-BYE, SILENCE, NO, ALL-GONE	*mamma* (mommy) *pappa* (baby food) *acqua* (water) *apri* (open) *sì* (yes) *no* (no) *più* (all-gone) *ciao* (bye-bye)

were conventional, culturally defined gestures, some apparently specific to the Italian repertoire (for example, bringing the index finger to the cheek and rotating it for GOOD; repeatedly opening-closing four fingers, thumb extended, for the Italian *ciao* = BYE-BYE; putting the index finger to lips for SILENCE); and other perhaps less culture-specific gestures (for example, shaking the head for NO, turning and raising the palms up for ALL-GONE). The class of representational words (rw) included for the most part content words that, in the adult language, are assigned to the classes of common and proper nouns, verbs, adjectives, adverbs (for example, *mommy, food, water, open*), affirmative and negative expressions (for example, *yes, no, all-gone*), interjections (for example, *bravo!*), greetings (*bye-bye*).

Extensive communication in both the gestural and vocal modalities was observed in all participants, although a substantial amount of variability among individual children was also evident. At both 16 and 20 months of age, children produced single signals in the spoken and gestural modalities and combinations of two or more elements within and across modalities.

In order to provide an accurate representation of the word and gesture production observed at 16 and 20 months, and to highlight individual differences in word and gesture usage, we report the data in terms of patterns exhibited by individual children. Figure 11.1a and b present the total number of different word and gesture types (both deictic and representational) produced by each hearing monolingual subject and by the hearing bilingual child at 16 and 20 months.

For the monolingual children we considered only gestures and words, while for Marco we also included signs (hereafter indicated in boldface small capital letters). In addition, to avoid overestimating Marco's sign production, we were quite conservative in the criteria used to distinguish signs from gestures. Communicative gestural signals were defined as signs only when: (a) they resembled adult LIS forms; and (b) their form differed from those produced by monolingual children. All of Marco's manual signals that failed to meet these criteria were classified as gestures. Thus, for example, although the LIS sign for **GOOD** is executed by rotating the index finger on the cheek, instances of this form were classified as gestures for Marco because the gesture GOOD is produced in the same way by monolingual Italian children.

Figure 11.1a indicates that at 16 months two subgroups of monolingual participants can be distinguished. Five children had more extensive gestural than verbal vocabularies, six children had more word than gesture types, and one subject (no. 6) had exactly the same number of word and gesture types. Whereas the numbers of different gesture types within the repertoires of the various children were fairly similar (range from 5–14), variability in the production of words was much more apparent (range from 1–73) and statistically highly significant. Marco exhibits a pattern similar to child no. 6, with a slight preference for the gestural modality. When gestures and signs are considered together, a preference for the gestural modality becomes more pronounced.

As is evident in figure 11.1b, at 20 months a significantly larger proportion of participants had more different communicative signals in the vocal than in the gestural modality. In the case of Marco, when gestures and signs are considered together, the number of communicative signals produced in the vocal and in the gestural modalities are very similar (35 words versus 36 gestures + signs).

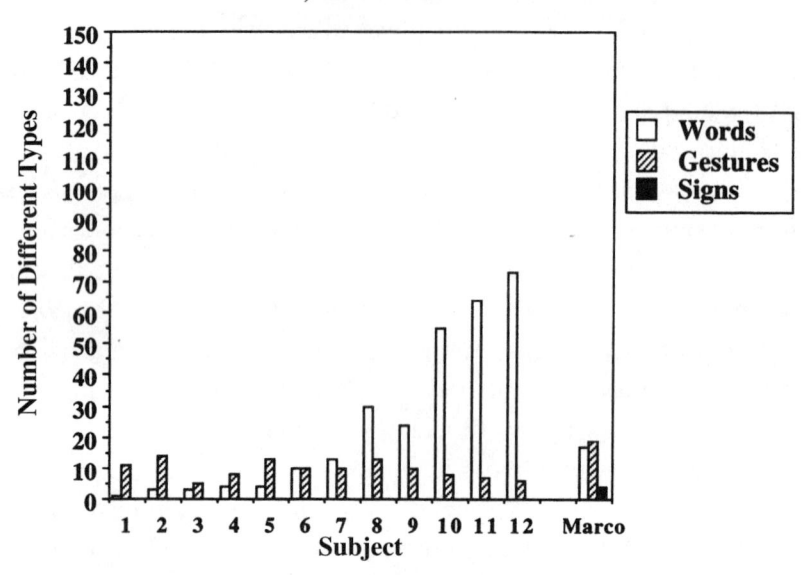

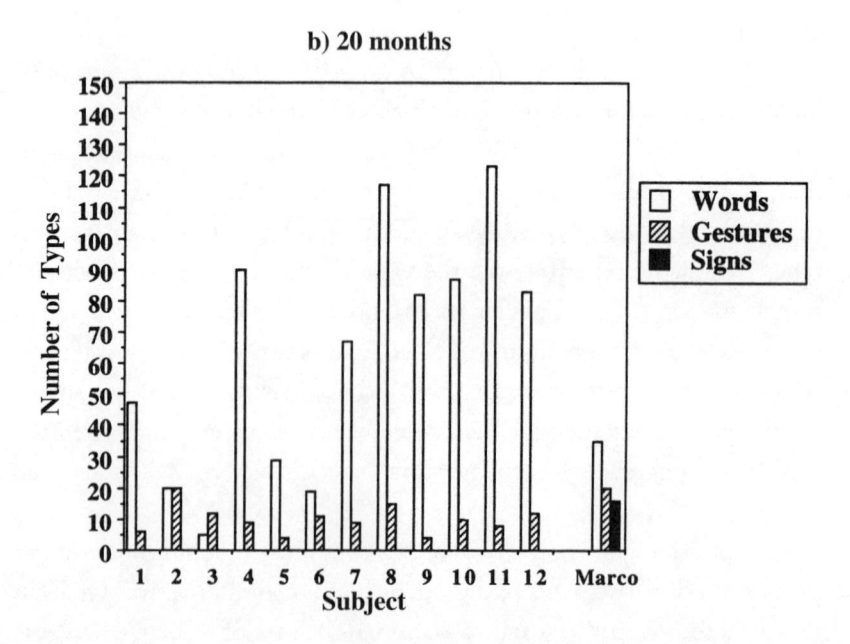

Figure 11.1. Number of word, gesture, and sign types produced by 12 monolingual children and by Marco

The data indicate generally that when both modalities are considered together, Marco's total vocabulary size falls within the range for the monolingual children (that is, both gestures and words). He was not, in other words, advantaged relative to children not exposed to sign language input. A more general look at the data confirms that hearing children make extensive use of the gestural modality even though they are exposed to a nonsystematic gestural input. The shift to a preference for the vocal modality occurs only later in the second year. Because Marco is also exposed to a sign language input, he can make greater use of the gestural modality, but the developmental pattern of gesture and word use is very similar to that of monolingual children (Volterra and Iverson 1995).

Exposure to sign language does appear, however, to have qualitative effects on gesture production. When the proportions of deictic and representational gestures produced by Marco were compared to those of the monolingual children, an interesting difference was observed. While monolingual children produced deictic gestures much more frequently than representational gestures (68 percent versus 32 percent at 16 and 80 percent versus 20 percent at 20 months) Marco showed an opposite trend and used more representational than deictic gestures (52 percent versus 48 percent at 16 and 62 percent versus 38 percent at 20 months) at both ages—a finding consistent with data also reported by van den Bogaerde and Mills (2000). This finding suggests that exposure to sign language may attune bilingual children to the ways in which representational information can be captured by the manual modality.

An interesting aspect of the data is that they also illustrate the gradual process of decontextualization that occurs in the course of symbolic development in all children. For example, we observed a decline from 16 to 20 months in the use of action-by-agent nominal gestures (for example, drinking from a toy cup) produced with the object-referent in hand and a concurrent increase in the production of form or movement-of-object nominal (for example, opening and closing the mouth for FISH) and predicate gestures (for example, holding the thumb and index fingers close together for PICCOLINE [tiny]), all of which were empty-handed. This finding supports Werner and Kaplan's

(1963) argument that, with the passage of time and growth in the cognitive and representational domains, the child's communication becomes progressively less bound to specific contexts. Action on the object may no longer be necessary as the child is now capable of representing the object in a symbolic fashion and distancing the symbolic vehicle (that is, gestures or words) from the referent.

Utterance Types

In the analysis of children's gestural and vocal productions, we classified as one-element utterances all gestures, signs, and words that occurred in isolation. Gestural and/or vocal units that were produced simultaneously, with some extent of overlap, or in immediate succession, were classified as combinations of two elements. Figure 11.2 shows the mean number of tokens and the standard deviation of each major utterance type across participants (one gesture, one word, one sign, and two element).

As is apparent in figure 11.2, in the monolingual children one-element utterances were produced more frequently than two-element utterances and one-element utterances were produced predominantly in the vocal modality at both ages. Marco presents a different pattern in the type of utterances produced. At 16 months, like the monolingual children, he produced more one-element utterances than two-element ones, with a majority in the gestural modality. At 20 months, his production of one-element vocal and gestural utterances was similar to that of monolingual children, but his production of two-element utterances increased sharply from 16 to 20 months of age and the size was more than the double of that of monolingual children. In contrast, Marco produced a very small number of single signs at both ages. The majority of Marco's two-element combinations consisted of one word + one sign. In the following two sections we analyze two-element combinations from structural and semantic standpoints.

The data from the monolingual children also reveal large individual differences (see the SD values), and somewhat different developmental patterns. Looking at individual production, we can see that at 16

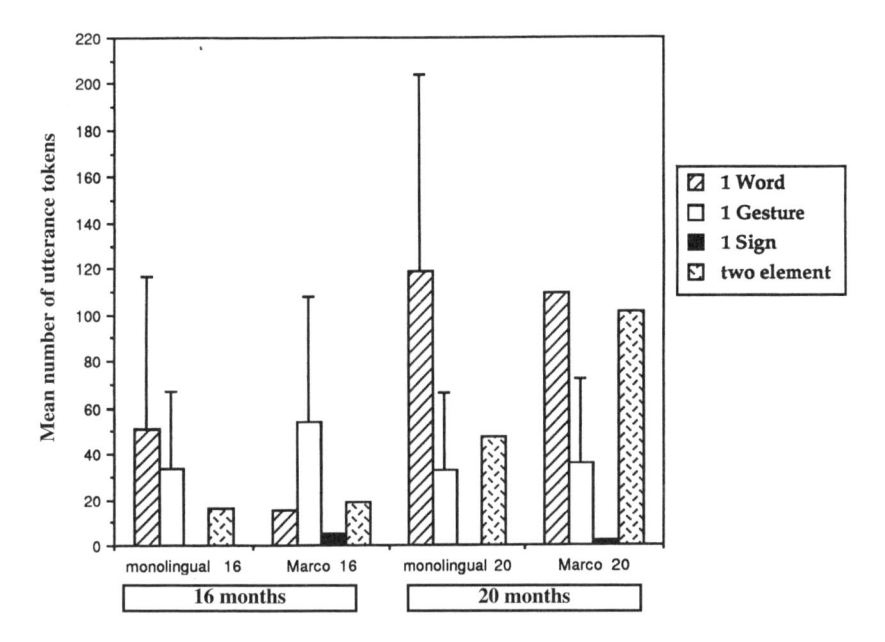

Figure 11.2. Mean number of tokens of different utterance types produced by 12 monolingual children and by Marco

months, eight children showed a clear preference for the gestural modality while at 20 months, only two children exhibited this pattern, and most produced more one-representational word utterances and had thus shifted to the vocal modality. Thus, although on the average one-representational word utterances were at both age points more frequent than the other utterance types in the individual production of most monolingual children, this pattern held true at 20 months, but not at 16 months.

Two-Element Utterances: Modality

All the children's utterances were categorized into three major classes according to modality of production. We illustrate our coding scheme only with respect to those two-element utterances that we actually observed in the children's production, described in table 11.2.

Combinations of a gesture and a word, in which each element was produced in a different modality, were classified as crossmodal (for

TABLE 11.2. Two-Element Combinations: Modality and Components

MODALITY	COMPONENTS	COMBINATIONS
Crossmodal		
	DG-rw	(1) POINT (to flowers) – *fiori* (flowers)
		(2) SHOW (a cup) + *acqua* (water)
		(3) POINT (to a pigeon) – *nanna* (nap)
	RG-rw	(4) BYE-BYE – *ciao* (bye-bye)
		(5) BIG – *grande* (big)
		(6) ALL-GONE – *acqua* (water)
	DG-dw	(7) POINT (to toy) – *eccolo* (here it is)
		(8) POINT (to game) – *te* (you)
	RG-dw	(9) YES – *questo* (this)
Unimodal		
Gestural		
	DG-RG	(10) POINT (to drawing of fish) – FISH
		(11) POINT (to a closed box) – OPEN
	DG-DG	(12) POINT (to bottle of water) – POINT (to glass)
		(13) POINT (to toy) REQUEST (same toy)
Vocal		
	rw-rw	(14) *piccolo – miao miao*, (little-kitty)
	dw-rw	(15) *questa – pappa* (this baby food)
		(16) *questo – c'entra* (this goes in here)
	dw-dw	(17) *eccoli – qua* (here they are here)
		(18) *qua – mia* (here mine)

example POINTING to flowers while producing the word for "flowers"). Combinations of two gestures were classified as gestural utterances (for example POINTING to a drawing of a fish while producing the gesture for FISH). Combinations of two words were classified as vocal utterances (for example *piccolo miao miao* = "little kitty").

Table 11.3 presents the total number, mean, and standard deviation across participants of the different types of crossmodal and unimodal two-element combinations observed in the monolingual children at 16 and 20 months of age. The data in table 11.3 show that crossmodal

TABLE 11.3. Total Number, Mean, Standard Deviation, and Distribution Across Subjects of Different Crossmodal and Unimodal Two-Element Combinations Produced at 16 and 20 Months of Age by the Monolingual Children

	16 MONTHS (N = 12)				20 MONTHS (N = 12)			
	Number of Combinations	Mean	SD	N Subj	Number of Combinations	Mean	SD	N Subj
Crossmodal	**181**	**15.08**	**17.45**	**11**	**401**	**33.41**	**23.48**	**12**
DG-rw	122	10.17	13.22	11	243	20.25	15.22	12
RG-rw	52	4.33	4.65	9	76	6.33	4.92	11
DG-dw	7	0.58	1.73	2	80	6.66	10.89	7
Unimodal	**14**	**1.17**	**1.19**	**7**	**166**	**13.83**	**15.47**	**11**
Gestural	**9**	**0.75**	**1.13**	**5**	**9**	**0.75**	**2.30**	**2**
DG-RG	7	0.58	1.00	4	3	0.25	0.87	1
DG-DG	2	0.17	0.39	2	6	0.50	1.45	2
RG-RG	0			0	0			0
Vocal	**5**	**0.42**	**0.67**	**4**	**157**	**13.08**	**15.93**	**10**
rw-rw	5	0.42	0.67	4	117	9.75	14.03	10
dw-rw	0			0	34	2.83	3.07	7
dw-dw	0			0	6	0.50	1.24	2

Note: Combination types are described in the text. N Subj. = number of subjects producing each combination type at each age. Numbers in bold show group totals for each major type.

combinations were produced more frequently than unimodal ones at both 16 and 20 months of age. This difference was highly significant at 16 months and remained significant at 20 months of age. The most frequently produced subtype was the DG-rw combination, which increased substantially and significantly by 20 months of age. This combination type was also produced by 11 participants at 16 months and by all participants at 20 months.

Given the predominance of crossmodal combinations of the DG-rw subtype, we examined the different deictic gestures combined with a representational word in more detail. At both ages, the number of combinations including POINT was significantly higher—roughly three times greater—than the number of combinations including REQUEST or SHOW.

Unimodal combinations, which were almost absent at 16 months, increased markedly by 20 months of age. This developmental change, however, was due primarily to the growth and differentiation of two-word combinations. As expected, there was a sharp and highly significant increase of combinations of two representational words. In addition, two new vocal combinations (dw-rw and dw-dw) appeared for the first time. In contrast, as noted, unimodal gestural combinations were observed in very small number at both ages.

The data in table 11.3 highlight an additional difference with respect to combinations of two representational elements: we found both crossmodal (RG-rw) and unimodal vocal (rw-rw) combinations, but unimodal gestural combinations of two representational elements (RG-RG) were never observed, either at 16 or at 20 months of age.

We next compared the production of crossmodal and unimodal utterances observed in the bilingual child, Marco, at 16 and 20 months with the means obtained from our group of 12 monolingual children.

At 16 months, Marco's relative distribution of combinations across structure types was generally quite similar to that for monolingual children. Indeed, the total number of gesture + word combinations produced by Marco ($n = 15$) fell within the 95 percent confidence interval for the monolingual distribution. Both Marco and the monolingual children produced relatively few gesture + gesture ($n = 3$) and word + word combinations ($n = 1$) at this age. By 20 months, however, Marco's overall production of gesture + word combinations ($n = 67$) fell more than two standard deviations above the group mean for monolingual children. In fact, Marco produced more gesture + word combinations than any of the monolingual children. (for further details see Capirci et al. n.d.).

With respect to word + word combinations ($n = 6$), however, Marco's production fell within the 95 percent confidence interval for the monolingual distribution. Gesture + gesture combinations remained infrequent for both Marco and the monolingual children. In addition, at both ages, Marco combined two representational gestures and one sign-one gesture ($n = 3$), structures that were never used by his monolingual peers.

These findings suggest that the constraint on production of two-word combinations cannot be explained by the greater degree of difficulty of vocal relative to manual production because combinations consisting of two elements within the manual modality do not appear before other combination types. Instead, the appearance of crossmodal combinations prior to combinations of two linguistic symbols (that is, word + word and sign + sign) suggests that the difficulty lies in the production of two symbolic linguistic elements in the same modality.

Two-Element Utterances: Information Conveyed

Table 11.4 illustrates the classificatory criteria used in analyzing the information conveyed by the different two-element utterances observed in the monolingual children, and the corresponding notation. The examples of utterances given in table 11.4 are the same as those reported in table 11.2, with numbers that show this correspondence (for example example (4a) in table 11.4 corresponds to example (4) in table 11.2).

Equivalent combinations included only crossmodal productions of two representational units that typically referred to the same referent and conveyed the same meaning—noted "RG = rw" as in example (4a). The complementary and supplementary classes included both crossmodal and unimodal combinations. Complementary combinations—like the equivalent ones—typically referred to a single referent, but had one distinctive feature, denoted by an ampersand (&) between

TABLE 11.4. Two-Element Combinations: Information Conveyed

MODALITY	COMBINATION	INFORMATION
Equivalent		
Crossmodal		
	RG = rw	(4a) BYE-BYE = *ciao* (bye-bye)
		(5a) BIG = *grande* (big)
Complementary		
Crossmodal		
	DG & rw	(1a) POINT (to flowers) + *fior* (flowers)
		(2a) SHOW (a cup) + *acqua* (water)
	DG & dw	(7a) POINT (to toy) + *questo* (this)
Unimodal		
Gestural	DG & RG	(10a) POINT (to drawing of fish) + FISH
	DG & DG	(13a) POINT (to toy) + REQUEST (same toy)
Vocal	dw & rw	(15a) *questa* + *pappa* (this + baby food)
	dw & dw	(17a) *eccoli* + *qua* (here they are + here)
Supplementary		
Crossmodal		
	DG + rw	(3a) POINT (to drawing of pigeon) + *nanna* (sleep)
	DG + dw	(8a) POINT (to game) + *te* (you)
	RG + rw	(6a) ALL-GONE + *acqua* (water)
	RG + dw	(9a) yes + *questo* (this)
Unimodal		
Gestural	DG + RG	(11a) POINT (to a closed box) + OPEN
	DG + DG	(12a) POINT (to bottle of water) + POINT (to plastic glass)
Vocal	rw + rw	(14a) *piccolo* + *miao miao* (little + kitty)
	dw + rw	(16a) *questo* + *c'entra* (this + goes in here)
	dw + dw	(18a) *qua* + *mia* (here + mine)

the two combined elements (for example, DG & rw): they always included one deictic element (gestural or vocal) which provided non-redundant information, singling out or disambiguating the referent indicated by the accompanying representational element or by another, co-occurring deictic element. For example, in utterances (1a), (2a), and (10a) in table 11.4, the DG point or show complemented the rw and RG they accompanied and singled out the referents "flowers, water, fish." The demonstrative dw "this" played a similar role in utterance (15a). A slightly different, but still complementary relationship was observed when the two combined units were both deictic. In crossmodal combinations of this kind, as in example (7a) the DG provided the necessary information for identifying the toy to which a child referred with the ambiguous demonstrative 'this.' Unimodal combinations of two DG (or two dw) were included in the complementary class when they referred to a single referent, and each of the combined units simply integrated the information provided by the other. In examples (13a) and (17a) the request DG and the dw *eccoli* ("here they are") primarily fulfills an ostensive function, while the accompanying point in (13a) or the locative dw *qua* (here) in (17a) specify the location of the referent object.

Supplementary combinations differed from the other two types in that they referred either to the same or to two distinct referents, but in all cases each of the combined elements added information to the other one—hence the '+' character in our notation (for example, DG + rw). Unimodal combinations of two representational words provide the clearest illustration of this class of utterances, as in (14a), but eight other different subtypes were identified. Combinations of two deictic elements (DG or dw) were also classified as supplementary when one of the combined elements provided additional information with respect to the other: in example (12a) the second DG appeared to indicate a locative relation of "inside"; in (18a) the two dw specified a location-possession relation. We recognize that, beyond their similarities, the various subtypes differed at both the symbolic and the semantic level.

Note that two different gestures, or a gesture and a word can be (and often were) produced simultaneously. In the examples illustrated in tables 11.2 and 11.4, as in all the examples of gestural or crossmodal utterances given throughout the paper, the distinction between sequential and simultaneous productions is not represented, and the order given reflects only arbitrary transcription conventions. In utterances composed only of words, instead, the order in which words occurred is preserved (for example, as in *nonna + viene* [grandma comes]). It must be noted, however, that in some cases children combined two or more vocal items always in the same sequence in what appeared to be frozen phrases. Contextual information and criteria of productivity were used to distinguish true combinations from frozen phrases. Clearly formulaic expressions such as *mamma mia* (Mother of God) were also coded as one-word utterances.

Table 11.5 shows the total number, mean, and standard deviation across participants of equivalent, complementary, and supplementary combinations of two elements observed in the production of our monolingual children at 16 and 20 months. The number of equivalent combinations was smaller relative to the other two combination types. This difference was significant with respect to complementary combinations at 16 months, and highly significant with respect to both complementary and supplementary combinations at 20 months. The small increase in equivalent combinations from 16 to 20 months of age was not significant. At 20 months, there was a significant increase in production of both complementary and supplementary combinations. At both age points there was no significant difference in the number of complementary relative to supplementary combinations.

With regard to developmental changes in production of different combination subtypes, it is evident that within the complementary class, crossmodal combinations of a deictic and a representational element (DG & rw) were the most frequently produced and the most evenly distributed across participants at both ages. They also increased significantly over time. At 20 months, the second most frequently produced type were crossmodal combinations of two deictic elements (DG & dw), which had also significantly increased from 16 to 20 months. Unimodal complementary combinations of a deictic and a representational word (dw & rw) appeared only at 20 months.

TABLE 11.5. Total Number, Mean, Standard Deviation, and Distribution Across Subjects of Equivalent, Complementary, and Supplementary Two-Element Combinations Produced at 16 and 20 Months of Age by the Monolingual Children

	16 MONTHS (N = 12)					20 MONTHS (N = 12)			
	Number of Combinations	Mean	SD	N Subj	Number of Combinations	Mean	SD	N Subj
Equivalent	**46**	**3.83**	**3.81**	**9**	**66**	**5.50**	**3.85**	**11**
RG = rw	46	3.83	3.81	9	66	5.50	3.85	11
Complementary	**82**	**6.83**	**6.97**	**10**	**251**	**20.92**	**14.85**	**12**
DG & rw	67	5.58	6.19	10	144	12.00	9.32	12
DG & dw	7	0.58	1.73	2	72	6.00	10.57	7
DG & RG	6	0.50	1.00	3	2	0.17	0.58	1
DG & DG	2	0.17	0.39	2	1	0.08	0.29	1
dw & rw	0			0	28	2.33	2.81	7
dw & dw	0			0	4	0.33	1.15	1
Supplementary	**67**	**5.58**	**8.51**	**7**	**250**	**20.83**	**19**	**11**
DG + rw	55	4.58	7.5	7	99	8.25	7.74	9
RG + rw	6	0.50	1.00	3	10	0.83	1.53	4
DG + dw	0			0	8	0.67	1.23	3
RG + dw	0			0	2	0.17	0.58	1
DG + RG	1	0.08	0.29	1	1	0.08	0.29	1
DG + DG	0			0	5	0.42	1.16	2
rw + rw	5	0.42	0.67	4	117	9.75	14.03	10
dw + rw	0			0	6	0.50	1.45	2
dw + dw	0			0	2	0.17	0.58	1

Note: Combination types are described in the text. N Subj. = number of subjects producing each combination type at each age. Numbers in bold show group totals for each major type (e.g. at 16 months, 9 out of 12 children produced equivalent combinations, and all 9 children produced the RG = rw type; 10 children produced complementary combinations, all 10 produced the DG & rw subtype, 2 children also produced the DG & dw subtype, 3 the DG & RG subtype, 2 the DG & DG subtype, etc.).

Within the supplementary class, at 16 months of age the most frequent type were crossmodal combinations of a deictic and a representational element (DG + rw). The mean number of these combinations doubled at 20 months, but this increase was not significant. Crossmodal supplementary combinations of two representational elements (RG + rw) were produced at both ages in roughly the same, small number. In contrast, unimodal combinations of two representational words (rw + rw), which appeared in a very small number at 16 months, underwent a highly significant increase at 20 months of age.

The data in table 11.5 also show that in addition to these combinations, the children produced as many as 8 other subtypes of both complementary and supplementary utterances, of which 7 appeared for the first time at 20 months. Because these other types were represented in very small numbers ($n =$ from 1 to 8 across participants) and were used by very few children ($n =$ from 1 to 3), they will not be discussed in any detail.

Figure 11.3 shows the distribution of equivalent, complementary and supplementary utterances in the production of the twelve monolingual children (mean number) at 16 and 20 months, compared to the distribution of the same utterance types in the production of the bilingual child, Marco, at the same age points.

At 16 months of age Marco produced about the same number of equivalent, complementary and supplementary combinations produced by monolingual children. At 20 months, the pattern of complementary and supplementary combinations looks quite similar for Marco and the monolingual children, but Marco produced many more equivalent combinations. Almost all of Marco's equivalent combinations ($n = 60$) consisted of sign = word (44 percent, $n = 27$) and gesture = word (54 percent, $n = 32$). All of the sign-word and approximately half of the gesture-word combinations conveyed equivalent information (for example, WORK = "work"; PINOCCHIO = "pinocchio"; NO = "no"). This finding suggests that Marco's sign-word combinations convey redundant information and thus are not similar to word-word combinations.

Why might Marco make such great use of equivalent sign = word combinations? We suspect that it is in part a reflection of the nature of the input to which he was exposed (see also van den Bogaerde and

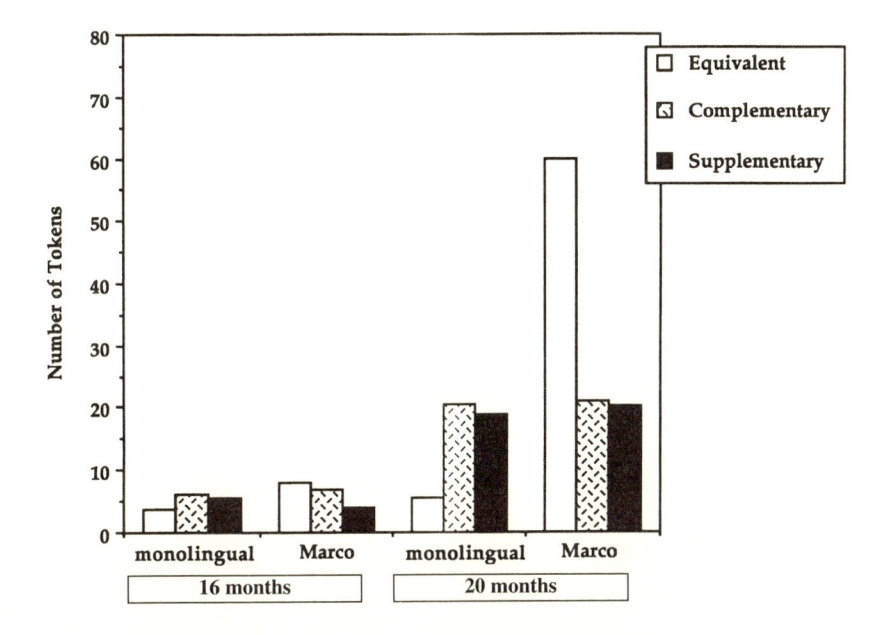

Figure 11.3 Number of equivalent, complementary, and supplementary combinations produced by 12 monolingual children and by Marco

Mills 2000). Although Marco's mother used both LIS and spoken Italian when communicating with her son, she often used signs and words simultaneously, a tendency that increased as Marco grew older. Thus, Marco's extensive use of informationally redundant sign-word combinations may be the product of extensive experience with simultaneous communication in everyday interactions.

Taken together, these findings suggest that exposure to sign language does not affect the informational content of early two-element combinations. There is, in other words, no evidence of an advantage in the production of supplementary combinations.

The Role of Input

Data on the role of input come from a study designed to provide infomation on maternal use of gesture during mother-toddler interactions and to assess whether maternal use of gestures changes as children's speech becomes progressively more complex. Our twelve upper-middle-class Italian mother-child dyads were videotaped in their homes for 45 minutes when children were 16 and 20 months of age. The children were the participants in the previous study (described in the preceding section).

The gestures produced by the mothers were classified as deictic (for example SHOWING and POINTING), representational (for example, SPIN, CIAO), or emphatic (for example, moving the head from side to side in time with accompanying speech). The distributions of maternal gesture types at both observations are presented in figure 11.4.

As is evident in the figure, the majority of gestures produced by mothers at both observations were deictic (most commonly POINTING), or representational while emphatic gestures were much less common. These distributions are different from those that have been reported for mother-adult conversations (Bekken 1989), in which deictic and metaphoric (included in our emphatic category) gestures were produced with roughly equal frequency (32 percent and 28 percent of total gestures respectively). Comparison of maternal gesture patterns at

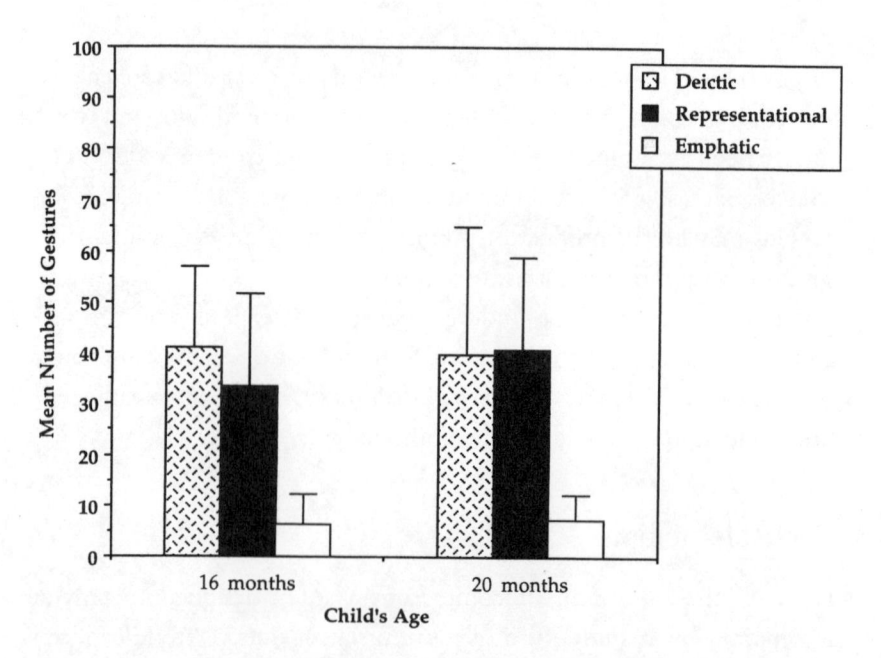

Figure 11.4. Mean number of deictic, representational, and emphatic gestures produced by mothers at the two observations

16 months with those at 20 months revealed no significant differences in the production of any of the three gesture types over time. The finding that emphatic gestures were produced so infrequently in this sample is especially interesting given the large repertoire and extensive use of such gestures in Italian culture (Kendon 1995; Magno Caldognetto and Poggi 1995).

All utterances containing both speech and gesture were categorized as *reinforce* (for example, YES + "Yes, I know that Mommy is ugly."), *disambiguate* (for example, POINT to floor + "Put it over there."), or *add* (for example, POINT to toy telephone + "pretty") according to the informational role played by gesture with respect to speech). At both observations a majority of maternal gestures served to reinforce the message conveyed in speech (53.25 at 16 months and 56.67 at 20 months). Utterances in which gesture disambiguated the verbal message were somewhat less frequent (respectively 16.5 and 19.0 at 16 and 20 months), while utterances in which gesture added information to that conveyed in speech were relatively uncommon (4.17 at 16 months and 3.0 at 20 months). No significant statistical differences were found in the number of utterances in each of the three categories across observations.

While we did not specifically observe the mothers in our study in interaction with another adult, it must be noted that the rate of maternal gesture production in our Italian mother-child interactions (15 percent of all utterances) was much lower than that previously obtained for American mothers interacting with other adults (24 percent of all utterances; Bekken 1989). This suggests that Italian mothers are also gesturing less with their children than they would with another adult. This is particularly striking in the light of the fact that at both observations, the proportion of maternal utterances containing gesture was much lower than that for children. The relatively low rate of maternal gesture was not, in other words, a simple reflection of low gesture rates in the children with whom they were speaking.

In summary, analyses of maternal gesture production reveal that when mothers gestured, their gestures tended to co-occur with speech, consisted primarily of deictic gestures that served to indicate referents in the immediate context, and were redundant with information conveyed in speech. Mothers' gestures, in other words, rarely provided information that was not already present in the verbal message. This is in marked contrast to what is typically reported for adult-adult interactions, in which gesture generally complements or supplements information conveyed in speech (McNeill 1992, 2000).

Because young children seem still uncertain between the two systems, gestural and vocal, mothers may shift the burden of communication to speech and use gestures primarily to highlight and reinforce aspects of their verbal message. In effect, mothers appear to be using a kind of "gestural motherese" characterized by fewer and more concrete gestures redundant with and reinforcing the message conveyed in speech. Not only are mothers' gestures tightly linked to the immediate linguistic and extralinguistic context, but they appear to be used with the goal of underscoring, highlighting, and attracting attention to particular words and/or objects. Gestures that cannot be used for this purpose—such as the emphatic gestures widely used by Italian adults when speaking to other adults—are virtually eliminated from the communicative repertoire when mothers speak to their children.

Discussion

The observation of a proportionate decline in the production of gesture relative to speech at 20 months is consistent with the notion that gesture fails to develop into a full-fledged linguistic system in hearing children exposed only to speech. This decline, however, cannot be interpreted as the beginning of the demise of gesture because the overall token level of gesture production actually increased at this age. We would like to suggest that the change in gestural production between 16 and 20 months was not due to a decline in the absolute level of gesture production, but rather to a change in the way gesture was used. Some evidence for this hypothesis is provided by the finding that the increase in gesture production was qualitatively different than that observed for word tokens. Neither acquisition of new gestural lexical items nor enhanced use of representational gestures was responsible for the rise in production of gesture tokens. Rather, the observed increase was primarily the result of substantial growth in the use of pointing. In fact, pointing was the deictic gesture used most often at both 16 and

20 months, a result that supports suggestions that pointing, which helps establish situations of joint attention, plays a special role in the course of initial lexical acquisition (Bruner 1975; Lock et al. [1990] 1994) and also in later stages of linguistic development such as the period of transition to two-word speech.

Taking into account the data reported here, we now address specifically the three questions raised at the beginning of the chapter.

1. When children move to two-word speech, is the use of gesture and gesture-speech combinations a robust developmental phenomenon, exhibiting similar features across different children and cultures, or are there significant individual differences?

    With respect to cultural differences in early gesture production and potential effects on the use of gesture at the onset of two-word speech, our results are consistent with previous findings from smaller samples of Italian and American children. We found that first utterances are mainly crossmodal: a string formed by a gestural pointing and a spoken symbol, not yet a string of symbols. In particular: (a) unimodal combinations of gestures constituted a very small proportion of the two-element utterances produced and, in particular, there were no combinations of two representational gestures; (b) the most frequent type of two-element combinations were crossmodal utterances of deictic gestures and representational words, which continued to play an important role at the onset of two-word utterances. Taken together, these findings suggest that the use of gesture in the transition to two-word speech, specifically in the context of crossmodal gesture-word combinations, is a robust feature of communicative development, even across potentially significant individual and cultural differences.

    In line with previous studies, we found that at 16 months when two-word utterances were essentially absent from the children's repertoires, crossmodal two-element combinations were already very frequent and included supplementary utterances referring to two distinct elements. In other words, children demonstrated the cognitive capacity to combine two ideas (using a single word and a single gesture) at this young age, even though they did not yet produce utterances of two spoken items.

This question can be further clarified by examining data on combination production in the bilingual signing/speaking child. If the constraint is specific to the vocal modality, then we should find that combinations produced entirely within the manual modality (that is, gesture + gesture, gesture + sign, sign + sign) emerge before other combination types that contain words (that is, gesture + word, sign + word) in the bilingual child. Alternatively, if the difficulty with two-word combinations lies in the general problem of within-modality coordination of two elements, then we might expect to see gesture + word and sign + word combinations precede the emergence of other combination types.

Our findings suggest that the constraint on production of two-word combinations cannot be explained by the greater degree of difficulty of vocal relative to manual production because combinations consisting of two elements within the manual modality did not appear before other combination types. Instead, the appearance of crossmodal combinations prior to combinations of two linguistic symbols (that is, word + word and sign + sign) suggests that the difficulty lies in the production of two symbolic linguistic elements in the same modality.

2. Is the information content of children's crossmodal, gesture-word utterances (which are apparently used at both the one-word and the two-word stage) comparable to that conveyed by two-word utterances?

The development of gestural and gesture-word combinations was clearly related to word-word combinations. Children's supplementary combinations expressed a variety of basic semantic relations; in particular, the relations expressed via crossmodal supplementary combinations were highly similar to those that have been widely described in the English literature for children at the early two-word stage (Brown 1973; Maratsos 1983). The relations expressed included those of

Notice: (HI + *mamma*/"mommy"), (*ciao* + *mamma*, "hi + mommy");

Recurrence: (REQUEST + *altra*/"other"), (*ancora* + *altro*, "more + other");

Nonexistence: (ALL-GONE + *pappa*/"baby food"); (*no* + *acqua*, "no/all-gone water");

Agent-Action: (POINT [to oven] + *scotta*/"burns"), (*mette* + *mamma*, "mommy + puts");

Action-Object: (POINT [to toy to be taken away] + *toglie*/"takes_ away"), (*lo* + *toglie*, "takes it away");

Action or Entity and Location: (POINT [to toy] + *giú*/"down"), (*vai* + *dentro*, "go inside");

Possession: (POINT [to daddy's cup] + *pap^*/ "daddy"), (*mamma* + *penna*, "mommy's + pen");

Attribute and Entity (POINT [to balloon] + *grande*/"big") (*questo* + *grande*, "this + big").

Two-element combinations that incorporate a gestural component may thus allow young children to overcome the limits of their linguistic resources. In particular, our results suggest that these gesture-word combinations serve three different functions for young children as they attempt to communicate. First, the redundancy provided by representational gestures in equivalent combinations may function to reinforce the child's intended message and seems to help the child who is both vocally uncertain and still moderately unintelligible to ensure that her message is understood. Second, the gestural indication contained in complementary utterances provides disambiguating information that helps to locate and identify the single referent in the child's utterances. Third, in supplementary utterances, the gesture and the word refer to two distinct elements and, as a result, the child's intended message is extended.

3. What is the role of linguistic input in the structuring and information conveyed by two-element combinations?

Although exposure to an enhanced gestural input did not appear to influence the overall pattern of gesture-word combination, some of our data suggest that a rich gestural culture may have an effect on the number of representational gestures that children use, for example in the case of the hearing child exposed to Sign Language. In addition, we observed that the repertoire of representational gestures produced by our Italian sample appeared to be larger than that reported for American children by Goldin-Meadow and Morford (1985, [1990] 1994). In contrast, the types and number of deictic gestures produced appeared to be relatively similar across the two groups.

We noted that although our hearing participants were not exposed to a formal gestural linguistic input (that is to a sign language), they produced a considerable number of single-gesture utterances and used deictic gestures productively in crossmodal combinations with words at both 16 and 20 months. This result supports the view that the general ability to produce single representational signals in communication and the capacity to combine communicative elements are not directly determined by exposure to a modality-specific linguistic input (Caselli and Volterra [1990] 1994; Volterra and Iverson 1995). When the combinatorial and the representational capacities were used simultaneously, however, the effects of exposure to a vocal linguistic system became apparent: representational elements were combined in the spoken modality, but never in the gestural modality. The early verbal/gestural communicative system of the hearing child exposed to a single spoken language does not develop into two distinct languages. When this system begins to evolve in a differentiated manner, verbal communication is elaborated into a linguistic system, but gesture never acquires some of the properties that are characteristic of language.

As the verbal system begins to emerge as the primary mode of linguistic communication, gesture shifts from a position of relative communicative equivalence with respect to speech to one of secondary support system integrated with speech. The finding that maternal gesture production does not mirror developmental changes in children's communication suggests at the very least that these radical changes in children's developing communicative systems are not simply a direct reflection of changes in maternal gestural input. Indeed, maternal gestural input seems remarkably insensitive to these changes.

Conclusion

The data we have presented and discussed support the views recently proposed by a number of investigators. Long before children learn to speak, they are able to communicate, meaningfully and intentionally, with their caretakers. In learning a language, children are acquiring a more effective and elaborate means of doing something that they can already do in a more primitive fashion.

Taken together, the findings discussed here highlight the remarkable similarities between production in the gestural and the vocal modalities during the first stages of language acquisition. They also raise an interesting issue with regard to the communicative and linguistic value of early words and gestures.

This body of work has shown that different types of gestures are used productively as independent items or in combinations with other gestures and/or words. Such gestural productions appear to exhibit symbolic and combinatorial properties similar to those attributed to children's early one- and two-word utterances.

The argument developed here is that there is continuity from preverbal to early verbal combinations. The transition is largely from cross-modal to unimodal utterances. As Lock (1997) has suggested,

> The combinatorial ability is a general one that has a developmental continuity and can be applied to combine content items that emerge from a different strand of development where the endpoint of the strand, through an incremental process of small changes, appears as a developmental discontinuity. The approach here is to look for principles of continuity at an abstract level. How these principles are realized in development is a separate issue. For example, suppose we think at a simplistic level about the issue of temporal organization in manual gesture versus speech. Two manual gestures can be produced

simultaneously, one by each hand. This provides opportunities for the way in which combinations might occur in this medium. By contrast, two words cannot be said at once, and this provides constraints on how meanings are expressed, in that words can only be combined sequentially. The organization of the delivery systems of meaning has, therefore, to be discontinuous between the two modalities. But at an abstract level, there can still be continuities between how "elementary particles" of meaning are combined, irrespective of the communicative modality being used. To get at these continuities requires looking at things in a new way.

Recently, some authors have begun to consider data on the development of gesture and speech and its implications for both the neural organization of language and language evolution. With regard to the neural organization of language, Iverson and Thelen (1999) have speculated that

> The speech-gesture-language system is a particularly transparent manifestation, we believe, not only of the sensorimotor origins of thought, but also of its continued embodiment throughout life.... For the systems involved in speech, gesture, and language to be so linked together, they must be represented in the brain in compatible means; that is, the representations of the mental aspects of language must be able to mesh seamlessly with those involved in the control of movements. We suggest that as these aspects are linked initially, when language emerges, so they remain coupled throughout life.

With respect to the question of whether human language evolved from manual gestures, an issue that has been of considerable interest in the past two centuries, Deacon (1997) has argued that

> Though children's language development likely does not recapitulate language evolution in most respects (because neither immature brains nor children's partial mapping of adult modern languages are comparable to mature brains and adult languages of any ancestor), we can nevertheless observe a progressive assimilation of nonverbal supports

to more flexible and efficient vocal forms as their language abilities develop. These facts suggest that gesture comprised a significant part of early symbolic communication, but that it existed side by side with vocal communication for most of the last 2 million years. Rather than substitutes for one another, gesture and speech have co-evolved complex interrelationships throughout their long and changing partnership. (Deacon 1997, 354–55)

We conclude this chapter as we began it with a quotation taken from Stokoe's recent writings, a quotation that we believe is consistent with the premises underlying our work. "Not only is a human brain necessary for language, but also human society and culture are necessary for language to have evolved, to be acquired and to operate. The social and the biological aspects of language together make it unique to have evolved."

References

Abrahamsen, Adele. 2000. Explorations of enhanced gestural input to children in the bimodal period. In *The signs of language revisited: An anthology to honor Ursula Bellugi and Edward Klima*, edited by Harlan Lane and Karen Emmorey, 357–99. Mahwah, N.J.: Lawrence Erlbaum Associates.

Armstrong, David F., William C. Stokoe, and Sherman E. Wilcox. 1995. *Gesture and the nature of language.* Cambridge: Cambridge University Press.

Bates, Elizabeth, Laura Benigni, Inge Bretherton, Luigia Camaioni, and Virginia Volterra. 1979. *The emergence of symbols: Cognition and communication in infancy.* New York: Academic Press.

Bates, Elizabeth, Luigia Camaioni, and Virginia Volterra. 1975. The acquisition of performatives prior to speech. *Merrill-Palmer Quarterly* 21: 205–26.

Bekken, Kaaren. 1989. Is there motherese in gesture? Ph.D. diss., University of Chicago.

Bruner, Jerome S. 1975. The ontogenesis of speech acts. *Journal of Child Language* 2: 1–19.

Butcher, Cynthia, and Susan Goldin-Meadow. 1993. From one word to two: Exploring the changing role of gesture. Paper presented at the Biennial

Meeting for the Society for Research in Child Development, New Orleans, La.

Camaioni, Luigia, M. Cristina Caselli, Emiddia Longobardi, and Virginia Volterra. 1991. A parent report instrument for early language assessment. *First Language* 11: 345–59.

Capirci, Olga, Jana M. Iverson, Elena Pizzuto, and Virginia Volterra. 1996. Gestures and words during the transition to two-word speech. *Journal of Child Language* 23: 645–73.

Capirci, Olga, Jana M. Iverson, Elena Pizzuto, and Virginia Volterra. Forthcoming. Gestures, sign, and words in early language development: The role of linguistic input. *Bilingualism and Cognition*.

Caselli, M. Cristina. 1983. Communication to language: Deaf children's and hearing children's development compared. *Sign Language Studies* 39: 113–44.

———. [1990] 1994. Communicative gestures and first words. In *From gesture to language in hearing and deaf children*, edited by Virginia Volterra and Carol J. Erting, 56–57. Reprint, Washington, D.C.: Gallaudet University Press.

Caselli, M. Cristina, and Virginia Volterra. [1990] 1994. From communication to language in hearing and deaf children. In *From gesture to language in hearing and deaf children*, edited by Virginia Volterra and Carol J. Erting, 263–77. Reprint, Washington, D.C.: Gallaudet University Press.

Deacon, Terence W. 1997. *The symbolic species. The coevolution of language and the human brain*. New York: W. W. Norton.

Folven, Raymond, and John D. Bonvillian. 1991. The transition from non-referential to referential language in children acquiring American Sign Language. *Developmental Psychology* 27: 806–16.

Goldin-Meadow, Susan, and Marolyn Morford. 1985. Gesture in early child language: Studies of deaf and hearing children. *Merrill-Palmer Quarterly* 31: 145–76.

———. [1990] 1994. Gesture in early child language. In *From gesture to language in hearing and deaf children*, edited by Virginia Volterra and Carol J. Erting, 249–62. Reprint, Washington, D.C.: Gallaudet University Press.

Goodwyn, Susan, and Linda Acredolo. 1993. Symbolic gesture versus word: Is there a modality advantage for the onset of symbol use? *Child Development* 64: 688–701.

Iverson, Jana M., Olga Capirci, and M. Cristina Caselli. 1994. From communication to language in two modalities. *Cognitive Development* 9: 23–43.

Iverson, Jana M., Olga Capirci, Emiddia Longobardi, and M. Cristina Caselli. 1999. Gesturing in mother-child interaction. *Cognitive Development* 14: 57–75.

Iverson, Jana M., and Esther Thelen. 1999. Hand, mouth, and brain: The dynamic emergence of speech and gesture. *Journal of Consciousness Studies* 6: 19–40.

Kendon, Adam. 1995. Implications of recent research on gesture and sign languages for the gesture theory of language origins. In *In search of language origins: Selected papers from the seventh meeting of the Language Origins Society* [web page], edited by Edward Callary. Available: http://baserv.uci.kun.nl/~los/Meetings/Dekalb

Lock, Andrew. 1980. *The guided reinvention of language.* New York: Academic Press.

———. 1997. The role of gesture in the establishment of symbolic abilities: Continuities and discontinuities in early language development. *Evolution of Communication* 1 (2): 159–93.

Lock, Andrew, Andrew Young, Valerie Service, and Penelope Chandler. [1990] 1994. Some observations on the origin of the pointing gesture. In *From gesture to language in hearing and deaf children,* edited by Virginia Volterra and Carol J. Erting. Reprint, Washington, D.C.: Gallaudet University Press.

Magno Caldognetto, Emanuela, and Isabella Poggi. 1995. Conoscenza e uso di gesti simbolici: Differenze di sesso e di età. *Atti del Convegno Internazionale di Studi "Dialettologia al Femminile,"* 399–412. Padova, Italy: CLEUP.

Masur, Elise Frank. [1990] 1994. Gestural development, dual-directional signaling, and the transition to words. In *From gesture to language in hearing and deaf children,* edited by Virginia Volterra and Carol J. Erting, 18–30. Reprint, Washington, D.C.: Gallaudet University Press.

McNeill, David. 2000. *Language and gesture.* Cambridge and New York: Cambridge University Press.

———. 1992. *Hand and mind: What gesture reveals about thought.* Chicago: University of Chicago Press.

Morford, Marolyn, and Susan Goldin-Meadow. 1992. Comprehension and production of gesture in combination with speech in one-word speakers. *Journal of Child Language* 19: 559–80.

Nicolich, Lorraine. 1977. Beyond sensorimotor intelligence: Assessment of symbolic maturity through analysis of pretend play. *Merrill-Palmer Quarterly* 23: 89–99.

Piaget, Jean. 1945. *La formation du symbole chez l'enfant: Imitation, jeu et rêve, image et representation.* Paris: Delachaux et Niestlé.

Shore, Cecilia, Elizabeth Bates, Inge Bretherton, Marjorie Beeghly, and Barbara O'Connell. [1990] 1994. Vocal and gestural symbols: Similarities and differences from 13 to 28 months. In *From gesture to language in hearing and deaf children,* edited by Virginia Volterra and Carol J. Erting, 79–91. Reprint, Washington, D.C.: Gallaudet University Press.

Stokoe, William C. 1999. Il linguaggio umano: prospettiva evoluzionistica della lingua dei segni. In *Il cervello di Homo Sapiens, parte prima del volume terzo Sistemi Intelligenti,* edited by Emilio Bizzi, Pietro Calissano, and Virginia Volterra. Rome: Istituto della Enciclopedia Italiana.

Van den Bogaerde, Beppie and Anne Mills. 2000. *Input and interaction in deaf families.* Utrecht, The Netherlands: LOT.

Volterra, Virginia, Luigia Camaioni, Laura Benigni, and Elizabeth Bates. 1981. Le prime parole. *Giornale Italiano di Psicologia* 8: 243–63.

Volterra, Virginia, M. Cristina Caselli, Emiddia Longobardi, and Luigia Camaioni. 1993. Sviluppo gestuale e vocale nei primi due anni di vita. *Psicologia Italiana* 4: 62–67.

Volterra, Virginia, and Carol Erting, eds. [1990] 1994. *From gesture to language in hearing and deaf children.* Reprint, Washington, D.C.: Gallaudet University Press.

Volterra, Virginia, and Jana M. Iverson. 1995. When do modality factors affect the course of language acquisition? In *Language, gesture and space,* edited by Karen Emmorey and Judy S. Reilly, 371–90. Hillsdale, N.J.: Lawrence Erlbaum Associates.

Werner, Heinz, and Bernard Kaplan. 1963. *Symbol formation.* New York: John Wiley and Sons.

CONCLUDING THOUGHTS

The Future of American Sign Language

Carol A. Padden and Jennifer Rayman

In an earlier paper (Padden 1990), American Sign Language (ASL) was described as a kind of "collective memory" in which generations of deaf people "remember" the language through using it and passing it down to succeeding generations. This memory was sustained despite the fact that until very recently, there were no recognized grammars of ASL, and there were very few institutions for preserving and maintaining the language. The paper focused on changes of the last thirty-five years in which, as we all know, there was a surge of scientific and popular interest in sign languages, particularly in the United States. We now have grammars of ASL, and institutions dedicated to sign language study and preservation. As the paper described the impact of these changes on the American Deaf community, it stopped short of asking questions about what lies ahead for the future of the community and their language. How will this community continue to "remember" its language into the future?

It seems questions about the future of ASL and its community are very much on people's minds. When we lecture about sign language, we find this topic finds it way in questions and comments from our audiences: Will sign language survive the ambitions of technology and genetic engineering? While on the one hand the popular media is full of news of advances and achievements of medicine and biotechnology, there has also been a resurgence of cultural pride in Deaf communities around the world. Classes in ASL are remarkably popular in colleges and universities in the U.S., and sign language is featured in some of the most popular programs on American television. Even as we try to talk about the vibrancy of the deaf community today, the future is thrust in our faces as a warning. It is not hard to feel a sense of foreboding, as George Veditz must have when he gave his 1913 lecture exhorting the preservation of "the sign language." He warned of "'pharaohs who knew not Joseph' taking over the land and our American schools" (Veditz 1913). Then, a growing fascination with oral education in Europe was spreading to the United States, threatening to betray a tacit agreement between deaf people and their educators to allow the use of sign language in education. Now nearly a century later, schools for the deaf openly advertise ASL as the language of instruction, but their enrollments are far smaller than they used to be. A massive shift away from institutions and toward mainstreaming in public schools has removed much of the population that used to attend these schools. The role of deaf schools in the maintenance of ASL has always been regarded as important, but how can the language be maintained when deaf children are dispersed across numerous small public schools? At a time when awareness of the language is high, indeed the total number of people learning ASL (hearing and deaf) is greater than it has ever been in its history, the paradox is that the threat of language death is still there. In circumstances like these, how do we imagine the future of ASL?

Some of the most profound changes of the last thirty-five years can be traced to a shift in ideas about human languages in general, and sign languages in particular (Padden 1990). Where the idea of a sign language in the nineteenth century meant a language unlike any other (Baynton 1996), by the middle of the twentieth century, ASL joined the family of "natural languages," including spoken languages, allowing it to claim a status of equality. The twin concepts of "natural language" and then "human culture" in the scientific community filtered into a popular vocabulary that deaf people began to use for themselves (Humphries 1996). Using a rhetoric of inclusion into the family of languages and human cultures, there came also a rhetoric of civil rights that led to legislation to include equal access to employment, public utilities, and facilities. More recently, legislation has been passed to expand this access to include private and corporate facilities such as in hotels and small businesses. Aside from the expansion of rights, what is important about these acts of legislation is that they changed public spaces for deaf people.

Furthermore, along with these changes—indeed, as a result of them—there was a significant shift in deaf people's work lives. Deaf people began to be employed in places they had never been before, and they began to circulate in spaces they had never before visited. As they traveled in new spaces, they began to imagine different modes of interaction among themselves and with hearing people (Padden 1990). They began to take on new kinds of jobs, quite different from the "solitary" trades that characterized jobs for deaf people in the early part of the century. An example of this shift is illustrated in the work life of Don Padden (Padden's father). Shortly after he graduated from Gallaudet College in 1945, he was hired to join the faculty. But because his income was small, he supplemented his pay with a job as a printer at the *Washington Post* on weekends. He worked with a group of deaf men, all printers by trade. About 1965, he stopped, and his union card lapsed. At this time there was a shift toward professionalization in deaf education, when teaching became a class-conscious profession and teachers began to separate themselves from workers from other types of similarly paid jobs, such as printing. One important result of this shift was a growing divide in the deaf community, separating an emerging professional middle class from the working class of printers, bakers, shoe repairers, carpenters, and other kinds of labor that many deaf men and women continued to do at that time. The effect was to change how deaf people met together and on what terms (Padden 1990).

At almost exactly the same time as the growth of the deaf middle class came the dismantling of some of the traditional institutions of the American Deaf community. The massive shift toward public schooling of deaf children throughout the 1970s moved deaf children away from schools for the deaf to local school districts (Schildroth 1988). In the early 1970s, one of the largest schools in the country, Indiana School for the Deaf, had nearly 750 students; today it has 321. Utah School for the Deaf has about 40 students, as more students are enrolled in their local schools throughout the state. Despite campaigning by the deaf community, Nebraska School for the Deaf finally closed its doors in 1998 when enrollment dwindled to 28 students. Many of these schools were built in the period between 1850 and 1900, when institutions were ideally large, pastoral, and paternal. Often these schools were located in the center of the state, however isolated that place might be, reflecting the belief that resources were best located centrally so that travel was equidistant from its furthest corners. Today some of these locations are too distant by modern standards from urban centers where many deaf children live. Economics affected other schools; the Pennsylvania School for the Deaf's rolling estate was sold in 1975 to a small private college when the school could no longer afford to maintain its extensive lawns and its massively large buildings. To this day, alumni of the school continue to hold out hope that the campus can be bought back, but it is hard to imagine how to amass the large enrollments that the school once had.

The falling out of favor of such institutions led to dismantling the neatly separate physical boundaries that these schools helped to maintain. The Maryland School for the Deaf, located in what was once rural Frederick, had the stately look of many schools for the deaf—a large brick building supported by enormous colonial style pillars and a sharp-edged iron fence around the perimeter of the campus. The school was physically separate from the neighborhood, set aside by the enormity of the buildings, and the large sign at its entrance proclaimed it as an institution for the deaf. Residents of Frederick did not walk onto the campus, instead they walked carefully around it and next to it. The students left the confines of the school only under strict supervision. Now those boundaries have faded; the iron fence is only decorative. The school remains to this day pleasantly separate, as any school might be, but it is not forbidden territory. In fact, many of these schools have been rebuilt and redesigned to look more like public schools and less like asylums. The buildings are built closer to the ground and more sprawling, more decentralized than the older majestic buildings.

The spaces of these schools show that as physical boundaries changed and became more permeable, symbolic boundaries rose to prominence in a new way. Instead of iron fences, semantic boundaries of naming and categorization separated those who knew about the culture from those who did not. Some of these names were harsh, and just as barbed and pointed as the old fences. The language of the community makes fine distinctions between qualities of knowing the culture, whether one learned the language from deaf parents, or learned it later in life, whether one used more English in signing than other stylistic forms. Some deaf schools, too, began to describe themselves differently, not as "residential schools," harking to an era of forced isolation, but as bilingual schools, where the distinction between them and other schools is their teaching philosophy and commitment to ASL as a language of education.

The geography of deaf education has changed from sending children off to remote institutions to sending them to their neighborhood schools, in effect fractionating the ways they can meet each other. Deaf communities that developed around deaf schools will no longer have the school to anchor them if the school has closed. Deaf clubs built in those communities in the shadow of deaf schools have become curiosities and anachronisms, populated mainly by the old and nostalgic. More and more "places" of the community are borrowed spaces. Instead of meeting at deaf clubs owned by members of an association, we rent hotel space and host conferences about Deaf Studies and ASL teaching, but the spaces are not ours, they are rented for the weekend. Instead of being schooled in institutions for the deaf, many of us are educated in public schools, sometimes in portable classrooms next to the asphalt playground, again borrowing space from school districts. In Fremont, California, a group of deaf senior citizens has successfully petitioned the City of Fremont to award them city space next to the deaf school for the purpose of building a retirement home. Is this a last gasp of holding onto an experience that harkens to an earlier time, of spending one's last years in visible sight of a deaf school? Will the next generation of deaf people care as deeply about where they want to live?

The landscape has been altered, and we need to look upon it differently. The question is how? Cultural events in contemporary deaf communities have taken on a new prominence, as events formerly exclusively within the community are moved to public places to become visible to others. San Diego, California, is an example of a contemporary Deaf community held together more by events than by institutions. The reason in part is because San Diego has never had a residential school; its deaf children until 1953 were sent to Berkeley to attend the California School for the Deaf. When a second school in Riverside was built by the state, deaf students from the southern part of the state transferred there. In recent years, there has been yet another shift. Now fewer children travel from San Diego to Riverside, instead they remain in the county, placed in the programs that local school districts run for them. After public mainstreamed schools, there are community colleges as well as universities. Both San Diego State University and the University of California, San Diego, have programs for training teachers of the deaf. San Diego State University has a graduate program for training rehabilitation counselors of the deaf. Several community colleges offer ASL classes as well as interpreter training programs. The social services center, Deaf Community Services of San Diego, has a bookstore, provides interpreters and vocational counseling as well as several other programs. San Diego is also home to one of the leading Deaf publishing companies, DawnSign Press, as well as a long-standing sign language research program at the Salk Institute for Biological Studies. These "sites" are not primarily social spaces but rather educational or service spaces, yet the events they offer, ranging from classes with other deaf students to poetry readings, research colloquia, and other sign language events provide a context for signers to meet.

The availability and frequency of deaf cultural events remain somewhat sparse. There are weekly religious meetings such as those of The Deaf Christian Fellowship of the Southern Baptist Convention and the Deaf congregation of the Jehovah's Witnesses. Aside from religious worship, the only weekly gatherings available are a deaf bowling league popular among older members of the community and for younger deaf men and women, a Friday night coffeehouse event at Cafe Crema in Pacific Beach. At the latter, both hearing signers and deaf people gather to socialize. With no real institutional support to sustain gatherings, these kinds of coffeehouse gatherings exist unstably, sometimes disintegrating with the invasion of curious hearing people eager to meet deaf people and practice their sign language. Perhaps the only reason that Cafe Crema has lasted a few years is that one of its purposes from the beginning was to allow deaf and hearing signers to interact. It is public knowledge that this is not a Deaf-only event but this does not prevent irritations from arising when beginning signers ask deaf people to help them fulfill a homework assignment for their ASL or interpreting class. The forum of the coffeehouse allows for the building of relationships within the community, as a venue for the symbolic work that takes place in conversations about deaf culture and identity as well as personal anecdotes that position the boundaries between deaf and hearing people. Other regular events include a monthly Deaf pizza night and open-captioned movies along with some events sponsored by the local chapter of the Southern California Recreational Association of the Deaf.

In areas like San Diego, culture circulates in more elusive ways through quasi-institutions and events in the discourses of the community. Nostalgically, we look to a once vibrant past when neatly bounded places such as the deaf clubs were sites for playing cards, telling stories and sharing jokes, even meeting future spouses. Hearing people rarely ventured inside these spaces except for those born or married into the culture. As the places for regular gatherings and cultural performances have become fewer and fewer, concerns about the maintenance and circulation of cultural forms that bond people together in communities of shared identities become greater. Physical boundaries that once created a cohesive sense of place in the community have been replaced with less obvious boundaries. The security once found in places that belonged to us is no longer to be found.

This leads to the question of whether fluid communities like San Diego's can sustain a sign language. Can fluid communities bear the burden of what Veditz beseeched the community to do in 1913, to find ways to "to keep and pass on [the language] to coming generations?" San Diego's community exists in the shadow of other more durable and institutionalized communities like Los Angeles, Washington, D.C., New York, San Francisco, and Chicago. For much of American Sign Language's remarkably long history—spanning nearly 200 years—

there was a steady growth in the number of deaf schools, which led to the establishment of deaf clubs and deaf associations in nearly every state. The result has been a strong national presence in maintaining a sign language with little regional variation for a long period of time. But these institutions are fading; some are being reinvented, others are being closed outright. If deaf children don't live in residential schools, but live at home with their families and attend local public schools borrowed from others, is there still a sense of "there" anymore, as William Leach asks about the dispersal of space in modern American life (Leach 1999)? Will the new geography of education and social life, dispersed over a large and diffuse area, lead to a splintering of a national community and then eventually to the demise of the language? If the language continues to exist, will it survive only in regionalized form, as the strain to hold a national variety together starts to fall apart?

One way to imagine the future is to look at research on present-day sign languages of different ages. Wendy Sandler, Irit Meir, and Mark Aronoff have begun describing the sign languages of Israel. Even within a small country like Israel, there can be several sign languages, of different ages and of different origins. Israeli Sign Language, the national sign language, is between 40 and 50 years old, and can be traced to the German Sign Language used by deaf immigrants arriving in Israel from Berlin and other cities between 1935 and 1945. In recent years, immigrants from Russia, Morocco, Algeria, and Iraq have brought an influx of sign languages from those regions, adding to the vocabulary of Israeli Sign Language. Also interesting in this region of the world are sign languages of very recent origin, as in the case of the appearance of a deaf family in a Bedouin community. Traditional and of Muslim faith, Bedouins keep apart from the Israeli social system, thus creating conditions for the independent development of a home sign language. There are also a number of Arab and Druze villages where because of intermarriage, the incidence of deaf members in these villages is higher than it would be in a larger population. Over time, it appears that a local signing system has developed linking the deaf people in the villages. Religious ties have made possible development of a separate signing system, but over time proximity to the Israeli deaf community and access to Israeli schools has brought deaf Arabs and Druzes into contact with Israeli Sign Language.

When new sign languages were described by the anthropologists William Washabaugh (Washabaugh 1986; Washabaugh, Woodward, and DeSantis 1980) and Rolf Kuschel (Kuschel 1974), their examples were cases of sign language creation in geographically remote areas of the world, from Providence Island in the Caribbean to Rennell Island in the Pacific. In the case of Israel, the new languages are being created within a small space, demarcated by ethnic and religious boundaries, as Arab and Bedouin communities stay separate from the rest of Israel. Within the United States, Susan Goldin-Meadow and her colleagues have documented sign inventions by deaf children without access to ASL because their parents did not elect to send their children to schools where they would interact in a deaf community. A deaf child is born into a family of speakers, and in full view of parents and relatives, creates an independent sign language out of the gestural material of the world around the child. The parents for any number of reasons, do not know about a community of signers, or are shielded from this community, and the child continues to develop a sign language to communicate with siblings, friends, and parents (Goldin-Meadow 1993; Goldin-Meadow and Mylander 1983; Goldin-Meadow and Mylander 1984). The story of new sign languages, indeed about language communities and groups, shifts from sign languages on islands surrounded by oceans to sign languages separated only by area and a few miles.

The phenomenon of sign languages created within one generation, like Israeli Sign Language and home signs by American deaf children is age-old, as conditions of distance, either symbolic or geographic, of deaf people from each other make it possible for it to happen again and again through history. When we compare the structure of American Sign Language, which is at least 200 years old, with recent sign languages such as Israeli Sign Language, or very new sign languages such as those in small Bedouin and Arab communities, we can see both backwards and forwards as we project into the future how sign languages will change.

At least one lesson can be learned from this work on new sign languages: sign languages are easily amenable to invention. Even today, new sign languages are still being created, by ethnic groups separated by custom or by families separated by ideology in the case of hearing families who do not want their children to associate with signers. A single deaf child in a hearing family can contrive a workable system, which might become the raw material of a sign language or a deaf family in an Arab village can find other deaf members in a neighboring village and join signing resources. The iconicity and the visual nature of gestures may be both the basis of how sign languages are created and how they can survive over time. Gestural candidates for such concepts as "up" or "down," or body parts such as "eye" or "head" seem to produce iconically obvious sign candidates. Once incorporated in a grammar, iconically transparent signs rapidly become conventionalized and quickly lose their gestural or iconic rigidity. Clearly there is a great difference between sign languages that have survived many generations and those that are brand-new. But, it could be argued that iconicity is the saving feature of sign languages: It remains durable in all sign languages, overlaid by conventionalized and grammatical forms, even obscured by them, but it never entirely disappears (Taub 1997; Aronoff et al. forthcoming).

There is also another lesson from new sign languages. Sign languages can be invented many times over, but grammatical development and complexity seems to depend on the presence of an institutional core. When Nicaragua's newly stable government built a school for deaf children at Bluefields, the children who began to attend the school developed a sign language out of the individual home signs of the children (Horgan 1995; Osborne 1999). The continued presence of young children at the school over time created not only children whose own forms were more complex, but the language available for newer arrivals at the school was richer, contributing in turn to grammatically rich productions by children who came more recently to the school (Senghas 1995). The development of the new language was swift, attesting to the flexibility and the resources of the visual mode, and it recreated in modern times what must have been the start of sign languages like ASL, which likely had regional forms before the first permanent school was founded in Hartford, Connecticut, in 1817. The disappearance of the sign language on Martha's Vineyard, which co-existed with the Hartford and New England varieties, is most likely due to migration as the language accompanied the deaf residents who left the island for the New England mainland (Groce 1985; Lane 1999). The new school at Bluefields not only brought a community of children and adults together, it created social and cultural conditions for sustaining development of a grammar.

In the modern age, technologies of communication and transportation have yielded a fluid geography of communities and identities. In this environment, where people who share linguistic and ethnic backgrounds are dispersed throughout urban areas, a sense of community and identity becomes fragile. Indeed, the very concept of a shared culture rooted in a physical place may begin to break down. Telecommunications and other technologies of travel and communication have enabled communities to stretch farther over time and space; in effect, communities are no longer defined by the unity of space. One can hop on a plane and travel from Los Angeles to Washington, D.C., in a matter of hours or send an email message half way across the globe in seconds. Vast distances that once required lengthy time to communicate across have been shortened and time and space compressed. Postmodern anxieties about time-space compression have yielded concerns about the maintenance of community. If our sense of "place" is not derived from a physical space, how can our community be maintained? Will the future promises of an America, where more and more deaf people have access to text pagers allowing for real-time digital print conversations between remote parts of the world, weaken deaf communities tied to specific localities?

The observation that communities are not tied to particular geographical neighborhoods is not really new, nor is it directly tied to the penetration of all kinds of telecommunications devices into the daily buzz of different relationships. Communities are not necessarily isometric with places. Doreen Massey writes that "'places' have for centuries been more complex locations where numerous different, and frequently conflicting communities intersected" (Massey 1994). Religious, political, and ethnic communities have experienced this flux and dispersion long before the telephone and the Internet stretched relationships over time and space. These technologies have not necessarily brought with them a change in the fundamental practices of community but instead may have made more visible some of the cultural work that must go on to create identity and community. Community and identity are not static—they require continual re-creation. They are not necessarily natural inhabitants of a place unified in space. Pan-ethnic communities such as those of Native Americans and Latinos as well as the Deaf community are examples of such fluid communities that require extensive cultural work through explicit talk and performance to remain cohesive (Sommers 1991; Weibel-Orlando 1999). Though we may not have a visible neighborhood to provide a sense of stable ground for the maintenance of Deaf culture, our stories, and our discourse carry the burden of forming the symbolic structure of our way of life. Cultural events provide a chance for this kind of cultural work, constructing "places" out of the temporary and boundaries out of words.

The anxieties many of us have at present about holding communities together are valid. In increasingly complex and diverse societies, the fabric of community life appears to be fragile indeed. But, perhaps identities and communities have always been fragile. Their fragility has just been obscured by other stabilities of place and institution. When we look at how different communities, despite lack of geographical cohesion, have managed to maintain and create community, we can see the symbolic work of remembering, rebuilding, and recreating the culture through various practices.

It is through cultural performances of ceremony, ritual, and festival in display events that we meet together to self-consciously and unself-consciously reflect upon our identities and connections to the community. Within the symbolic work of such performance, social tensions can be played out and resolved temporarily. Symbols and emblems are woven in and out of the action of performances to stitch deeper meanings into the fabric of interconnectedness between peoples. Borders are hemmed in and seams mended, emotions pricked. Whether at the signed poetry performance, the coffeehouse discussion or the church service, deaf people and their hearing allies continually worry about the positioning of those symbolic boundaries and the survival of American Sign Language. The hope of their own survival into an uncertain future is symbolically and literally tied to the survival of American Sign Language. Just as Veditz and his compatriots worried about the survival of their language almost 100 years ago, in some way, our constant anxiety about the demise of sign language (and its culture) has served as the salvation from peril. This constant anxiety and expectation of the demise of the culture, moves us forward into a constant cycle of rebuilding and preparing for the rebuilding of the culture. Acting out this anxiety in positive ways provides us with the hope that we will not let go.

We close with a description of a photograph on the wall of the president's residence at Gallaudet University. It was taken most likely in the late 1880s or early 1890s, a panoramic wide shot of the main grounds of the campus, from the President's House to Faculty Row and includes the old Gymnasium and College Hall. A party of young men are standing, scattered around the lawn, nattily attired with walking canes and dark suits. As we look at their profiles and haughty arrangement across the lawn, we are struck by a sense of ownership that these men had of the land. The space of Gallaudet University is extraordinary indeed, 100 acres of land where deaf people have congregated since the founding of the university in 1864. Their confidence in place is palpable. But this stiffly proud collection of white men seems an anomaly, for now Gallaudet admits women and students of color. The old buildings in the photograph still exist, but interspersed among them are high-rise dormitories and modern brick structures. The pastoral campus of the waning years of the nineteenth century is gone as is segregation by race and gender. What we have to look forward to in the future is not that communities become fluid, but that as communities change and shift, they need to exist in the face of durable and stable places like Gallaudet. As communities become more fluid, the stability of places like this campus become even more significant.

As we face the challenges of maintaining cultural identity in the face of technological innovation, population diversity, and migration, we need to write a new description of the community that recognizes forces of regeneration and renewal and, at the same time, recognize the need for stability of place in different forms. As we continue to describe sign languages, especially those newly created and those existing for longer times, we will see that the human dimensions of language capacity and grammatical structure depend deeply on cultural institutions such as the school and the deaf associations, whose crucial role is to make possible durability and complexity.

References

Aronoff, Mark, Irit Meir, Carol Padden, and Wendy Sandler. Forthcoming. Classifier complexes and morphology in two sign languages. In Perspectives on Classifiers in Sign Language, editied by K. Emmorey. Mahwah, N.J.: Lawrence Erlbaum.

Baynton, Douglas C. 1996. *Forbidden signs: American culture and the campaign against sign language.* Chicago: University of Chicago Press.

Goldin-Meadow, Susan. 1993. When does gesture become language? A study of gesture used as a primary communication system by deaf children of hearing parents. In *Tools, language and cognition in human evolution,* edited by Kathleen R. Gibson and Tim Ingold, 63–85. Cambridge: Cambridge University Press.

Goldin-Meadow, Susan, and Carolyn Mylander. 1983. Gestural communication in deaf children: Noneffect of parental input on language development. *Science* 221(4608): 372–74.

———. 1984. Gestural communication in deaf children: The effects and noneffects of parental input on early language development. *Monographs of the Society for Research in Child Development* 49(3–4): 1–121.

Groce, Nora E. 1985. *Everyone here spoke sign language: Hereditary deafness on Martha's Vineyard.* Cambridge: Harvard University Press.

Horgan, John. 1995. A sign is born. *Scientific American* 273(December): 18.

Humphries, Tom. 1996. Of deaf-mutes, the strange, and the modern deaf self. In *Culturally affirmative psychotherapy with deaf persons,* edited by Neil S. Glickman and Michael A. Harvey. Mahwah, N.J.: Lawrence Erlbaum Associates.

Kuschel, Rolf. 1974. *A lexicon of signs from a Polynesian outlier island: A description of 217 signs as developed and used by Kagobai, the only deaf-mute of Rennell Island.* Copenhagen: Akademisk Forlag.

Lane, Harlan. 1999. The impact of sign language research on deaf communities. Paper presented at the National Conference in Celebration of the 80th Birthday of William C. Stokoe, Washington, D.C.

Leach, William. 1999. *Country of exiles: The destruction of place in American life.* New York: Pantheon Books.

Massey, Doreen B. 1994. A place called home? In *Space, Place and Gender,* edited by Doreen B. Massey, 157–73. Minneapolis: University of Minnesota Press.

Osborne, Laurence. 1999. A linguistic big bang: For the first time in history, scholars are witnessing the birth of a language—a complex sign system being created by deaf children in Nicaragua. *New York Times*, 24 October.

Padden, Carol A. 1990. Folk explanation in language survival. In *Collective remembering*, edited by David Middleton and Derek Edwards, 190–202. Thousand Oaks, Calif.: Sage Publications.

Schildroth, Arthur N. 1988. Recent changes in the educational placement of deaf students. *American Annals of the Deaf* 133:61–67.

Senghas, Ann. 1995. Children's contribution to the birth of Nicaraguan Sign Language. Ph.D. diss., Massachusetts Institute of Technology, Cambridge, Mass.

Sommers, Laurie Kay. 1991. Inventing Latinismo: The creation of Hispanic panethnicity in the United States. *Journal of American Folklore* 104(411): 32–53.

Taub, Sarah F. 1997. Language in the body: Iconicity and metaphor in American Sign Language. Ph.D. diss., University of California, Berkeley.

Veditz, George. 1913. *The preservation of the sign language.* Silver Spring, Md.: National Association of the Deaf. Film.

Washabaugh, William. 1986. *The acquisition of communicative skills by the Deaf of Providence Island.* Amsterdam: Mouton de Gruyter.

Washabaugh, William, James C. Woodward, and Susan DeSantis. 1980. *Providence Island Sign: A context-dependent language.* Washington, D.C.: Gallaudet University Press.

Weibel-Orlando, Joan. 1999. *Indian country, L.A.: Maintaining ethnic community in complex society.* Rev. ed. Urbana: University of Illinois Press.

INDEX

AAVE. *See* African American Vernacular English
Abrahamsen, Adele, 215
action (*see also* gestures/gestural communication); hands and, 123; syntactic structure of language and, 46–47; theories of language origins and, 35, 36–38
Action Sequencing test, 204
adjectives: directionality and, 76n9
African American Deaf community, 154–56. *See also* Black Deaf community
African American Vernacular English (AAVE), 138, 144, 154
age: language variation and, 156
agreement affixes, 71–72
agreement verbs, 73
Ahlgren, Inger, 177
alphabet: onomatopoeia and, 66–67
American Annals of the Deaf (journal), 2, 14, 28
American Anthropological Association, 43–44
American Indian sign language, 14, 15
American Sign Language (ASL): accepted as a natural language, 53, 58, 191, 248; ape language projects, 44–45, 107–9, 112–13; aphasic individuals and, 199; changes in deaf education and, 248; cherological structure, 58–59; as "collective memory," 247; compared to new sign languages, 254–57; future of, 247–59; iconicity and, 53, 60–68, 78; issues of survival in fluid communities, 253–54; Long's dictionary of, 30n5; misconceptions about at Gallaudet College, 57; modality effects and, 59; morphological studies, 59–60; negative perceptions of, 2; pointing and, 60, 68–77; simultaneous communication, 57n; William Stokoe's studies and contributions, xii, xiv–xvii, 3–6, 29, 45–46, 58–59; sublexical structure, xv; —, variation in: *Dictionary of American Sign Language* and, 138–44; forms of, 137–38; historical overview of research concerning, 144; impact of research on the Deaf community, 157; location signs, 150–57; sociolinguistic research on, 145–50
Amer-Ind signs, 199
Amistad rebels, 19
Anatomy and Philosophy of Expression, The (Bell), 24

263

angular gyrus, 111
animal communication/gestures: compared to human language and gestures, 28, 124–25; compared to sign languages, 26–27
anthropological linguistics, xiv–xv
ape language projects, 44–45, 107–9, 112–13
aphasic individuals: sign communication programs and, 192, 197–99
apraxia, 201, 202
Arabs, 254
Aramburo, Glenn B., 164
Arbib, Michael A., 111, 126
area F5, 111
Aristotle, 101
Armstrong, David, 4, 5, 70, 97, 108, 112
Aronoff, Mark, 254
ASL. *See* American Sign Language
Aspects of the Theory of Syntax (Chomsky), 144
athletics: skilled movements, 97
Australian aboriginal sign language, 15, 43
australopithecines, 91
Ayres, J. A., 18

Barringer Crater, 54–57
Barringer, D. M., 54, 55
Battison, Robbin, 144
BDAE. *See* Boston Diagnostic Aphasia Examination
Beattie, Geoffrey, 109
beauty: nineteenth-century notions of, 22–23
Bedouins, 254
Bell, Alexander Graham, 27–28
Bell, Sir Charles, 24

Bellugi, Ursula, 44–45, 46, 49n9, 59, 63–64
Bible: notions of facial expression, 24; notions of language origin, 24–25, 85
Bickerton, Derek, 105
bilingual children: modality combinations in two-element utterances, 225, 226–27; two-element utterances produced by, 232–33; types of utterances produced by, 223; word and gesture production in, 219–21
Bishop State Community College, 167
Blackburn, Deborah Webb, 199
Black Deaf community, 161–63 (*see also* African American Deaf community); impact of sign language research on, 163–69, 170
Black scholars, 166–67
Bluefields school, 256–57
Bolinger, Dwight, 61
Bonvillian, John D., 199, 203
Bornstein, Harry, 190
Boston Diagnostic Aphasia Examination (BDAE), 204
bow-wow theory, 85–86
brain: gestural theory of language origins and, 126; hand-brain co-evolution, 91–95; hand-brain relationships, 90–91; language organ concept and, 111–12; left-hemisphere injury, 110; speech-gesture-language system and, 242
Braun, Allen R., 111
Broadfield, Douglas C., 111
Broca's area, 111, 126
Bronowski, Jacob, 44, 45

Brown, Roger, 44
Bruner, Jerome S., 214

Cafe Crema, 252, 253
California: contemporary Deaf community in, 251–53
California School for the Deaf, 252
Camp, Henry B., 23–24
Cartesian worldview, 101
Cary, J. Addison, 21, 23
Casterline, Dorothy, 49n10, 138
Center for Sign Language and Sign-Supported Communication (Denmark), 173, 178, 186
Center for Total Communication (Denmark), 173
Ceylon, 15–16
chain of being, 101–2 (*see also* continuity of beings)
childhood autistic disorder: motor functioning in, 193, 200–1, 203, 206–7; motor impairments and sign learning in, 199–207; sign communication programs and, 191–92, 194–95, 207; signing hand preference, 202–3
chimpanzees: cultural transmission in, 107–8; evolutionary proximity to humans, 106; gestural communication in, 107–9; language projects, 44–45, 107–9, 112–13
Chomsky, Noam, xiv, xvii, 86, 87, 144; comparison of animal communication and human language, 124–25; on language acquisition, 44; language evolution and, 93–94, 102–4; language organ concept, 103–4
civil rights movement, xiii–xiv, 249
cochlear implants, 187

code switching, 178–79
Coelho, Carl A., 198
co-evolution: hand-brain, 91–95
cognitive grammar, 121–22
collaborative research: Black Deaf community and, 166
Communication through the Ages, 15
Condillac, Etienne Bonnot de (Abbé), xvi–xvii, 37, 86, 119
continuity of beings, 100–2, 103
Copenhagen School for the Deaf, 181
Coughlan, Jane, 109
Cours de linguistique generale (Saussure), 42
creationist narrative, 24–25
Croneberg, Carl, 49n10, 138–40, 141, 142, 157, 163
cross-fostering, 112–13
crossmodal utterances, 223–26, 237–39
"cultivated signs," 18–19
"cult of sincerity," 22–23
cultural performances: significance to the Deaf community, 251–53, 258–59
cultural transmission: in the Black Deaf community, 162–63; in chimpanzees, 107–8
Current Anthropology (journal), 44

Daniloff, Joanne K., 199
Danish language: bilingual teaching model for deaf education, 180–83; deaf bilingualism and, 184
Danish Sign Language: deaf bilingualism and, 175–76, 181–82; grammar book of, 174; research in, 173–75
Dar (chimpanzee), 108, 109

Darwin, Charles, 26, 27, 28, 85, 100, 101, 103, 110
Darwinism: evolution of language and, 85; views of gestures and facial expression, 28; views of sign languages, 25–27
David, Rand, 152
Dawkins, Richard, 105–6
DawnSign Press, 252
Deacon, Terence W., 242–43
deaf bilingualism: code switching, 178–79; the deaf experience and, 184–86; in Denmark, 172, 175–87; features of, 184; future challenges, 186–87; impact on deaf professionals, 186; language situation of deaf people, 175–80; teaching model for Danish, 180–83
deaf children: code switching, 178–79; in hearing families, 176–78; language acquisition, 125; language development and (*see* language development); language learning and, 179–80; social consequences of mainstreaming, 185–86
deaf clubs, 251
Deaf community: American Sign Language and, 247; changing geography of deaf education and, 248, 249–51; changing landscape of, 251–53; civil rights movement and, 249; demographic revolution in, 161; impact of modern technology on, 257; increasing fluidity of, 257–58; language variation research and, 144, 157; shift in work lives, 249; sociolinguistic variation and, 138–44; survival of sign language and, 253–54; symbolic recreation, 251–53
Deaf community Services of San Diego, 252
deaf education: bilingual model for Danish, 180–83; changing geography of, 248, 249–51; demographic trends of students, 161; International Congress on Education of the Deaf in Milan, 2; negative perceptions of, 1–2
deaf middle class, 249
Deaf President Now (DPN) movement, 6, 142
deaf professionals, 249; bilingualism and, 186
deaf schools: American Sign Language and, 156, 248; for Blacks, 162; decline in enrollments, 248, 250; impact of mainstreaming on, 248, 249–50; physical and symbolic barriers surrounding, 250–51
Deaf Studies programs, 167
deaf teachers: bilingualism and, 186; oralism and, 14; professionalization, 249
decontextualization: in language development, 214–15, 221–22
Degerando, Joseph-Marie, 38
deictic elements, 214, 217, 221; in maternal use of gestures, 234, 235–36; in two-element utterances, 225, 226, 227–32
"De l'Epée sign language," 28
DeMatteo, Asa, 63
Denmark: deaf bilingualism, 172, 175–87; sign language research in, 173–75; teachers of deaf children, 174
DeSantis, Susan, 144

Descartes, René, 101
Detmold, George, 142
dialects, 139, 140
Dictionary of American Sign Language (DASL), xv, 45; appendices on sociolinguistic variation, 138–44, 157; significance of, 141
Diderot, Denis, 37
directionality: of nouns and adjectives, 76n9; with numeral signs, 70–71, 72–73; with verbs, 71–72, 73, 75–77
discontinuity paradox, 93–94
Druzes, 254
Duffy, Robert J., 198
dyspraxia, 202, 203

Eco, Umberto, 127
education: emotions and, 20–21
Einstein, Albert, 127
Emerson, Carolyn, 167
emotional expression, 20–21, 29
Engberg-Pedersen, Elisabeth, 174
Erting, Carol J., 144, 157, 215
Essay on the Origin of Human Knowledge (Condillac), 37
essentialism, 101
ethology, 112–13
Evangelicalism, 20, 23
Expression of the Emotions in Man and Animals, The (Darwin), 28

facial expression, 24, 28
fallacy of the excluded middle, 101
fantasia, 35
feature-changing rules, 59
fine-motor functioning. *See* motor functioning
Fischer, Susan, 59
form board completion, 207

Fouts, Deborah H., 108
Fouts, Roger S., 108, 110
France: manual tradition and, 27
Fremont (CA), 251
Frishberg, Nancy, 62, 64, 65, 144
Fulwiler, Robert L., 110

Gallaudet College (*see also* Gallaudet University); diversity in communication modes at, xiii, 2; Linguistic Research Laboratory, xv; misconceptions about American Sign Language at, 57; William Stokoe at, xii, xiii, xv–xvi, 2–5, 57; vertical variation in American Sign Language and, 140
Gallaudet, Thomas H.: Amistad rebels and, 19; on education and emotion, 20; on facial expression, 24; on gestures and emotional expression, 21; "natural language of signs" concept, 17; on oratory, 21–22; romantic notion of sign languages, 24; sincerity of sign languages and, 22–23
Gallaudet University, 145, 259 (*see also* Gallaudet College); Deaf President Now movement, 6, 142; Kendall elementary school, 2; significance to the Deaf community, 5; Stokoe's legacy at, 5, 6
"Gallaudet University Communication Forum," 167
Gallaudet University Press, xvi, 6
Gallimore, Laurene, 167
Gannon, Patrick J., 111
"Gaps in the Mind" (Dawkins), 105–6

Gardner, R. Allen, and Beatrix, 44–45, 109, 112, 113
Garretson, Mervin, 142
generative linguistics, xvii
Georgetown University, 144
Gerlernter, David, 118
German Sign Language, 254
Germany: oralism and, 14, 27, 42
Geschwind, Norman, 111
gestural theory of language origins: cultural transmission studies in chimpanzees, 107–9; elegance of, 119; historical overview, 35–41, 43–44, 106–7, 119; implications for understanding gesture, sign, and language, 126–28; semantic phonology concept, 120–24; Stokoe and, xvi–xvii, 86, 87, 119, 126–27, 128; testable predictions from, 124–26; unifying power of, 120
Gesture and the Nature of Language (Stokoe, Armstrong, and Wilcox), 119
gestures/gestural communication (*see also* gestural theory of language origins; iconic gestures); in chimpanzees, 107–9; continuity with speech, 109–10; Darwinian views of, 25–26, 28; decline in studies of, 43; deep connection to language, 124–25; development in, 126; emotional expression and, 21; hand-brain evolution and, 91; meaning of term, 127; oratory and, 21–22; pointing, 68–77; praxic movements and, 98; semantic phonology concept and, 123–24; syntax and, xvii, 46–47, 97, 108–9; theories of universal language and, 38; —, language development and, 214–15; decline in use of gestures, 236; effect of exposure to sign language on, 221; maternal use of gestures, 233–36, 240–41; pointing, 236–37; studied in monolingual and bilingual children, 217–22; transition to two-word speech, 237–38; in two-element utterances, 223–27
Gilbert, Grove K., 54
glottogenesis. *See* language evolution; language origins
Goldin-Meadow, Susan, 125, 255
Goodman, Linda, 190
Gough, Bonnie, 59
gradualism, 102, 105–6
grammar books: of Danish Sign Language, 174
grammatical development: role of social and cultural conditions in, 256–57
grammatical function signs, 154, 156–57
Guiding Proposals Concerning the Teaching of Sign Language in the Folkeskole, 182
gulls, 105
Guy, Gregory, 145

habitual movements, 97–98
Haislip, Michelle, 108
Halttunen, Karen, 22
hand preference: autistic children and, 202–3
hands: archetypal grammatical role of, 123; evolutionary tool-making and, 92, 94–95; gestural communication and, 91; hand-brain co-evolution, 91–95; hand-brain

relationship, 90–91; hand-mouth relationship, 109–10; "hand-thought-language" nexus, 126; language origins and, 95–99; praxic movements, 97, 98; rehearsed movements, 95–97; significance in human life, 89–90; "3-jaw chuck" grip, 91

Hand, The (Wilson), 126

Harnad, Stevan, xvi

HBCUs. *See* historically Black colleges and universities

hearing families: bilingual deaf children and, 176–78

herring gulls, 105

Herzog, Martin, 143

Hewes, Gordon, xvi, 43–44, 49n9, 85–86, 107

historically Black colleges and universities (HBCUs), 167

Hockett, Charles, xvi, 46

Holloway, Ralph, 111

home signs, 255

hominids: hand-brain co-evolution, 91–95

Homo erectus, 92, 94–95

honesty: nineteenth-century notions of, 22–23

horizontal language variation, 139–40, 156, 157

Howe, Samuel Gridley, 14

Humphries, Tom, 162

Hurd, Angela, 195

iconic gestures: in chimpanzees, 107–8; Stokoe's language evolution studies and, xvi–xvii, 119, 126–27, 128; syntax and, xvii, 97, 108–9

iconicity, 47, 53, 78; arbitrary nature of signs concept and, 60–61, 62–63, 65, 67–68; creation of new forms and, 66; formation of new sign languages and, 256; metaphor-linked, 66; modality effects and, 63; onomatopoeia and, 61–62, 65, 66–67

iconic signs: aphasic individuals and, 199

Ideals, 101

imagination: Vico's theory of language origins and, 35

Indiana School for the Deaf, 250

inscriptions: Vico's theory of language origins and, 35, 36

Institute of Psychology (Italy), 216

intellect: oralist association with speech, 27

International Congress on Education of the Deaf in Milan, 2, 42

Israel: sign languages of, 254–55

Iverson, Jana M., 242

Iwaszuk, Wendy, 108

Johnson, Robert E., 75, 150–52, 157

Jorio, Andrea de, 40

Kanner, Leo, 194

Keep, John, 20

Kendall elementary school, 2

Kendon, Adam, 15, 69, 125, 215

Kimura, Doreen, 125

Klima, Edward, 44, 49n9, 59, 63–64

Koreber, A. L., 15

Kuschel, Rolf, 255

Labov, William, 143, 144, 147

landmarks, 73

Langacker, Ronald, 73, 121

language: chain of being concept and, 101–2; compared to animal communication, 124–25;

language (*continued*):
modality of expression and, 46; Stokoe's notions of, 47; structured heterogeneity concept, 143; sublexical structure, xv; viewed as speech, xi–xii, 16

language acquisition, 125; chimpanzee research, 44–45; mentally retarded individuals and, 195

language development, 126; analysis of utterance types in children, 222–27; bimodal period, 215; decontextualization process, 214–15, 221–22; impact of maternal use of gestures on, 233–36, 240–41; language evolution and, 242–43; neural organization and, 242; pointing and, 236–37; role of gestures in, 214–15; transition from crossmodal to unimodal utterances, 241–42; transition to two-word speech, 215, 237–38; two-element utterances, 223–33, 237–40; words and gestures produced in infancy, 217–22

language evolution (*see also* language origins); child language development and, 242–43; Noam Chomsky and, 93–94, 102–4; discontinuity paradox, 93–94; gradualist approach, 102, 105–6; hand-brain relationship and, 91–95; language organ concept and, 103–4; punctuationalist approach, 102, 104–5

Language in Hand (Stokoe), xvii

language organ, 103–4; neurological basis, 111–12

language origins (*see also* gestural theory of language origins; language evolution); ape language projects, 44–45, 107–9, 112–13; ban on studies in, 42; biblical presentation, 24–25, 85; bow-wow theory, 85–86; Darwinian perspective, 85; evolution of speech apparatus and, 102; gradualist approach, 102, 105–6; hand-brain relationship and, 91–95; hand movements and, 95–99; human tool use and, 99; language organ concept and, 103–4; modality of expression and, 46; punctuationalist approach, 102, 104–5; studies of sign languages and, 38–41, 43–48; theoretical perspectives, 85–87

Language Origins (Stokoe), xvi

Language (Sapir), xi

Law of the Excluded Middle, 101

Layton, Thomas L., 195

Leach, William, 254

left-hemisphere brain injury, 110

Lenneberg, Eric, 44

L'Epée, Charles Michel de, 37–38

lesser black-backed gulls, 105

Lettre sur les sourds et muets (Diderot), 37

Liddell, Scott, 71, 75, 127, 150–52, 157

"linguistic Darwinism," 25–27

Linguistic Research Laboratory, xv

linguistics: anthropological, xiv–xv; Noam Chomsky and, xiv, xvii, 86, 144; language viewed as speech, xi–xii; Saussure's science

of signs, 42–43; sublexical structure of language, xv; syntax and, xvii
Linguistic Society of Paris, 42, 85
Linstok Press, xvi, 49n10
location signs: variation in, 150–57
Lock, Andrew, 241–42
Locke, John, 36–37, 37
London Philological Society, 42
Long, J. Schuyler, 30n5
Loulis (chimpanzee), 107, 108
Lucas, Ceil, 166, 167
Lucy (hominid), 91

mainstreaming: impact on American Sign Language, 248; impact on deaf schools, 248, 249–50; social consequences, 185–86
Mallery, Garrick, 26, 39–40, 43
Mandel, Mark, 63
Man (journal), 15
Mann, Horace, 14
manual dyspraxia, 203
manualist tradition: articles published in *American Annals of the Deaf,* 14; biblical notions of language and, 24–25; "cult of sincerity" and, 22–23; in France, 27; gestures and emotional expression, 21; nineteenth-century sign languages and, 18; romantic notions of sign languages, 23–24; sign languages viewed as natural, 17, 19
Marbury, Nathie, 167
Markowicz, Harry, 144
Martha's Vineyard, 256
Maryland School for the Deaf, 250
Massey, Doreen, 257
Maxwell, Madeline, 163
McNeill, David, 125

Meggitt, Mervyn, 15, 43
Meir, Irit, 254
mentally retarded individuals: acquisition of spoken language skills, 195; sign communication programs and, 191–92, 195–97
Merrill, George P., 55
metaphor-linked iconicity, 66
Metaphysics (Aristotle), 101
Meteor Crater. *See* Barringer Crater
Metzger, Melanie, 71
Milan Congress, 2, 42
Mills, Anne, 221
Milroy, Leslie, 147
mirror neurons, 111–12, 126
modality effects, 59; iconicity and, 63; sign languages and, 53
modality of expression, 46
Moja (chimpanzee), 108
monolingual children: modality combinations in two-element utterances, 224–26; two-element utterances produced by, 231, 232; types of utterances produced by, 222–23; word and gesture production in, 219, 220, 221
morphology: studies of American Sign Language, 59–60; variation and, 138
mothers: impact of gestures on child language development, 233–36
motivated signs, 122
motor functioning: childhood autistic disorder and, 193, 199–207
Motor Imitation test, 204
Mountford, C. P., 15
mouth: hand-mouth relationship, 109–10
Movement Copying test, 204

movements: habitual, 97, 98; rehearsed, 95–97; super-praxic, 98
Müller, Max, 85
musicians, 89, 97

NAD. *See* National Association of the Deaf
Namir, Lila, 49n9
NAOBI. *See* National Alliance of Black Interpreters
National Alliance of Black Interpreters (NAOBI), 162–63, 164, 166
National Association of the Deaf (NAD), 139
National Black Deaf Advocates (NBDA), 162, 164, 166
National Congress of Jewish Deaf (NCJD), 139
National Fraternal Society of the Deaf (NFSD), 139
National Research Council (Italy), 216
National Science Foundation, 145
natural languages: as conceived by linguists, 17; sign languages as, 17–25
natural selection, 103
NBDA. *See* National Black Deaf Advocates
NCJD. *See* National Congress of Jewish Deaf
Neapolitans, 40
Nebraska School for the Deaf, 250
neuro-imaging, 198
"New Light" evangelicals, 20
Newport, Elissa, 77, 125
new sign languages, 254–57
New York Evening Post, 26
New York Times, 93

NFSD. *See* National Fraternal Society of the Deaf
Nicaragua, 256
Nielsen, Kirsten, 185
nonspeaking individuals (*see also* aphasic individuals; childhood autistic disorder; mentally retarded); sign communication programs and, 190–99
notions: in semantic space, 121–22
nouns: directionality and, 76n9
numeral signs: directionality and, 70–71, 72–73

Observer's Paradox, 155–56
Oceana (journal), 15
Oliver, Susan, 144
onomatopoeia: bow-wow theory of language origins, 85–86; iconicity and, 61–62, 65, 66–67; semantic phonology concept and, 122
oral dyspraxia, 203
oralism: association of speech with intellect, 27; cochlear implants and, 187; decline in sign language studies and, 14, 27–28; Germany and, 14, 27, 42; limited efficacy of, 183; rise of, 14
oratory, 21–22
Original Signs (Armstrong), 4
Origin of Species, The (Darwin), 85, 100

Padden, Carol A., 76n, 79n, 162
Padden, Don, 249
Paget, R. A. S., 109
pan-ethnic communities, 260
pantomimic signs: aphasic individuals and, 199

pantomine, 108; Darwinian views of, 25–26; nineteenth-century notions of, 18, 19
paralinguistic elements, 68–69. *See also* pointing
parents, hearing: bilingual deaf children and, 176–78; sign language learning, 178
Parker, Sue T., 107
PDMS. *See* Peabody Developmental Manual Scales
Peabody Developmental Manual Scales (PDMS), 203–4, 205
Peet, Harvey, 21
Pennsylvania School for the Deaf, 250
"performatives," 214
Pettingill, Benjamin, 17–18, 18–19
phonology, 58, 59; variation in, 137–38
Pinker, Steven, 103, 105, 106
Plains Indians sign language, 15, 39–40, 43
planum temporale, 111
Plato, 101
pointing, 60; as articulatory instruction, 69; in child gestural production, 214, 236–37; directional signs, 70–73; gestural *vs.* grammatical analyses of, 76–77; linking signs with external entities, 72–75; notions of gestural modalities and, 70; as paralinguistic element, 68–69; theoretical frameworks, 75–77
praxic movements, 97, 98
premotor cortex, 111
"Primate Communication and the Gestural Origin of Language" (Hewes), 44
pro-drop languages, 138

Project Washoe, 44–45, 112–13. *See also* ape language projects
pronouns: directionality and, 76n9
Protestants: evangelical emotion, 20
public spaces, 249
punctuationalism, 102, 104–5

Rae, Luzerne, 18
reduplication, 59
referential gestures, 214
regional language variation, 139–40, 156, 157
rehearsed movements, 95–97
religion: evangelical emotion, 20
representational elements, 214, 217–18, 221; in maternal use of gestures, 234; in two-element utterances, 225, 226, 227–32
residential schools, 140
Reynolds, Peter J., 94, 95, 99
Riley, William, 144
Rimpau, James B., 109
"ring species," 105–6
Rizzolatti, Giacomo, 111, 126
Romanticism, 23–24
Roosevelt, Franklin D., 1

Salk Institute for Biological Studies, 45, 49n9, 252
Salk, Jonas, 45
San Diego (CA), 252–53
San Diego State University, 252
Sandler, Wendy, 254
Sankoff, David, 152
Sanz, Crickette M., 108
Sapir, Edward, xi
Saussure, Ferdinand de, 42–43, 60–61, 65
"savages," 26
Schlesinger, Izchak M., 49n9
Science (journal), 26, 27

Seal, Brenda, 201
Second Great Awakening, 20
semantic phonology, 119, 120–24
"Semantic Phonology" (Stokoe), xvii
semantic space, 121–22
semiologie, 42–43
Shuy, Roger, 144
Sicard, Roch Ambroise, 38
sign-based education (*see also* deaf education); negative perceptions of, 1–2
sign communication programs: for aphasic individuals, 192, 197–99
sign communication programs, for nonspeaking individuals: changing perceptions of sign language and, 191; for childhood autistic disorder, 191–92, 194–95, 207; impact of sign language research on, 207–8; increasing numbers of students in, 190; for mentally retarded individuals, 191–92, 195–97; outcomes research, 192–99
Signed Danish, 178
Signes et de l'art de penser, Des (Degerando), 38
sign inventions, 255
sign language acquisition, 125; chimpanzee research, 44–45
sign language dictionaries, 30n5, 141 (*see also* Dictionary of American Sign Language)
sign language research: civil rights movement and, xiii–xiv; decline in, 14–16, 43; in Denmark, 173–75; dissemination of research information, 169–70; impact on sign communication programs, 207–8; impact on the Black Deaf community, 163–69, 170; language origins studies and, 38–41, 43–44, 46–48; on language variation, 144, 157; William Stokoe's studies and contributions, xii, xiv–xvii, 3–6, 29, 45–46, 58–59, 191
sign languages: accepted as natural languages, 17–25, 53, 58, 191, 248; creation of new languages, 254–57; Darwinian views of, 25–27, 28; deaf bilingualism and, 175–76; demise of research tradition in, 14, 28; emotion and, 20–21; implications of gestural theory for, 127–28; inherent legibility of rehearsed movement and, 95–96; modality effects and, 53; negative perceptions of, xi–xii, 1–2, 16; nineteenth-century perspectives, 13–28; oralism and, 14, 27–28; oratory and, 21–22; role of social and cultural conditions in grammatical development, 256–57; romanticism and, 23–24; sign inventions, 255; spoken languages and, 53; viewed as nonhuman, 26–27
Sign Language Structure (Stokoe), 45, 58
Sign Language Studies (journal), xv–xvi, 6
Sign Language, The (Long), 30n5
sign language variation (*see also* sociolinguistic variation): *Dictionary of American Sign Language* and, 138–44; forms of, 137–38; impact of research on the Deaf community, 157;

location signs, 150–57; overview of research in, 144; sociolinguistic research, 145–50
signs: aphasic individuals and, 198–99; arbitrariness concept, 60–61, 62–63, 65, 67–68, 122; as articulatory gesturing, 125; autistic children and, 202; early studies of, 38; gestural theory and, 125, 126–28; iconicity and, 53, 60–68, 78; Garrick Mallery's notions of, 40; mentally retarded individuals and, 196; Saussure's science of, 42–43; semantic phonology concept and, 122–23; sign inventions, 255; Stokoe's conceptualization of, 119, 191; Vico's theory of language origins and, 35–36
Signs of Language (Klima and Bellugi), 49n9
Simultaneous Communication, 57n
Siple, Patricia, 49n9
Slavoff, Georgina, 203
Smith, Henry Lee, 141
Smith-Todd, Syble, 164
smoke signaling, 16
social language variation. *See* vertical language variation
Sociolinguistics of the Deaf community, The (Lucas), 167
sociolinguistic variation: defined, 138; Dictionary of American Sign Language appendices and, 138–44, 157; horizontal and vertical, 139–40; impact of research on the Deaf community, 157; in location signs, 150–57; research in, 144, 145–50
Sørenson, Ruth Kjaer, 173, 181

Southern California Recreational Association of the Deaf, 253
speciation, 100
species: Darwin's concept of, 100, 105; Dawkin's "ring species" concept, 105–6; essentialism concept, 101
speech: as articulatory gesturing, 125; continuity with gestural communication, 109–10; language viewed as, xi–xii, 16; mentally retarded individuals and, 195; notions of language origins and, 46; oralist association with intellect, 27; sign languages and, 53; Vico's theory of origins, 35–36
speech apparatus: appearance in humans, 102
standard sign language, 139, 140
Steklis, Horst, xvi
Stokoe, William C., 70, 157, 163, 173, 201, 243; anthropological linguistics and, xiv–xv; ape language projects and, 112–13; background of, xii–xiii; character of, 1; cherology concept, 58–59; concept of language, 47; conceptualization of signs, 119, 191; contributions to sign language studies, xii, xiv–xvii, 3–6, 29, 45–46, 58–59; criticism of language organ concept, 104; death of, xviii; *Dictionary of American Sign Language* and, xv, 138, 141; on evolution of speech apparatus, 102; at Gallaudet College, xii, xiii, xv–xvi, 2–5, 57; gestural theory of language origins, xvi–xvii, 86, 87, 119, 126–27, 128;

Stokoe (*continued*):
  gestural theory of syntax, xvii, 46–47, 97, 108–9; intellectual qualities, 118, 119, 128; language evolution studies, xvi–xvii, 86, 87; nineteenth-century tradition of sign language studies and, 13; semantic phonology concept, 119, 120–24; on sign language dictionaries, 141; *Sign Language Studies* and, xv–xvi
Stone, Collins, 19
stone tools, 92. *See also* tool making
structured heterogeneity concept, 143
super-praxic movements, 98
surgeons: rehearsed movements, 95–96
surrogates, 74
Sweden: code switching by deaf children, 179
sympathetic mouth movements, 110
Syntactic Structures (Chomsky), 144
syntax: gestural theory of, xvii, 46–47, 97, 108–9; nineteenth-century sign language studies, 19–20; variation and, 138

Talbot, Benjamin, 20
Tatu (chimpanzee), 108
technology: impact on the Deaf community, 257
Teitelbaum, Philip, 204
telecommunications technology: impact on the Deaf community, 257
Tennessee Archaeologist (journal), 15
Thelen, Esther, 242
"3-jaw chuck" grip, 91

Tilghman, Benjamin, 54
tokens, 74–75
Tomkins, William, 16
tongue, 110
tool-use: hand-brain co-evolution and, 92, 94–95; language origins and, 99
Trager, George, 141
trajectors, 73
Turner, Charles, 24
two-element utterances: frequent appearance of crossmodal combinations, 237–38; impact of linguistic input on, 239–40; information content and, 227–33, 238–39; modality combinations in, 223–27
Tylor, Edward B., 25–26, 38–39, 42

Understanding Language through Sign Language Research, 49n9
Uniformitarian Principle, 54–57
unimodal utterances, 225, 226, 227
Universal Indian Sign Language (Tomkins), 16
universal language, 38
University of California, San Diego, 252
Utah School for the Deaf, 250

Van de Bogaerde, Beppie, 221
VARBRUL program, 152
Veditz, George, 248, 253
verbs: directional signs and, 71–72, 73, 75–77; trajectors and landmarks, 73
vertical language variation, 139, 140, 157
Vico, Giambattista, 35–36, 119
visual signs, 18

vocal gestures, 47
Voegelin, C. F., 15
Volkerpsychologie (Wundt), 40–41
Volterra, Virginia, 215

Walbiri sign language, 43
Washabaugh, William, 255
Washington State School for the Deaf, 156
Washoe (chimpanzee), 44–45, 107, 108, 112–13
Weinrich, Uriel, 143
Wernicke's area, 111
Wescott, Roger, xvi, 61
West, La Mont, 15, 43

Whitney, William Dwight, 25
Wilbur, Ronnie, 62, 64
Wilcox, Sherman E., 4, 70, 97, 108, 109, 112
Wilson, Frank, 126
Wilson, Paula S., 190
Wolfram, Walt, 144
Woodruff, Lucius, 20–21, 23
Woodward, James, 144, 163, 166
words: arbitrariness concept and, 18, 60–61, 62–63, 65, 67–68
Wright, Frank Lloyd, 118
Wundt, Wilhelm, 40–41, 42

Yale, Caroline, 27